Teaching and Performing
Ideas for Energizing Your Classes

Second Edition

by William M. Timpson and Suzanne Burgoyne

Atwood
Publishing
Madison, WI

Teaching and Performing: Ideas for Energizing Your Classes

Second Edition

by William M. Timpson and Suzanne Burgoyne

© 2002 by Atwood Publishing
2710 Atwood Avenue
Madison, WI 53704

www.atwoodpublishing.com

ISBN: 1-891859-43-9

Cover design by Brian Gunning

Library of Congress Cataloguing-in-Publication Data

Timpson, William M.
Teaching and performing: ideas for energizing your classes / William
M. Timpson, Suzanne Burgoyne. --2nd ed.
p.cm
Previous ed. Entered under title.
Includes bibliographical references (p.) and index.
ISBN 1-891859-43-9
1. College teaching. 2. Performing arts. I. Burgoyne, Suzanne. II. Title
LB2331.T34 2002
378.1'2--dc21

                                                        2002011783

Dedication

To Nick Burlak —
actor, director, producer, and performer in the most dramatic of roles on the world's stage of history. May your courage, energy, and charisma inspire others.

Acknowledgments

There are many people and organizations to thank for support and assistance on this project — which has been a truly creative journey from its very inception. For starters, we need to recognize the groundbreaking work that went into the 1982 publication of *Teaching as Performing*, which Bill Timpson co-authored with David Tobin, and acknowledge the receptivity, support, and ideas that came from the teachers and professors who participated in various workshops and courses. Fortunately, we were able to capture much from these early years on videotape. Throughout this early period of development, Professor Barbara Nelson (Colorado State University) also helped us frame our ideas within a larger context of effective communication and instruction.

Once this work shifted into a focus on teaching and performance in higher education, Bill received invaluable help and ideas from colleagues at Colorado State University, the University of California-Santa Cruz, and the University of Queensland in Brisbane, Australia. When Suzanne Burgoyne joined the project, she drew on her own circle of colleagues at Creighton University and the University of Missouri- Columbia. A special debt of gratitude must also go to Christine Jones of Colorado State University and Waldo Jones of the University of Northern Colorado, both of whom added much to the first edition of this book.

Equally important as the teachers in our lives have been people from all walks of life who have worked with each of us on a variety of staged productions over the years — people who have given so much of themselves: their time, their energy, and their talents. In particular, we want to acknowledge the staff, cast, and crew of the Larimer Chorale, Fort Collins Opera, Foothills Civic theatre, Canyon Concert Ballet, and Open Stage theatre, as well as university theatre productions at Creighton University and the University of Missouri-Columbia.

We also want to acknowledge the contributions of the staff and television crew at the Office of Instructional Services, Colorado State University, — in particular, Sally Hibbitt, Joe Schwind, Mike Ellis, Larry Preuss, Bill Kruse, Fred Rosenkranz, and Pres Davis — for helping us preserve so many superb performances on videotape. These tapes have been broadcast nationally and are available for purchase through Colorado State University.

As this manuscript moved toward completion, we also received valuable feedback from a variety of readers. We applaud each of you. For her contributions on film references, Gloria Campbell deserves special recognition.

We also extend our heartfelt appreciation to our earlier editor at Magna Publications, Bob Magnan, and our current publisher, Linda Babler at Atwood Publishing, for their support, guidance, and patience as this manuscript evolved through various stages and revisions. Bob took the lead in providing both general and editorial support for the first edition.

Finally, we want to thank all those students and workshop participants whose positive responses have encouraged us to produce this second edition. While the essence of the text remains unchanged except for minor organizational and stylistic modifications, as well as updates to our references, we have drawn on our use of the first edition as well as other experiences to add some important refinements.

Table of Contents

Foreword from the Lectern

Bill Timpson

In the late 1970s, I was actively developing a variety of workshops on teaching. I hoped that fresh ideas might attract new "students" from among college faculty. Some who enrolled were colleagues from my own campus at Colorado State University. One offering that quickly proved both popular and practical addressed the parallels between teaching and the stage. Having performed in a community dance troupe, local ballet productions, various choirs, musicals, and operas, I knew firsthand the associated benefits to my own teaching. Whenever teaching was discussed as art and science, I could always weigh in on both sides, wedding my experiences on stage with my graduate training in educational psychology.

What became an experimental offering on campus evolved first into an article and then a book for Prentice-Hall. Written with my colleague, Dave Tobin, and published in 1982, *Teaching as Performing* introduced teachers at all levels to related skills and practices from the stage. My first workshops later became a fixed component of a regular graduate course on communication and presentation skills. Over a four-week period each spring semester, teachers would plan, script, and stage one particular idea. With a performer's approach to voice and movement, costuming, sets, lighting and props, characterization, and direction, they would rehearse their pieces both in and out of class and get feedback from their classmates. On the last day of class, these teachers would then give their performances in front of their classmates, friends, and, at times, television cameras brought in to capture a visual record for future reference.

Over the years, I have found the results of these workshops intriguing, challenging, and even dramatic as these teachers have pushed themselves to produce something both creative and meaningful to their own students. Along the way, these same teachers have also pushed me and my own understanding of the performing processes that underlie dynamic and engaging instruction. In many ways, these performances have also served as benchmarks of exemplary instruction. Rehearsed and refined over time, these "staged" lessons have proven challenging and renewing, giving these teachers a viable way to rekindle their own excitement by finding fresh and creative ways to approach familiar material.

My colleague Suzanne Burgoyne and I now offer you this extension of that first book as well as our 1997 first edition of *Teaching and Performing*, with some new examples and updated references. Suzanne brings to this task a lifetime of work in academia and the theatre, including acting and directing at the university level; maintaining an active research interest in translating a Belgian playwright; and leading workshops on performance skills for her colleagues at Creighton University and the University of Missouri-Columbia. I myself bring a background in stage work to my ongoing scholarly work on postsecondary instruction. I'm also an active consumer of good film and theatre, dance, and music.

Case Studies

In what follows, I summarize interviews with four colleagues who bring a lot of the performer's skill and élan to their teaching. I think you'll find their comments intriguing and useful as a lead-in to this book.

Janice Moore

Dr. Janice Moore is a professor of Biology who has an enviable publication record and a real gift for teaching. She's a senior scholar who actually enjoys teaching large introductory classes. She is successful with them, in part, because of her extensive performance background. I've known Janice for several years and I've watched her lecture. Her expertise, skill, energy, and joy in teaching are quickly evident. Even the smallest of mollusks looms larger when she lectures: its evolution miraculous, its mysteries foundational to understanding our universe. Knowing that she had an extensive background as a performer intrigued me. So I wanted to explore her insights into the teaching/performing connection.

From an early age Janice regularly sang solos in church services. In high school she received awards for public speaking. At Rice University she parlayed her singing talents into a rock band, performing every day one summer and intermittently thereafter. In college she acted in some melodramas, and wrote and directed several one-act plays for an intercollegiate competition, noting with some pride her first and second place awards.

As we talked, Janice offered a number of observations and insights about the connection between teaching and the stage:

William M. Timpson: What did you bring over to teaching from performance?

Janice Moore: All of it! I can usually get students' attention and keep it. Students can see me as enthusiastic, interesting. On the negative side, they do say they want more AV stuff, but I know that I always saw slides and films as distracting when I was a student. They also want me to be more organized. I don't hand out lecture notes. I do believe that students think more if they have to pay attention.

WMT: What do you do with stage awareness?

JM: With a lower-division class of two hundred, for example, I don't need to update my notes at the same rate as I have to for upper-division classes, so I can think about teaching more. At the beginning, I'll joke, talk about the weekend, show some empathy, get their attention. If I see students are drifting off, I'll stop and ask what's going on. I'll try something different. On stage you can't depart from your script or song, but I can change my physical relationship with the audience. In class I can do the same thing. I'll move out toward my students. Out front there are fewer obstructions. I can project more energy.

WMT: What about preparation?

JM: There is no better preparation for teaching than performing because the challenges are the same — getting people's attention and holding it. (I note for you, the reader, Lowman's [1995] conclusion that the two most important qualities for university teachers to achieve in class are intellectual excitement and rapport with students.)

WMT: Energy?

JM: As a teacher I imagine myself as a student. I know that I felt timid. I think of myself as a student for two minutes or so before class —

ideally I should do it for five minutes. In this way I remind myself what it's like to be in my own class, to whom it is that I'm talking. Whereas a performance audience will pull for you. They want a good show. They're your friends. In that sense performance is more satisfying; unfortunately, not all students want to be in class. Students often assume an antagonistic relationship with their teachers. Histories and values clash. As students, we typically were the interested ones. It's important for a performer to get in tune with an audience, for a teacher to be in tune with students, but it's more difficult to relate to students. As a teacher, you have to welcome all student questions; there are more individual interactions. That's different for a performer, except for the rare instance with a drunk.

WMT: Costuming?

JM: Absolutely the same for performing and teaching. For example, I always wear a dress when I teach. It's always "Dr. Moore" with undergrads. I'm not just another student. It's part of the act. Students may like teachers who dress and act like them, but I think the subtle barrier is important. In my classes, my authority equals my expertise and contributes to their motivation to learn. Primates learn better from superiors, not subordinates or equals. Admittedly, there may be gender differences here. Women professors have less perceived authority. Consequently, they must dress the part more. I also believe that it is disrespectful of audiences to dress sloppily. Male teachers should wear a sport coat and tie, or a vest. Something "non-student."

WMT: What about preparation time?

JM: Here, there is a big difference. You cannot perfect a lesson. You give it once a year. It's more like writing for a newspaper with its daily deadlines than trying to perfect a novel.

WMT: Props?

JM: I do need to use more. As a student, however, I didn't like to sit in the dark and try to take notes. That's why I don't like slides. I use overheads, but in a lit room. Yet I know that some students miss the lecture and could use something up on a screen. If the overheads are detailed, however, students are just copying; they're not thinking. I could just as easily provide a handout. Sometimes I do provide little toys as prizes — gimmicks for winning a quiz, for example. I'll give out a wind-up crab or something else funny and weird. I suppose I could do more to make things more interesting with multimedia. Again, this is much like newspaper deadlines. I have produced multimedia shows — for conference presentations, for example — but that can require a great deal of prep time.

WMT: In the theatre, we talk about "raising the stakes," making it important for an audience to care. What do you do in class?

JM: I'll use the building block concept. For example, "Pay attention to this. You'll see it again." Or, "This will be on the exam," although I rarely use that one.

WMT: What do you do for a hook, that theatrical device used to engage the audience early on in a production?

JM: I may say something like, "This is important or neat because ... " to get their attention. I use a review the same way, although sometimes I forget.

WMT: Any use of warm-up before teaching?

JM: On my good days — when I'm energetic, upbeat, feeling good — I may tease students or joke with them. I'll pay attention to them, talk to some. On bad days — when I'm down or tired — I'll just start the lecture. Teaching takes a different kind of energy. As a performer, you can fake it. You can certainly fake some things as a teacher, but it's hard to do the personal interactions when you're cranky. On bad days you can just do your job and teach, whereas as a performer you get more positive feedback. An audience can pull you up and out. Students don't do that as much. They're like a nameless crowd. Yet some teacher "performers" can get sucked or hooked into pleasing students, and this, then, becomes a goal. For me the goal always has to be teaching; the performance is simply a way to do it.

WMT: Do you think there are any gender differences relevant to the teaching/ performing connection?

JM: As I said, women professors are not seen as authority figures, hence teaching is more difficult for them.

WMT: Any other insights into the impact of performance on teaching?

JM: I'm in demand as a speaker. I play with my audiences. Whenever I talk about my cockroaches, audiences love it. I give very playful research seminars. My attitude is that my audiences should have a good time. I know that I'm having a good time and that's a key. It gives me energy, makes me enthusiastic. If I'm not having a good time, no one else will.

Carol Mitchell

Dr. Carol Mitchell is a friend and colleague in the English Department at Colorado State University. A folklorist by training, she has toured the Middle East and has created a new course on goddesses in literature. She is an intriguing character study for this book because, unlike Janice Moore, she has not performed. But she thoroughly enjoys her teaching and brings a lot of the performer's skill and attitude into class — i.e., costuming, energy, self-awareness, and "stage presence" (awareness of what's happening beyond the "script" or lecture content). In fact, she really isn't that interested in traditional performance; she likes the spontaneity of creating something new in class over the demands of memorizing lines for the stage.

Carol is energetic, intense but friendly, and fun to be with. She is alive with ideas, someone who combines a genuine love of teaching with an active intellectual interest in folklore, Asian literature, mythology, and goddess studies. As a high school English teacher, she learned how to keep the interest of her students or suffer the consequences (if students found her boring, they would quickly create their own diversions). Her frequently tinted hair, sometimes a deep blue and at other times with a bit more purple, sets her apart as she walks across campus.

William M. Timpson: Do you think about your costumes?

Carol Mitchell: I do make great use of costuming in class. In my Asian Lit and Folklore classes, I'll wear different examples of clothing I've collected over the years. It's not uniformly true, but some students do respond positively, mostly the females. It adds some interest. For others, mostly the males — and this tends to be a classic gender difference — what I wear is of only passing interest. More generally, though, what I wear does affect my teaching. They are watching me. I like clothes; I like jewelry. Clothes are an art form. When I think I look good, I have more confidence and perform better. Earlier in my career, when I was teaching high school, I felt I had to dress up more because I was so close in age to the students, and short, and I looked young. I still believe that my high heels made a difference, especially among the males. At the university, I know now that no one will confuse me with being a student, but I still wear more formal clothes — "different" slacks from what the students will wear, for example. I am in charge; my class is not a democracy.

WMT: Talk about being center stage.

CM: I enjoy being the center of attention when I'm teaching, so I have to be careful to give students enough chance to talk to each other. Yet they have limited knowledge, and I am the expert here; I do know more. Being center stage fuels my enthusiasm, which, in turn, helps me energize students about the material. But I don't teach in a vacuum; student feedback is critical. The way the class clicks makes a difference. Teaching is very dynamic; so is all performance. My Asian Lit and Goddess classes are giving a lot back to me, and I tell my students how important that is for me, how much I appreciate it. One class, my worst ever, just would not respond, no matter what I did. It was so strange because in previous years I had never had this kind of problem. I liked the material. So I finally gave up on them as a group and concentrated on teaching to those two or three who were responding. That made all the difference.

WMT: What do you do about preparation before class, and about reflections after?

CM: At least a half-hour before class, I know I'm getting up for it. I know that's what I do. I'm reviewing my notes, but not just to refresh my memory. I'm also getting in the right mood. And I do get "high" from teaching, especially after good classes. I'm "up." But it is a "downer" when I feel class has gone poorly.

I'm not conscious of reflecting on my teaching right after class; often students are coming up after class. I'm more likely to think about it at home, sometimes when I'm getting ready for bed. For example, recently I had this interaction with a particular student in class about religion. I was claiming that Christianity, with its linear conceptualization of time, began with creation and then moved through the cataclysmic second coming and a transformation of the earth into heaven, while other religions saw life and the earth in a more cyclical fashion with a continuous repetition of life, death, and reincarnation. Anyway, she didn't agree, and it seemed to me that we were just talking past each other. It was later that night that I got this insight into why we were missing, so I started off the next class with that same issue, but it wasn't planned.

Whether I think about teaching also depends on the people around me. If I know that someone else enjoys talking about teaching, I'll often talk about it. It's fun to chat about. In fact, we have a group that gets together weekly for dinner, and we often talk about our teaching.

WMT: Do you think about sets or props?

CM: I prefer to have classes with movable desks and chairs. It's really frustrating to be stuck in a classroom with everything bolted. It's hard to do any group work. I also tend to avoid using a podium; I like to use the front table of class. If I have a small class, I'll often pass around pictures. For some classes, I now do more with slides. I can point out the details, although slides can be distracting. Some students have a hard time looking at slides and listening to me at the same time. I know that I play with my glasses, and that's been a change. And sometimes I have a book I refer to.

WMT: Are you conscious of your movements in class?

CM: I move around, in part, to give students something to watch, but I also want to have them keep their focus on me. We are a culture that focuses on action, not being. Accordingly, staying rooted behind a podium is a problem. I am conscious of my movements. Sometimes, if I notice some students who are chatting or seem inattentive, I'll walk toward them, and that will usually correct the problem. Having taught high school, I have no problem confronting discipline. Periodically, I will note the effect of a certain gesture, but rarely is there any time during class to stop and reflect but for just the briefest of moments. There's just too much going on. I could never plan to repeat it; I guess it just gets stored somewhere in my unconscious and plays out in the future.

WMT: Are you conscious of the role you play when you teach?

CM: I'm really not a different character in class. It's all one, integrated, the teacher and me, although I'm a bit more formal when I teach. However, there was this one time — this was funny — when the teacher in me took over outside of class. I was in a bar with a friend and someone I didn't know sat down next to me. Soon we were in a conversation, and before I knew it I was giving a lecture until I stopped myself and we both laughed. You see, the teacher is me.

WMT: What do you do with humor in class? with emotions?

CM: I do enjoy myself in class and humor is part of it. I often tease my students and joke with them. I tell jokes about myself, mostly off the cuff. I like to hear laughter in my classes. But I also can exhibit the full range of emotions. My students have also seen me angry, sad, serious. I want to respond as a whole person, and I want them to do the same, to react holistically, integrating mind and body, not divorcing their emotions. At the university, we focus too much on the intellect alone, on reason. Nothing is that simple or unconnected.

WMT: It's fun to watch you teach. You have such enthusiasm.

CM: I like teaching. It's especially fun again now that I've had my sabbatical. I had a great break — reading, travel. I needed that space from teaching. The public and the legislature really don't realize how draining teaching can be. Schoolteachers need their summers off to recover, to get their emotional energy back. The U.S. just does not want to recognize the emotional needs of people.

Greg Dickinson

Tall and gangly, Greg Dickinson has a voice that booms. His easy style connects with students and his enthusiasm is infectious. Greg is enthralled with the power of speech to shape ideas and history. As a child, he was always taken by the influence his minister father could command from the pulpit — a real power to explain, elucidate, and persuade. Active from an early age in church, Greg found that he himself was often taking the lead in discussions in Sunday school; he liked to be "up front." In public school, he got even more opportunities to be "up front" through Speech and Drama. He admits that he struggled with learning lines for high school productions. Somehow, though, he avoided the often debilitating adolescent curse of self-consciousness.

William M. Timpson: So how do you connect your experiences on stage with what you do in class?

Greg Dickinson: I'm actually kind of stiff on stage. I'm more natural in a dialogue sort of setting ... when I'm acting with the audience as compared with acting to other actors and pretending that the audience isn't there. I never knew how to negotiate that (fourth wall between the actors and the audience).

WMT: So sticking to a script was too constricting?

GD: Yeah, although I'm fine with a speech I write myself, when I can connect directly with the audience. I've also done a kind of "Reader's theatre" through the church and that was fun. My dad was well known in the region through church activities, and it was fun for me to have people tell me how much I sounded like him. I actually had fantasies about having a job and traveling the country giving speeches. Why I didn't become a politician, I don't know.

WMT: So what is it about connecting with an audience that is so compelling for you?

GD: I like the laughter, the body language, leaning forward. But I really like that moment of enlightenment, that "aha!" Those are the moments I'm looking for. As a rhetorician, I look for the three-way connection between speaker, topic, and audience. But unlike actors, I get to play myself.

WMT: One enduring area of resistance with respect to linking teaching with performance is the fear that instructors have about not being genuine — that they are experts and not entertainers.

GD: From my discipline, I would agree that it's not about entertainment per se; it's about this connection. You demonstrate your commitment to a topic, that you're passionate about it and you want your audience to be passionate about it as well. So it's about making these human connections so that we engage the material more thoroughly.

WMT: Let's extend this discussion. As a public speaker, could you represent either side of an argument, like a hired gun?

GD: Not me, but that's a question in rhetorical theory. I think I could make good arguments on both sides of an argument. I could even fake an argument on one side. But one of the things that works for me in the classroom is that I am genuinely excited about the material. If there's one comment I get from students it's that "this professor is so excited about his material."

WMT: Now I could see you getting excited about a great speech, even though you disagreed with the content.

GD: There are speakers with whom I agree and those with whom I don't. But what I'm passionate about is their respective abilities to negotiate the issues — issues of truth and power and language.

WMT: Such as educating an audience to be able to listen to a Hitler or any other charismatic speaker, and not get caught up in the energy of it all but be able to think through the message?

GD: Absolutely — those critical listening skills with which you try to see what's going on.

WMT: Talk about other issues that performers pay attention to. Set, for example. Does the room matter?

GD: The room matters a lot in the way it either aids or detracts from my ability to connect with an audience. In a large lecture setting, I need space in which to move, to get myself into fairly close proximity to all the students fairly quickly, whether that's up the sides or up the middle or across the front. That's important to me, to be able to move toward students who may not be paying close attention. Or, when there's a group that is really involved, I might move away from them so that there's this energy exchange across the room, and hopefully some of that energy infects the other folks. I'm very conscious of not moving toward those who are engaged because that narrows that energy band.

WMT: And that's a real license you have that a performer in a scripted play lacks.

GD: You want to be able to move in a way that responds to how a particular audience is acting on a particular day. That's very rhetorical, constantly adjusting what you need to say and do. It's what the classical rhetoricians called *kairos*, which literally means time or timing, trying to bring the "right" speech to the "right" audience at the "right" time and in the "right" way. The best speakers bring a wide knowledge of all these factors.

WMT: Are you aware of props? Do you make use of them?

GD: Very little. I'm a little bit of a "technophobe," afraid that the technology just won't work very well. But more importantly, I'm so committed to making a connection with who I am and who they are and often the props get in the way. We start paying more attention to the prop, like an overhead that shifts the audience focus to copying. I do think about doing more with a plan for the class at the very beginning, but even that can get in the way of a connection in the here and now. I need to find a way to negotiate that. So I'll use the board to note a concept that has emerged in our discussion, something they said or I said, but I don't necessarily know ahead of time what that key concept will be or what relationships will be identified. I end up with lots of arrows on the board.

WMT: What about costuming?

GD: I'm very conscious of the clothes I wear, but I never do the "scene" thing where, because it's Greek day, we do the togas. I don't have any problem with that, but it would take me time to find the toga and I would be embarrassed to wear it. In that sense I'm not an actor. I don't have much interest in taking on another character. I'm big. I can be articulate. I move around a lot. I want less formal clothing that says I'm approachable. I'm also gentle. I can also listen. I tell new teachers that I have an excess of authority and so I consciously dress more casually. I tell my students to call me Greg. I have a lot of power, and I can give away power and still have a lot. If these new teachers walk into their classrooms with a deficit of authority, then they may want to use clothing in a different way. If they are female, small, and non-white, then "Doctor" and the suit may be important to gaining authority.

WMT: So your talents and interests in all this developed early. It seems to come easily for you. And you enjoy it. However, it might be easy to fake it, to wing it, to come to class less than fully prepared. Is that a danger you have to watch?

GD: I think I'm reasonably good at all this, but I'm very conscious of developing these skills. It's not as if they are just there. I think a lot about it. Over the years, I've moved away from certain kinds of behaviors and added more. Like an actor who has a real proclivity for performing but must work at it and practice. To be a skilled rhetorician takes a lot of thought and practice. For me there is the danger of saying that I've prepped this material before and I don't have to prepare, but it never goes as well. I need to remake my commitment to the material every semester. What I carry into the room is a very deep commitment to that material, and students pick up on that excitement. If I don't reinvigorate myself, then it becomes more of an act. I, then, find myself being less articulate, not asking as good questions. So even though I've read this material many times, I have to read it again or, at least, scan it, look over my margin notes. I never use lecture notes or a script, but I do spend time thinking about the key issues, what I'm excited about.

WMT: But why wouldn't you use a script or prepared notes?

GD: Because, especially in my large class, I want to use an inductive method. I want the insights to come through the conversation with students. And I'm clearly taking the lead in that conversation, but they are also involved. If I have any script, it's about the questions I want to ask. We'll start with key passages from the text. We'll reread it. I'll ask what it means, we'll start to talk, and then I'll expand on what they say. In some sense, the script is provided by the reading itself. At times, this feels like it comes from my religious background: "The verse for today is…" Let's turn today to page 561 and unpack it. That sort of hermeneutic method.

WMT: Do you enjoy the spotlight, being center stage? And how do you balance that with eliciting what students think?

GD: This is the joy of the spotlight: being up front and pulling from students ideas they didn't know they had. It's not the spotlight of, "Let me tell you the truth." It's the spotlight of, "Watch us," but under my baton, just like a conductor, because I have thought through this. They articulate their positions as best they can and then I rearticulate those positions in ways that are more meaningful, more coherent, more connected to our readings. I help my students feel smarter. And they feel part of that process. For me, that's what's really exciting.

WMT: Rehearsal and direction are so central to any staged production. You mentioned the reference to an orchestra or a band conductor. How do you get feedback?

GD: That's why I invite my colleagues from the department in to observe my classes on a regular basis, almost every semester. Sometimes I'll have very specific things I want them to think about — for example, gender issues in the classroom or that nature of questioning. I urge my TAs to do this but they never do. I also take time out three or four times a semester to ask my classes, "How's it going folks? Give me some feedback." I very seldom get much but I sometimes do. I'm always looking for it. I don't rehearse much, except for the final day of class when I write a speech that celebrates what we've done for the semester, four to five minutes of praise and blame: what we've struggled with, our successes, and why it's been important. It's a way of summarizing the class, both intellectually and in terms of what it's meant for our sense of community. I redefine rhetoric, building it from the work we've done together. So I write this speech and rehearse it quite a bit.

WMT: So given your field and the work that goes into perfecting your craft, what do you say to colleagues in other disciplines who stick strictly to prepared notes, paying little attention to delivery or any connection with students?

GD: I move around a lot in class and try to generate some excitement about the material, but there are lots of other ways to operate. At core, I would urge them to demonstrate their commitment to the topic and to students as human beings. I knew a professor who sat during her classes — she had to — but cared so much about the material and so much about her students. Admittedly, her classes were small. But there's that triangle we spoke about earlier, the connection between student, material, and instructor. For her, it was a quiet intensity that also worked. I couldn't teach that way. And that may not work in a larger class. I think that what happens with boring instructors is that they refuse to take the risk to show their commitment to the material and to the students. And that's a risk I'm willing to take. I think all good teachers risk themselves. We go in and say, "I care about this, and if you laugh at me, that's going to hurt."

WMT: And from your discipline, can the quiet introvert who much prefers the library learn to play to the big hall?

GD: Absolutely! But that's a really important question in rhetorical studies. I think you can always get better. It may be that some instructors will never be the most compelling, but they can certainly get to the place where they're not boring. It's a matter of bringing more of themselves into their teaching and at the same time asking where the students are on this material. Our own excitement is not enough. What we bring has to be understandable to the students. Anybody who is willing to step outside their own shell can do that.

Eric Aoki

A professor of Speech Communication, Dr. Eric Aoki focuses more on identity issues and cross-cultural communication. Energetic and friendly, Eric is ever alert to student responses, reinforcing their ideas, and connecting them to course readings. His classes ask students to look deeply at their own issues, their sense of self in the context of diversity. Communication becomes that much more critical as the students learn how to navigate a bigger and more complex world.

Eric Aoki: If you look on top of my bookshelves you'll see some trophies. Those were for speech contests in sixth, seventh, and eighth grades, where I first got to speak about issues that intersected the personal and the public spheres — from topics like "who's your hero and why?" to war. There's an energy required to present your ideas, to do the research and pull materials together. I grew up in a farming area and talked to a lot of farmers who were passionate about issues. And that was my entry into an arena where you get up and build a voice for yourself, and you begin to understand how much strength and power and connection a voice can have with people.

William M. Timpson: So how do you balance this passion you bring for particular issues with a longstanding academic value for neutrality and objectivity?

EA: I can appreciate the attempt for objectivity we make about knowledge in our classrooms. That was the dominant paradigm for my own educational career. But for my graduate studies on the ethnography of communication — the stories that people tell — I began to get into an analysis of subjectivity and objectivity. So in my classes, I'll typically ask students to question, to be critical of the information I give them. I want my students to see that every course on this campus has a political agenda, and that we should talk about degrees of objectivity and subjectivity. I want to let students in my classes speak their "positionalities," as I describe it, their experiences.

WMT: So there's a lot of emphasis on self-disclosure?

EA: Yes. I want to expose my students to the multiplicity of identities we all represent. My students see me in suits. They see me in jeans. They see me in different cultural garb that I pick up as I travel the world. I try to show them that I am not a stagnant identity, that they cannot confine me to just one paradigm. I have many and different identities.

WMT: Have you ever come into class as a character to make a speech?

EA: Sure, there is a character there, but it's different from the theatrical version of "in character." It's tied to some aspect of my own identity.

WMT: So is authenticity important to you?

EA: I do think that there is some aspect of performance inherent in what I do, but it's not something I don't know how to play out. Coming "in character" would feel like a mocking of the issues so central to my courses — the politic of subjectivity and self-disclosure, of identity construction and multiplicity. I do not censor the multiplicity that I allow myself to play out, the freedom to be many things in class and perform many pieces of my identity. So students see a performance of many subjective identities on my part.

WMT: Observing you the other day, I noticed how alert you were to students who wanted to participate, how willing you were to share the stage. Is that the stage awareness actors describe?

EA: When I was in graduate school in Seattle, I used to go to an interactive theatre where those on stage often dissolved the stage and people in the audience became a part of that stage. That's closer to what my class is; it's an interactive stage, and every performance might be slightly different depending on who decides to participate. Thinking about my class this way, I also want to mention that my stage also includes my home, because I invite my students over for dinner once a semester in groups of four to five. I also invite students out on the town every so often. Whoever wants to join me is invited. They get to see me as more than just a presenter in class. I always wanted to bring in a more intimate feel, to break the walls of the classroom down a little bit, something you can get at a small liberal arts college. And I think that that helps them want to participate in class.

WMT: In the class I observed, you had students in a circle. In the theatre, some halls allow for a performance "in the round."

EA: The circle is very purposeful for me. I let students know from day one about my politics, my methodologies, my biases. They are aware of my rationale and motives. They know that, when I teach cultural content, the circle makes us more accountable because we're looking at each other. When we're sitting in that circle, it's harder to say something about another identity when you have to look other people in the eye. It's about taking responsibility for our discourse in the class. In straight rows, looking at each other's backs, it's easier to make a comment without having to assume that face-to-face responsibility.

WMT: You must be talking about a certain kind of engagement because, as instructors, we can certainly get a high level of engagement with audiences sitting in straight rows.

EA: Sure. My seniors will joke with me, "Hey, Eric, I got four or so pages of lecture notes this semester," because I give lots of mini- notes. Instead of lectures, my TA and I produce frequent summaries of key concepts as handouts, maybe fifteen across the semester, because I want the students fully engaged in the classroom conversation. I tell them they can take notes but, most of all, I want them to pay attention. That's the big thing for me.

WMT: In some ways it's a more demanding climate for students in that they have to make eye contact with their classmates all the time. It's harder to retreat, to be private. Do you help students with the skills they need to function effectively in your kind of class?

EA: Yeah. We break down into smaller groups and that changes the degree of engagement as well. And we talk about communication because that's what we do in this department. I let them know that, for example, talking in a public setting is very different from talking one-on-one. Comfort and engagement can really vary.

WMT: Talk about timing and what you notice when you teach.

EA: It takes me about a half-hour to walk to campus, so I'll use that time to think about key issues for an upcoming class. And because I focus on issues, time is really a non-issue. This semester we've gone overtime because we've been deep into some issue and didn't even realize that class time was up.

WMT: What about the subtleties of time — slowing down for an important point that requires more reflection, or speeding up when things get exciting?

EA: I give them certain indicators at the beginning of class so that they can tell me if they need me to repeat something or slow down. I did a survey at the very beginning of one class and found out what kind of learners they were. A lot of students are "hearing" learners, and that sort of prompts me about what I can and can't do in class. In other classes I get more "visual" learners and, guess what, I'm at the board more. Those are the kinds of assessments I look for in terms of speech communication—an audience analysis—and that's what then prompts me to do what I do.

WMT: Talk about props.

EA: For me, it's all those things that can infuse a welcoming, inclusive, liberal arts kind of climate in my class. I'll bring in cookies, or we'll go to the Student Center and I'll buy them coffee or hot chocolate. The basic "Fs" of culture are *food, folklore,* and *festivities* — so food can be a wonderful "prop" for building a sense of community in class. When I share some British biscuits, that also says something cross-culturally.

WMT: Feedback and coaching: you've gotten your share through speech competitions.

EA: I've had such wonderful role models, such helpful mentoring and encouragement as I've worked to find my voice and identity as a teacher, a scholar, and an individual. At the University of Washington we had television cameras in our classrooms, and I'd often have them on and recording. My mentor would then spend many hours with me going over these tapes, looking at my body posture, my conversations, my use of material, the boards.

WMT: That's part of the tradition of speech communication — that you, as the speaker, are part of the speech.

EA: For example, this mentor would note how often I had my hands in my pockets in class, and comment on the sense of power I was projecting, the distance from my students. Now I do the same thing with my own graduate students. I ask them to videotape one or two classes, and then we sit down and review them together. I've had lots of visitors this semester, and I like encouraging that because I get so much value from the feedback. I like a system in which we're not afraid to do what we do no matter who shows up. I know that teaching well is tough, that it requires different energies and skills. I'm always interested in keeping it fresh, in learning something new.

WMT: Let's talk about what performers refer to as "set." One of your classes meets in a windowless, cinderblock, poster-less, off-white-colored room. What effect does that have on you and your students?

EA: My students notice it right away. They ask why we have to be in such dark places. That's when breaking down the teacher-student barriers becomes so important. So we talk about it, and that's why we end up holding some classes in the Student Center or out back in that amphitheatre-like space. That's why I like to have students over to my house.

WMT: So what would an ideal classroom space be for you?

EA: I like the new media some classes have — the projection systems, for example. I love showing movies on big screens; it has such a different effect. But I also like movable chairs because we do so many small-group activities. And good lighting makes a difference. I like windows and natural light. I'd also like different colors in the room, and posters. I've asked for these kinds of things but it just hasn't happened. So my hopes for something have been squelched. As another example, we made good use of bulletin boards in one class for displaying student work or pointing out study abroad opportunities that were being advertised. It's sad, though, that, in general, our classrooms are so sterile. Yet elementary classrooms are alive with color and postings.

WMT: I'm afraid it's partially about becoming adults — some kind of industrial mentality, keeping our heads down and focused on our work. As students move up through the grade levels and on into college, we seem to lose sight of some of the "softer" but no less important aspects of learning — what supports morale or stimulates creativity.

EA: I tell my students that many great speeches have taken place outside formal halls — in public squares, on soapboxes. In my office, I've almost overcorrected, plastering an entire wall with images and messages from magazines. If a student comes in searching for a topic I say, "Look at this wall for a few minutes and then let's talk."

Final Thoughts

Despite testimonials from gifted teachers like Moore, Mitchell, Dickinson, and Aoki, this mixing of performance and teaching may irritate some in higher education. Especially on those campuses where research is pre-eminent, interest in teaching may have limited career benefits. Those who receive awards for their teaching may even be viewed somewhat suspiciously as winners of "popularity contests." Accordingly, a focus on the performance skills of teachers might seem doubly dangerous, even heretical, especially for younger faculty on the tortuous tenure track.

Be that as it may, we still argue that every instructor can find something of value in this book. Whether you want to improve your own delivery or do more to inspire students, whether you want to engage students in critical and creative thinking or deepen their learning, we think you'll gain much from studying the place of performance skills and practice in teaching. Moreover, Suzanne and I both work at research universities, and we've found many ways to take our interests here and parlay them into articles, conference presentations, research, and now this book!

Ultimately, each of us has to be able to look in the mirror and feel good about our work as instructors. Can we improve? Do our students deserve better? We're convinced that performing skills can go far to help you sharpen your delivery, energize your teaching, and motivate and challenge your students. Break a leg!

Foreword from the Stage

Suzanne Burgoyne

I met Bill Timpson through the Kellogg National Fellowship program, a three-year fellowship for leadership training and interdisciplinary studies. The program is based on the philosophy that, as contemporary civilization demands increasingly focused specialization, it also requires leaders with a generalist perspective — leaders who have a view of the "whole picture" and can communicate across disciplinary boundaries. Each year, the Kellogg Foundation selected a class of forty to fifty mid-career professionals, from a variety of fields, who attended bi-annual seminars on such topics as public policy, technology, and change. The individual fellows also pursued independent study projects that took them outside their primary fields of specialization. Bill and I were Class II Fellows from 1981 to 1984.

I came to the program as a theatre professional interested in exploring how theatre techniques could be used for pedagogy in other fields. As an education professional with an interest in performance, Bill had already done work applying performance methodology to teacher training. With Bill's encouragement, I eventually developed "teaching as performance" workshops for faculty on my home campus and elsewhere. Together, Bill and I presented workshops for Kellogg Fellowship gatherings. In them we employed theatre-based methods to examine the particular social issues being considered in the seminar.

My belief that theatre has contributions to make in addressing the many challenges facing our civilization led me to apply for the fellowship. One of the problems inherent in over-specialization, however, is that people outside a given field usually don't know much about what's actually going on in that field — and they often hold stereotypical images of the field and its practitioners. Theatre, in particular, falls prey to such misunderstandings. When I applied for the Kellogg Fellowship, one of the interviewers asked, "Are you sure you're not just a frustrated actress?" And at the first meeting of Class II, a member of the advisory committee told me, "When we were planning this fellowship program, it never occurred to us that a theatre person might have something to contribute."

As Pineau points out, the prejudice against theatre also rears its ugly head whenever anyone suggests that theatre might have something to contribute to "the very serious business of education" (1994, 5). Pineau observes that "the ideology of American formal education has been constructed largely on models of technology, industry, and corporate bureaucracy" (1994, 4). Thus, analogies between teaching and the performing arts provoke disgruntled "critics such as Ralph Smith (1979) to claim that 'if the acting analogy were carried to its logical extreme, a teacher who took it seriously would never have to understand anything'" (Pineau 1994, 7).

Certainly those of us investigating the relationship between teaching and the performing arts have never advocated that the teacher become a "mere entertainer" in the classroom. Furthermore, Smith's comment reveals a naïveté about what a good actor actually does. In order to portray a role, an actor (like a teacher) engages in research, studying the historical period in which the play is set and the social, political, and cultural factors that influence the character. During rehearsal, the actors and director explore the characters' interactions with each other and with their environment — by acting them out.

By the time of the performance, actors can be convincing in their portrayals because their understanding of the play — and of why their characters act as they do — has moved from the intellectual to the experiential plane; the research has been assimilated and embodied by the actor. While an actor does acquire specific vocal and physical skills that enhance communication (and the teacher, too, can benefit from such training), the technical skills are not the heart of the actor's art any more than they are of the teacher's pedagogy. The heart of the actor's art has to do with a lifelong exploration of the nature of the human condition (Miller 1967, Bates 1987) — a "very serious business" indeed.

So why does the prejudice against theatre persist? Certainly, media hype perpetuates stereotypical and negative images of performers. The prejudice against theatre, however, has a long history, which Jonas Barish traces in *The Anti-Theatrical Prejudice* and calls "a kind of ontological malaise" (1981, 2). Studying manifestations of the prejudice in philosophers from Plato to Nietzsche, Barish observes that the actor is often equated with the liar — someone pretending to be what he or she is not. Even more fundamental to the problem, Barish argues, is that the protean actor, capable of transforming himself or herself into someone else, raises doubts about the stability of human identity.

For philosophers like Plato who advocate a stable society with everyone firmly implanted in fixed social roles, theatre is dangerous because the actor's ability to change roles suggests that other people, too, could change. Plato envisioned a highly specialized society, based on a "monolithic theory of personality ... [which] reduces each man to a single well-defined entity, firmly linked to his social role" (Barish 1981, 21, 23), and the ideal of an all-powerful state, which would form the characters of its citizens through education. As Barish points out, for Plato, individual freedom "carries the seeds of diversity and hence of disruption" (1991, 20).

In Plato's view, *mimesis* (imitation, theatre) is a powerful educational tool and must be controlled by the state. Believing that people become what they imitate, Plato would prohibit students from acting in roles other than those of persons of their own social and professional class, sex, and "moral outlook" (Barish 1981, 21). The educational system must suppress "anything in the intellectual diet that encourages freedom, curiosity, or exploration ..., [including] the whole realm of unstructured play, of spontaneous self-discovery, of casual and random improvisation" (1981, 19, 22). Students must not discover the possibility that they might become anything other than what the state has predetermined they should be.

While modern critics dismiss theatre as "mere entertainment," not "serious business," Plato wanted to banish the dramatic poet from his utopian Republic precisely because he viewed the theatre as a potent instrument of change, and thus a threat to social stability. Furthermore, Barish (1981, 8) observes, "The poets were being inflated into the rivals of the philosophers as the basis for intellectual training." Ironically, Plato testified to his belief in the power of drama by couching his attack on it in the form of a drama — a dialogue.

Whereas the ideal of stable societies and identities may offer an appealing image of security, that ideal was undermined in the twentieth century by new discoveries in all fields, by the ever-accelerating change that accompanies rapid technological development, and by an intense probing into the nature of human identity. Phenomenologist Bruce Wilshire (1982) argues that theatre serves as a laboratory for identity, necessary to the process of individuation for audiences and actors alike. Like Plato, Wilshire (1982, 230) proposes that theatre can stimulate change: "Theatre is an art which reaches out to encompass and thematize possibilities of personality change within the remarkably commodious matrix of identity of self."

In the twenty-first century, rapid change and self-conscious questioning of identity may promote the phenomenon noted by Wilshire, Barish, and others (see, for instance, Pineau 1994, and Abel 1963) that theatricality:

> seems increasingly to have become a major theme of our own culture....As the ancient distrust of the stage itself seems on the point of dissolving, the fascination with life seen under the aspect of theatre seems also to have become a central preoccupation of literature, philosophy, psychology, and sociology, not to mention the stage itself. (Barish 1981, 3)

Contemporary analogies between life and theatre contain dangers as well as possibilities. Wilshire (1982, xvi), for instance, critiques the use of the life-as-theatre metaphor in the social sciences insofar as he finds the metaphor tainted by the anti-theatrical prejudice:

> When we deliberately transfer the notion of role playing to off-stage life we carry with us, smuggled in, the notion of the fictionality of the actor's portrayal...we come dimly to believe that what we're doing offstage is an illicit version of what the actor is doing legitimately onstage, and so we attempt to flee our guilt and our responsibility for our unavoidable 'role playing.' This is a sort of schizophrenia that I think increasingly characterizes persons in our culture.

Barish (1981, 473) also acknowledges psychological dangers in the loss of a felt sense of stable identity, not the least of which is a reactionary "retreat into narrowness and fundamentalism." Drawing on existentialist philosophy, Barish suggests that if we are to "act" authentically on a world stage, we must choose to create our own characters instead of accepting the roles thrust upon us by others: "In this view, the intrinsic theatricality of our being leaves room for heroic possibilities" (1981, 476).

Futurists warn us that we must expect the pace of change to continue to accelerate. In "Our Medium Is Our Message: Potentials for Educational Theatre," Swanson (1980) cites Alvin Toffler (1974) in suggesting that theatre training offers one the means for learning to cope with the future. Borrowing the language of management, Swanson argues that educational theatre trains students to function well in ad hoc organizations, in which a group forms to perform a particular task (in the case of educational theatre, to put on a play) and then disbands. Furthermore, theatre students change roles and tasks from production to production; not only do actors change characters, but an actor in one performance may become a technical crew member in the next. Such experiences prepare students to deal with a changing world in which they may need to switch careers several times.

Pointing out that most educational systems imitate the structure of the manufacturing model, Swanson (1980, 63) proposes that "students are experientially programmed toward an intolerance of change by the regimented organization of schools." He cites a pilot study that was developed to test the impact of theatre on individuals, working from the concept of Milton Rokeach that people tend to be closed-minded (dogmatic or rigid) or open-minded (adaptable). Students were tested in order to discover whether one term's theatre experience would promote more adaptability than the regular classroom experience. The results of the pretests suggested that "students in regular classrooms became more rigid (less able to change)," while "theatre students became more open (more able to cope with change), strongly suggesting that theatre may be one important means of teaching students to cope with change" (Swanson 1980, 64).

In an era when organizational specialists attempt to train managers to function effectively in an environment of change, Swanson(1980, 64) notes the irony that:

> While businessmen are condemning theatre in schools as a luxury or a frill, their consultants are using techniques based on role playing, scenarios, and simulations (we [in theatre] call them "improvisations"). Many of the techniques for management and organizational development are thus adapted from theatre.

Not all change is positive, of course, and it would be as dangerous for educators to teach students to adapt unquestioningly to change as it would be to teach them to acquiesce unquestioningly to any current social order. Nor do I mean to suggest that theatre has all the answers. Debates about methodology, pedagogy, and goals abound in theatre, as in other disciplines. I do, however, mean to suggest that theatre is more than "mere entertainment," and that critiques of the contributions theatre can make to education often suffer from the distortions of the anti-theatrical prejudice and/or from lack of familiarity with current developments in the discipline.

For instance, McLaren posits three types of educators: the teacher-as-liminal-servant, the teacher-as-entertainer, and the teacher-as-hegemonic-overlord. Basing his discussion of the second type upon the separation of actors and audience and the presumed passivity of the latter, McLaren (1988, 165) critiques the teacher-as-entertainer:

> When students were actively engaged by the instructor but... remained isolated and unreflective viewers of the action, then the students were in the process of being entertained. The classroom was transformed into a theatre and the students constituted an audience. In this instance, the teacher assumed an entertainment role: as a propagandist—or, even worse, an evangelist—for dominant cultural, economic, or ethical interests.

While theatre can indeed function as a means of reinforcing hegemonic structures — and the new historiographers among theatre historians are busily analyzing how certain theatres have served that purpose (see, for instance, Postlewait and McConachie 1989) — performances can also critique a dominant social order and provide alternative role models and imagined futures (e.g., Hornby 1986).

The issue of the audience's relationship to the performance provides a fertile field of debate and experimentation within the discipline of theatre, and it is precisely within this arena that theatre may have the most to contribute to classroom pedagogy. How "unreflective" is an audience member? Drawing upon "reader response" theory, some scholars view the spectator as an active participant in the construction of meaning. Major twentieth-century theatrical theorist/practitioners from Brecht (1964) to Grotowski (1968) have sought means to jolt the spectator out of passivity and into active engagement.

Experiments with the arrangement of the theatrical space, from arena and thrust stages to environmental theatre, have explored the impact of spatial organization on audience/performance relationships. Theatre artists committed to social change often seek to involve audiences actively in the creation of the performance. For instance, Augusto Boal

(1979) has developed his method of "Theatre of the Oppressed," building upon Paulo Freire's (1970) *Pedagogy of the Oppressed.* Employing theatre games and role play, Boal helps audience members — whom he calls "spect-actors," — discover the nature of their oppression and empower themselves to overcome that oppression.

In order for our educational system to remain vital, disciplines must not become the narrow, rigid, carefully separated specialties that Plato envisioned. Systems theorists point out that closed systems, which "operate in relative isolation from the environment," usually "continue to operate in the same way in spite of environmental changes," and thus "suffer entropy — death from internal chaos." Open systems, on the other hand, are "in constant contact with [their] environment," and thus are "adaptive to environmental needs" (Swanson 1980, 62).

Things do change. Since Bill Timpson and I wrote the first edition of this book, more scholars and educators have been giving the relationship between teaching and performing serious consideration. Seymour Sarason, a Yale University professor emeritus of psychology, has devoted an entire book, *Teaching as a Performing Art*, to the subject. Arguing that teachers, like performers, should seek to engage their audiences on emotional as well as intellectual levels in order to promote meaningful and lasting learning, Sarason (1999, 54) concludes, "We [educators] have a lot to learn from those who are part of training programs in the conventional performing arts."

Whereas Sarason approaches the topic from a theoretical point of view, Jyl Lynn Felman, a women's studies professor at Brandeis University, takes an autobiographical stance in *Never a Dull Moment: Teaching and the Art of Performance* (2001), in which she describes her own teaching strategies derived from her view of the classroom as theatre. Gail Burnaford and David Hobson (2001), espousing four emerging paradigms for teachers in the new millennium, discuss the teacher as artist, along with the teacher as pedagogical researcher, navigator of technology, and collaborative learner. And, fortunately for me, the Carnegie Academy for the Scholarship of Teaching and Learning included the performing arts (though not the fine arts) in their select list of disciplines eligible for the PEW Carnegie fellowship program. At the first meeting of my interdisciplinary cohort of 2000-2001 Carnegie Scholars, Carnegie Foundation President Lee Shulman shared with me his belief that theatre folk indeed have contributions to make to the improvement of teaching.

Just as Bill and I continue to learn from each other's disciplinary perspectives, we hope you'll find our suggestions about the intersections between theatre and education stimulating to your own growth as a teacher. Much of actor training, though based upon theory, is conducted through active, experiential learning methods. We've included numerous exercises in this book; we encourage you to try them. We ask you to peruse these pages with an open mind—and not to succumb to the anti-theatrical prejudice.

Introduction

Teaching at the college or university level requires expertise and planning. Great teachers add energy, excitement, and sensitivity to the mix. Most teachers work in isolation, developing their skills through periodic feedback from students, both formal and informal, as well as their own intuitive feel and desire to improve. A few instructors actively seek feedback and direction from peers and other sources. Yes, great teachers are born and, yes, great teachers are made, but it's rather pointless to try to untangle the exact contribution of each. Every great teacher combines natural talents with skills developed along the way, attentiveness to student learning and an eagerness to improve.

And so it is with great actors. Training, direction, and regular feedback combine with natural gifts, alertness to audience reactions, and personal motivation to make performances memorable. Having worked with these ideas since the late 1970s, we believe that the performing arts contain methods and concepts that can help any teacher grow and help good teachers become great ones. Whatever discipline you represent, whether you teach regularly or only occasionally, lessons from the stage can help you increase your own self-awareness, sharpen your delivery, engage your students and audiences more effectively, and, ultimately, create deeper learning and promote critical and creative thinking.

Expertise and preparation are essential starting points for teaching in higher education, but an energetic delivery and the creative use of classroom time and resources can help you inspire your students. Indeed, even the best of lecture notes cannot guarantee learning when you're uninspired or you come to class prepared only to read your notes. In *What Students Really Think of Professors*, an analysis of class evaluation forms,

Linda Jackson and Michael Murray (1997, 80) include a chapter on the teacher as performer, observing that students applaud instructor enthusiasm as a motivator of learning, and chide professors whose lectures lack "umph." Drawing from our own training and experiences and that of the many teachers with whom we've worked on various campuses, we hope to offer you fresh insights into the art and science of effective instruction, as well as new designs for more engaging learning experiences.

Parallels Between the Classroom and the Stage

Teaching and performing are live public performances in which delivery, engagement, and feedback matter. Both require prior preparation. Indeed, effective teaching can be measured by some of the same basic criteria used to evaluate performers: Could the teacher be heard? seen? Was the material well organized? Did it hold together and make sense? Did the teacher's timing increase student engagement? Did the teacher make good use of the classroom space and other available resources? How did the teacher respond to the audience? Developing a sustained analogy between teacher and performer in *Teaching as a Performing Art*, Seymour Sarason (1999, 9) observes that we make certain assumptions about the performer:

- That "the artist wants to perform."

- That the performer "has rehearsed for the occasion."

- "That the artist will give his or her 'all' to the performance and will not leave us with the impression that he or she has gone through the motions, relatively devoid of personal feeling or involvement."

Can students make the same assumptions about their professors?

Good teaching is more than giving information. In this day of desktop publishing and Internet resources, class notes are easily updated, reproduced, and made available to students to copy; put on reserve at the library; or included on a course web site. Why not use class time for interactions, debates, discussions, questions, role plays, activities, opportunities to practice new skills — all meaningful ways to develop students' talents? Few members of the general public would attend performances during which scripts are merely read. They want more, and so do students. Great teachers use many of the skills of great performers to bring their lecture notes — their "scripts" — to life.

Instruction and Entertainment

Resistance to the notion that performers have anything substantial to offer teachers is understandable. "I'm not an entertainer," a professor might protest. Arthur Frank (1995, 29) mocks, justifiably, "the recent remarks of Alberta's former Education Minister, who wanted lectures given by professors to be replaced by videos scripted by academics but delivered by professional actors." Trained and rewarded as subject area experts, many professors bristle when judged on delivery. Except, perhaps, for a public speaking course, few have had formal training in presentation skills. Some even dismiss teaching popularity as pandering to students, and as valuing form over substance and entertainment over instruction.

Student learning, however, should top any list on teaching effectiveness. To succeed in stimulating student growth, we contend, requires more than subject matter expertise. It requires some mastery of delivery — more so in large classes — as well as skill in engaging the minds and hearts of students, in challenging them to consider new possibilities and rethink old ideas, in helping them learn better how to learn your subject.

While instructors who want to remain narrowly defined solely as subject matter experts may find such ideas threatening, others will embrace lessons from the stage that can help them develop new ways to engage students — or any other audience. With training, practice, and a commitment to ongoing feedback, you'll make rapid progress, we can confidently assure you. As a student and now as an instructor, you already have a wealth of classroom experience upon which to draw. Reflecting on his own experiences and observations of teaching, Sarason (1999, 4) points out:

> Resistance to changing one's style of performing the role is the constant enemy of deepening understanding of the role. The burned out teacher tends to be one whose performance has been routinized, like an actor in a long-running play who once "lived" the role but now goes through the motions.

Performance Anxiety and Fun

One common fear for most of us involves public speaking, an unavoidable hazard for teachers. Members of the general public often find the prospect of being up in front of any group, especially a large one, intimidating or even terrifying. Similar anxieties arise for performers. In a recent article in the journal *Pedagogy*, Princeton University English professor Elaine Showalter (2001) describes reading a book on stage fright to enhance her confidence. For performers — and teachers — a key strategy is to learn how to channel energy and feelings in a constructive direction, a process that can turn debilitating anxiety into useful motivation.

The flip side to stage fright, as Showalter observes, is the joy of performing: "Appearing before an audience is in some sense being nurtured and fed by them" (2001, 450). Excitement can come from the interaction between performer and audience, whether you're working through complex material or probing understanding, connecting different viewpoints or citing relevant sources, telling stories of discovery and dead ends or noting shifting paradigms, correcting misconceptions or answering questions, reminding people of old truths or inspiring those people with new insights. The energy exchange can be thrilling for you and your students alike.

The Making of Teachers and Actors

Because instructors are "born" *and* "made," each of us has the potential to improve. Some of us may come blessed with more "natural" talents — for example, a resonant voice, clear diction, ease with physical movements, or the ability to think easily on our feet. The great ones among us, however, also have a will to improve and perfect their craft — an openness to feedback, additional professional training, practice. And so it is with great actors. As Sarason (1999, 136-137) observes:

> Among the major attractions of the career is that there will always be challenges and self-testing, diversity of roles, new learning....[The] performer has to take lifelong learning seriously. Self-improvement is the name of the game.

In one regard, however, the traditions of the classroom and the stage differ remarkably. Unlike performers, instructors typically work in isolation from each other. By contrast, actors, dancers, and musicians routinely rehearse under the watchful eye of a director, choreographer, or conductor. Feedback is immediate and frequent. New ideas are rehearsed over and over again. As this book unfolds, you will read repeated nudges from us about the benefits of feedback, support, and assistance from your peers. Borrowing a phrase from the theatre, we hope you can "suspend your own disbelief" and experiment with some of the ideas we offer.

Cross-Fertilization and Creativity

We believe that viewing your teaching through the eyes of the performer will give you fresh insights as well as ideas for improvement. The study of creativity, for instance, demonstrates the benefits of cross-fertilization and incubation. Breakthroughs often result when the mind's focus is elsewhere: Jean Piaget developed his notions of a developmental hierarchy in learning and cognition after formal studies in biology and philosophy; James Watson came to his groundbreaking work in behavioral psychology from a career in business; and Albert Einstein wrote some of his most important papers in mathematics while working at the patent office in Vienna.

Plan of the Book

We begin your journey by comparing the requirements for planning and performance that instructors and actors face. Each must do substantial amounts of "homework," and this process demands one set of skills — among them research, study, organization, and preparation. Yet, in class and on stage, other skills become crucial as well. We want to help you see the parallels. We then revisit the lecture and the discussion as mainstays of instruction. In these teaching modes, we propose that lessons from the stage can guide you toward fresh ideas for better engaging students, and for challenging them to think, consider new possibilities, and develop new skills.

In Chapter Five, we explore energy, creativity, and spontaneity, all qualities that are central to the vitality of instruction. Since performers also need these attributes, performance training offers methods that you too can use to develop them. While volumes have been written about the value of behavioral objectives for teachers, for example, few resources exist to guide teachers toward essential subjective qualities. We agree with Sarason's (1999, 105) argument that:

> The teacher is more than a mechanical conduit of information, but rather is a stage setter who seeks to get the actors to use themselves and their experience to make the substance of the script a part of their psychological bloodstream; the script has to become propelling, believable, personal, not a routinized, impersonal experience the consequences of which enter the file-and-forget category of experience.

In the following two chapters, we argue for the place of "drama" in both the development of thinking and discovery learning. Finally, we end the book by identifying and describing a range of exercises and scenes for study — material for ongoing practice.

Come along, then. The bell has rung. The curtain is rising. The lights come up. We know you'll find this adventure challenging and rewarding, much like the experience we seek for students. Enjoy!

Chapter 1:
Planning and Performance

Higher education requires instructors to be skillful in both planning and performance, in preparation of organized class notes as well as in delivery of engaging instruction. The contrasts between these two areas are striking. While planning requires study and quiet reflection, teaching is active and often interactive, even pressured. While planning builds upon years of schooling and experience, teaching focuses on the present, the "here and now," and typically accommodates a wide range of factors, from the expected to the unpredictable.

For example, student questions and comments can run the gamut from the predictable—"Will this be on the exam?"—to the personal—"What do you think?"—to the blunt—"Do we have to come to class?" In many classrooms, chairs are bolted to the floor, but in some you may find them scattered all over the room. Occasionally, you may have to scramble when equipment malfunctions.

Think for a moment about the contrasts between planning and performance. Most instructors work quite independently on their plans for class, often at their offices, but also at home or in the library. Yet teaching itself is highly interdependent, a function of the relationships you have with your students and the learning experiences you can design and facilitate. While planning tends to be private, teaching is intensely public and, at times, in front of critical audiences of "paying customers." While you may have a great deal of flexibility about your planning—when, where and how—you must meet your classes at set times. *The show must go on.* Planning enables you to conceptualize and manage your classes effectively, especially in large classes where you may supervise teaching assistants or coordinate guest lecturers and the grading of exams. Performing allows you to improvise, to adapt to what's happening in the class, to seize the "teachable moment."

In sum, successful teaching requires skill in both planning and performance. You must come prepared as the expert yet ready to think on your feet. Actors prepare by analyzing their characters, doing research, learning their lines and movement; this intense preparation frees them to live "in the moment," making discoveries through focusing on their partners, reacting spontaneously to what other actors do. The excitement of live performance arises from the interaction between human beings onstage. In her discussion of teaching as a performing art, Felman (2001, 158) emphasizes the relationship between planning and performing for teachers:

> The pedagogy of improvisation is not a breeze, something to substitute when you haven't had the time to prepare properly. On the contrary, good, effective improv only follows good, effective preparation....without an assiduous command of the material and an ability to synthesize and create on the spot, the improvisation itself becomes merely an irreverent and professionally irresponsible response to the technical demands of teaching. Although some educators are more adept at improvisation than others, it remains a skill with specific techniques to be honed and learned through practice.

Unfortunately, instructors in higher education rarely receive formal training in the performance aspects of their teaching. Actors, dancers, and singers, however, come from traditions which systematically address both planning and performance. In this chapter, we want merely to suggest lessons teachers can learn from performers. In later chapters we will go into increasing depth.

Individuals are selected for permanent positions in higher education for their capacities as experts — and at universities, in particular, for their potential as scholars, researchers, grant writers and managers. Rewards at the research campuses have long been skewed heavily toward publications and grants. Yet the pressures to teach well are also growing. Lessons from the stage, we believe, can give even the most dedicated scholars new ideas, concrete practices and techniques, for translating subject matter expertise into dynamic, engaging instruction and thus enhanced learning.

Commonly, instructors draw on their training and experiences to begin planning long in advance of their first class meeting. They may have to research an area if it involves new material or catch up on other reading to stay current with the field. They may also have to select a text or create a class reader. They certainly have to think through that semester's requirements and assignments, matching announced dates and deadlines with the campus calendar. Yet, all too often, competing demands require a different kind of response; at times, you may end up pulling out old class notes and dusting them off shortly before class. On such occasions, while the course material itself seems substantially the same, you may find your own enthusiasm waning after repeated offerings.

Like teachers, performers also begin to plan long before a production debuts. Once the show is cast, formal rehearsals start and preparation becomes increasingly intense. Even for nonprofessional productions, six weeks seem necessary. Because these nonprofessionals (95% of performers are not paid) are typically obligated to jobs and families, they perform in addition to those responsibilities. Consequently, they must squeeze three to four rehearsal hours daily out of their evening and weekend schedules for a six week period, with even more time needed closer to opening.

The performer doesn't have a captive audience. Audiences must be courted, built. How demoralizing to put countless hours and a lot of work into rehearsals over several weeks and play to an empty house. Lackluster performances simply will not do. A lot is at stake; every performer must take personal responsibility to come prepared, energized, focused and fit for every show. Don't teachers also have the responsibility to give their best to their audiences?

Whatever your own area of expertise, and whatever the importance of your planning and enthusiasm, we want to draw on our own experiences with performers to offer the following suggestions:

- Be aware of the conditions that allow you to be most productive when you're planning.

- Schedule time to review past classes and rethink what you'll do in the next semester.

- Once the semester does begin, take a few minutes before each class and focus on your physical readiness with some simple exercises that get your heart rate and energy up.

- You can also quiet yourself and remember moments when you felt especially excited about the material, paying careful attention to the details of those memories, the classroom itself, your actions, even your attire. Once you re-experience these moments, note the accompanying feelings and try to bring them with you to the class session.

- Put reminders in your notes to rev up your energy level, and to move more to animate a particular point or stir up a lively discussion.

- Get to class early and set up so that you're able to begin class right on time. Convey a sense of urgency about what you want to accomplish, about achieving all you have planned.

- Be ambitious about what you want to accomplish during each class period so that your expectations can fuel your own sense of urgency.

- Observe other classes and chat with colleagues about their approaches to preparation and performing.

Warm-Up

For actors, getting ready for a role or even for rehearsal is quite different from getting ready for a performance. When planning, actors must research their characters, learn their lines, and speculate about their characters' possible motivations or relationships with the other characters. Once the production is at hand, however, warm-up becomes much more serious, intense, and focused. Here, actors must make a conscious transition to get into the characters they will portray. This metamorphosis inevitably requires intellectual, emotional, and physical *warm-up*. Using the "green room" behind a stage to concentrate and to begin moving and interacting in character, and reviewing lines and cues, are essential practices for most actors.

Although you may not think of them as warm-ups, you probably have your own idiosyncratic routines that help you prepare for and perform in your class sessions. When planning, for example, you may reserve certain days and times for writing at home or for research at the library. You may need quiet and focus to be most productive. You may need your references, your word processor, or a copy machine close at hand. Like many of us, you may need at least one good jolt of java to get yourself going.

For teaching, you warm up in quite different ways. You may like to review your notes right up until class, spending most of your time on the content, trying to get the wording just right or the ideas to fit within the allotted time period. You probably take little if any time for emotional or physical preparation. Given our experiences with performers, we suggest the following strategies that will help you warm up for each teaching session:

- Be aware of what you need to be efficient, productive, and creative, whether you are researching a topic or getting ready to teach.

- For an upcoming class, review the names of your students so that the class time can have a more personal feel. If the class is large, remind yourself to learn a few new names each day and to use the names you do know. A periodic role call can tell you who's present and give you a chance to practice names.

- Reflect on the dynamics of previous classes and what you could do differently to improve them in future sessions.

- Put your notes aside and get physically ready for class. A few stretching exercises can do wonders to loosen your muscles and release pent up tension. Humming can warm up your voice so that you minimize strain and you become primed to provide more vocal variety. Using a favorite song can help lift your mood and put you into a better frame of mind. *Just whistle while you work!*

Lesson Plans and Scripts

You write your notes in advance of class just as scripts are secured long before any "performance." However, instructors can depart from their "script" at any moment, to pick up on a particularly good question, to review a troubling concept or spark a discussion, to tie into something in the news that day. Consequently, they must come to class fully prepared but alert to student needs, in much the same way that actors improvise.

Lessons from the stage can prove useful. Consider the following: First, to perform well, actors must memorize their lines and cues. Second, performers often make extensive use of the margins of their scripts for notes and reminders to themselves. Third, actors take time to get into character, to add physical and emotional preparation to their review of the scripts. Otherwise, productions run the risk of being wooden, a series of recited lines instead of the kind of dialogue that appears "believable" to audiences.

For teachers, then, we recommend the following:

- Know your material well enough so that you can address your students directly and make eye contact with them. This will allow you to notice students who seem lost, or those who may be drifting off. It will also free you from enslavement to the podium, permitting you to roam freely around the class. Your proximity to students can make a difference. "Overlearning" your material can give you a great deal of freedom to create spontaneous and engaging learning experiences.

- Give yourself wide margins on your notes so that you can jot down reminders to yourself.

- Again, we remind you to put your plans aside just before class and allow yourself some time to concentrate on your physical and emotional readiness.

- Reflect on what you do differently. Check with students about their reactions. Plan to give these changes a longer run and see how effective they are over several class sessions. Theatre work involves trial and error, and performers learn quickly to be aggressive about taking risks. Consider doing the same thing yourself.

Roles

For teachers and performers, getting ready for a production may differ greatly from what you need to do once class begins or the curtain goes up. Preparation requires study, reflection and training. Once you find yourself on the classroom or theater stage, however, different roles come into play.

Instructors in class have extensive, varied, and complex role demands — ever changing, shifting and blending. As grader, you play the judge. When you handle logistical decisions, you play the manager. When students are in crisis, you may play the counselor. When students struggle to understand despite your best efforts, you may have to shift gears, play magician and pull completely new ideas out of your hat.

From our experiences on the stage, we recommend the following strategies:

- Be conscious of the varied roles you must play. Awareness alone can make a huge difference. Perhaps different hats, real or imagined, can help you make the shifts required. Each role may have a different look and emotion — a "thinking" hat for pauses; an "investigator's" hat for when asking questions or probing students' understanding; another hat that lets you speak clearly; and yet another hat for facilitating group discussions. Being conscious of your "writing" hat may, then, help you shift gears when out of class, signaling to others when you are busy and not available.

- Talk with respected colleagues about the roles they play. Observe them in their classes to see those roles in action.

- Write out the requirements for these roles so that you can be more clear and focused about each.

- Seek feedback from others — colleagues and students in particular — about your effectiveness in the various roles you play.

- Read. Take classes. Join relevant discussion groups on the Internet. Make your own professional and personal development a high priority. Invest in yourself.

Movements and Blocking

Your movements — or lack thereof — constitute what the performer thinks of as *blocking*. On stage, the blocking required for a production is carefully plotted far in advance, refined in rehearsal, and then practiced until all movements appear easy and natural. Once the curtain rises, directors and actors expect to remain faithful to their plans. Unlike the classroom, there's no place for spontaneous improvisation on stage unless some slip-up happens — a line gets dropped or a cue missed, and everyone must scramble to cover the mistake.

In class what you do physically can add or detract from what you say and impact what students learn. However, preparing for physical engagement and following through are two very different challenges. Before class begins, you can make notations about blocking in the margins of your class notes. For instance, if you want to add variety and break your dependence on the lectern, you can remind yourself to move toward a student when a question arises — you might create a more personalized conversation from which others can learn. If a discussion develops, you might want to cross to the middle of the room.

Note the different "feel" when you do break your usual pattern. Reflect on it. Put your thoughts in writing. How do you think students will react? Ask them? Or take a few minutes and have them write their reactions. You will benefit from the feedback and they will appreciate your concern for their learning. Indeed, we believe that eagerness for feedback is one of the major lessons teachers can draw from the stage.

That's the planning side of it; now what happens once class begins? At times you will have to leave your prepared notes and interact more spontaneously. You can discipline yourself to become more aware of your movements and how they may impact students and learning. You develop your *metacognitive abilities, a split consciousness* that allows you to watch yourself while you teach, a skill which performers must hone to succeed on stage. With training, experience, practice and concentration, actors become quite proficient. So can you. Timpson's (1999) *Metateaching and the Instructional Map* offers more on this notion.

For example, you can never predict exactly when or where questions will arise. Indeed, you may want to stimulate questions or encourage students who rarely participate. Your own movements can make a difference, sparking more engagement from some students when you draw closer to them. Being closer may also allow you to notice subtle reactions, confusion or agreement. On the other hand, moving away from a speaking student may allow you to energize others across the room and stimulate reactions from them. Pay attention, also, to whether you might be obstructing someone's view. Varying your movements provides variety and relief from the usual routine which has you up front and focused on your notes.

Equipment and Materials as Props

For their part, actors and directors must think through the props they want to use and work with them carefully so that each adds something important to the performance. There should never be any random, spontaneous use of props on stage. However, performers do need to learn how to think on their feet when some mistake occurs, such as a mislaid prop. As in the classroom, cultivating a *stage awareness* and maintaining high levels of concentration combine with experience to give actors the wherewithal to survive. *The show must go on!*

When you plan, consider the equipment, materials and other items which can help illustrate certain concepts or function as catalysts for learning activities. From pointers to big chalk for a large lecture hall, from slides to films, videos and materials for demonstrations, these "props" can have a positive impact on learning. As with your blocking, you need to plan in advance and make sure you have the props you need.

Once class begins, you have a great deal of freedom to decide exactly when and how to use each prop; and you always have the opportunity to shift plans. However, you may also have to deal with surprises along the way: equipment which fails; all those items you either forgot to bring or wished you had. Thinking on your feet is a skill you can cultivate with planning, awareness, experience, practice, and creative resourcefulness. Once again, feedback and risk taking, so important on stage, become essential mechanisms when you decide to refine your teaching.

Lighting

As with props, performers must determine the kinds of lighting they want. While classical musicians typically work with one set lighting pattern, rock groups often use a splashy, pulsating range of lighting options, including lasers, strobes, whirling spots and every kind of color imaginable. Dancers use light changes to enhance moods and movements. At times, choreographer Randy Wray would break from the classical ballet tradition of constant and bright lighting, and use very vivid colors to evoke particular feelings. Amidst all the bright and flashy entertainment options available today, he knew that his ballets had to be creative to compete for his share of the local audience. For plays, directors may want to illuminate the entire stage at one point, but then dim the lights and focus a bright spot on one of the actors in the very next moment. A wide variety of more subtle changes, often imperceptible to those in the audience, can augment a story as it unfolds on stage.

Teachers rarely pay much attention to lighting so this may seem a trivial note. However, sometimes your planning can make all the difference, for instance, when sunlight makes a video almost invisible, and scheduling another room would help. You may sense when you should dim the lights to make it easier for students to see an overhead, slide or Powerpoint presentation; at the very least, you could ask them if the lighting is okay. Ideally, you have the kind of class climate which allows students to interrupt you if they cannot see. If students are making presentations, you may want to take the lead with adjusting the lights since they may be inexperienced in a teaching role. Variation in lighting can also help keep students alert, as changes can recapture flagging attentions.

The next time you are in a theater or watching a movie or television, notice the effects of lighting on the story. Of course, directors work lighting out in meticulous detail far in advance of any performance. While you will always have freedom to improvise in class, you may be able to resolve problems or create some special moments by thinking through your needs for lighting in advance.

Costuming

Costuming is so important to a staged production, film, or video that producers and directors go to great lengths to get it right — although getting it right can prove to be quite expensive. What fun to see a period piece from the nineteenth century come alive with fancy gowns, capes, and hats. All of this investment can help an audience "suspend their sense of disbelief" more effectively and engage more fully in a performance.

Although the classroom can feel quite informal, your clothing can and does have an impact on your students. When she gave back exams, one professor of sports and exercise sciences found that, by switching from her usual sweats to a suit, she could eliminate some of the hassling with students about exam questions, grades, and the like. Her students seemed more likely to haggle with her when she dressed more casually. The interviews featured in our *Foreword from the Lectern* describe the awareness different instructors have about their clothing/costuming.

As mentioned, costuming is designed long in advance of any stage production's opening. We draw the following lessons for teaching:

- Be aware of the impact of clothing generally on others and on yourself, when it may be important to "look professional," or when formality may inhibit your own creativity or put an unnecessary barrier between you and your students. For example, you may feel uneasy about going outside to sit on the grass and hold class on a warm spring day when you're wearing good clothes.

- Experiment. Test your assumptions and hypotheses about clothing. Check it out with others, especially your students.

- Simple "costume" changes can help you in various roles you may want to play in class, from debates to dramatizations. If you decide to wear a costume, you need to plan to acquire it in advance. However, you can also call on the imagination of your students when you need them to "see" a certain piece of clothing, when, for instance, you discuss someone from the history of your discipline and need to fill in some of the background details.

Energy and Concentration

For performers, the differences between preparing for a role and actual performance can be like night and day. The progression of the rehearsal process, however, links the two. Everyone may be relatively calm at the outset, but emotions peak as opening night draws near. Once the curtain rises, the cast wants a relaxed but alert attitude that reflects confidence in preparation and attentiveness to what is happening on stage.

An important shift also happens for the instructor between the preparation required ahead of time and what actually occurs in class. The rehearsal process helps the performer make this kind of shift. Be aware of your own energies and abilities to concentrate in class, especially since learning depends so much on the enthusiasm you bring to the material and to your students.

True enough, when you prepare for class, you may have to deal with distractions and interruptions, from answering the phone to chatting with a colleague, from responding to a student who drops in to juggling various administrative duties. Once class begins, you must deal with other stresses. You want to cover certain material and achieve particular goals. You certainly want a good plan for that day. You may find it helpful to monitor the reactions of your students while watching the time you have available. When you begin a discussion, you face an additional element of uncertainty, not knowing exactly what students will ask or how the focus will shift, what you will need to do to keep everyone engaged or what you can use for a future exam.

Of course there are important differences between audiences in the theater and students in a class, and we don't want to minimize them. Attending one performance is far different than slogging through difficult material week after week in a campus course. Unlike performers, however, teachers don't have to present the same material day after day; they have license to shift gears, improvise or create something new. Despite these differences, we believe that instructors can profit from understanding how performers sustain their energy and concentration.

Audience Response

Through experience, instructors and performers alike learn to anticipate audience reaction. However, both groups have to deal with the unexpected as well. Felman (2001, 152-153) argues that:

> The 'unexpected moment' is one of the most unrealized pedagogical opportunities in the academy....The applied benefits of the 'unexpected moment' include the following opportunities for the professor: the immediate incorporation of new theories arising from the discussion itself, the chance to make previously unrealized connections on the spot, and the development of an emotional rapport with the students based on the seemingly informal exchange that simply does not occur in the traditional lecture-style format....The act of professorial improvisation calls forth in the student a passionate engagement in the material heretofore not experienced in the classroom.

One dramatic difference between a set theatre performance and a classroom is the amount of freedom the teacher has to shift gears. Bettina Aptheker (Women's Studies) often shifts into a relevant example or anecdote when she feels student attention flagging. All of a sudden, she becomes more animated, often more personal. She's telling a story and can add the kind of emotion and rich detail which engage students.

Sandy Kern (Physics) also departs from his plans when students appear confused. His use of common examples can make difficult concepts or principles more accessible for students. In a spontaneous way, he'll use imagery, objects, gestures and diagrams—whatever comes to mind—to describe new and different examples. It really is demanding, he says, to do that in the moment when the need arises, but why press on when students don't get it?

Gil Findlay (English) typically lectures in an up tempo manner, but regularly indulges in long and personal digressions to illustrate issues from the readings (e.g., autobiographies). Students seem to enjoy these insights into the personal life and thoughts of a favorite instructor. In this way Findlay becomes more human, more real, less of an authority figure, someone with hopes and dreams deferred, joys and tragedies, worries, good and bad days. Over time, and with his encouragement and modeling, students begin to shift away from a preoccupation with class as some graded hurdle to jump, and they and accept the challenge—if you listen to them, an unfortunately rare opportunity in their college experience—to look deeply within their own stories and begin to sort out what is most meaningful, essential or problematic.

Our advice: start with your own awareness of your students and how their level of engagement impacts learning. Expand from there to experiment actively, to probe student reactions and solicit feedback. You'll find further suggestions as the book proceeds.

Exercises

1. Throughout this chapter we have emphasized the importance of self-awareness as a starting point. To guide you in this process, rate your skills in the following areas. Which factors seem to affect your performance most?

Activity/Skill	Rating (High/Medium/Low)	Comments
Library research	H M L	
Anticipating problems	H M L	
Arranging for trips, speakers, etc.	H M L	
Arranging for equipment	H M L	
Vocal projection	H M L	

Activity/Skill	Rating (High/Medium/Low)	Comments
Clarity of speech (enunciation)	H M L	
Enthusiasm	H M L	
Response to questions	H M L	
Facilitation of discussion	H M L	
Thinking on your feet	H M L	
Awareness of audience	H M L	
Awareness of self	H M L	
Awareness of roles	H M L	
Awareness of movements	H M L	
Awareness of props	H M L	
Awareness of lighting	H M L	
Awareness of costuming	H M L	
Awareness of energy	H M L	
Awareness of concentration	H M L	

2. Interview several colleagues about their skills in both the planning and performance requirements of teaching. Seek out those with especially good reputations as teachers. Observe them in class.

Chapter 2: Warming Up

Few instructors take time to warm up before class. Trained to be experts in content, most concentrate on information and neglect other elements which could add immeasurably to their lectures. An adequate warm-up can make a difference in how you approach a class, in how you deliver a lecture or lead a discussion, as well as how students respond. You can also lessen the likelihood of vocal strain. Moreover, a few minutes of stretching and humming can be both energizing and relaxing, giving you a few minutes to think about your students, your goals and the rhythm you want that day. Knowing the effectiveness of their stage work depends on physical and mental preparation, performers are very disciplined about exercise and warm ups.

Typically, actors arrive at the theater at least an hour before the curtain rises so they will have time for warm-ups. For musicals and operas, leading actors and chorus members gather together for body and voice stretching. Because dancers have to express everything through their bodies, they often take even longer to warm up. Warm-ups not only prepare the voice and body but the mind, focusing intellect and emotions on the task at hand.

Along with promoting physical flexibility, warm-ups exercise the physical and vocal range you have available. Actors must project to be heard clearly in all corners of a theater. They must enunciate clearly or risk sounding muffled. Their voices need to reflect the emotions of their characters. Nothing is deadlier than a flat monotone. And if performers must sing, they must be able to reach the notes required with ease and accuracy. Even the best of scripts and scores will fail miserably if delivered poorly.

A few breathing and stretching exercises can give you more of the flexibility and focus you need to maximize your effectiveness as a lecturer. We believe that taking time for warm-ups can also help you enhance your own sense of satisfaction in class. Certainly, teaching and learning are serious matters requiring careful planning and execution, but the energy and care you convey, the extent to which you can find personal fulfillment and enjoyment in your teaching, can add the fuel you need to inspire.

General Warm-Up Exercises

1. Sit comfortably, breathe deeply, and concentrate on your own physiology for breathing, feeling the air enter, fill your lungs, and leave. Or focus on a sound silently repeated over and over. Or think of the color spectrum, imagining each color in turn, located somewhere between your eyes. Each of these exercises can help create that relaxed but alert state that physiologists refer to as alpha, where brain waves are rhythmic and synchronized. Many health professionals and devotees of meditation promote this mental state, especially as a therapeutic antidote to periods of high activity and stress.

2. Try neck rolls, although you may want to avoid rolling far to the back since new evidence from physiologists has raised some concerns about this exercise, especially as people get older. You could also try a sun salutation, a common yoga exercise, where you lie face down on the floor and slowly raise your head up by pushing off the floor with your arms, curving yourself upward until your arms, neck and head are fully extended.

3. Warm up your mouth and face. Alternately tighten and stretch the various muscles. Wiggle your mouth in different directions. Pucker everything to kiss a prize pig at the local county fair. Open as wide as possible in feigned terror.

4. Do other stretching exercises, bending at the waist or going up on tip-toe with arms raised toward the sky, then swinging down to the ground. Add your voice to follow these lifts and bends. Do this exercise at work with your office door open and enjoy the reactions of those passing by.

Note: See Chapter 8, "Performance-Enhancing Exercises," for an extensive description of additional exercises and activities.

Vocal Warm-Up Exercises

For your voice, a few minutes of warm up can help you improve your projection, variety, enunciation, intonation and inflection. Add in some understanding of vocal mechanics, perhaps some training or experimentation with feedback, and practice; add a new measure of concentration and who knows what you could do!

Note: Some of the following exercises are essentially repeats of others described in this text, but with some modifications or additions specifically for the voice.

1. The musculature in your jaw, throat, face, lungs, and diaphragm combine to determine the sounds that you can make. Rotate your neck and head. Feel the tension leave and your muscles relax. Tighten and relax the different muscle groups in your face, neck, shoulders and stomach.

2. Now go up on your toes with your hands above your head. Stretch to the sky with your hands and let your voice push against the top of your range. Now swing your arms down to the floor as you bend your knees while your voice drops to its lowest note; then repeat several times.

3. With your hands above your head, bend left then right, forward then back. Try a "wooshing" sound as your breath comes in and out. Any sound will do.

4. Wiggle and waggle your lower jaw. Lots of articulation problems stem from lazy jaws. Try a tongue twister or two:

Sally sells seashells by the seashore.

Did a big black bug bite a big black bear?
If a big black bug bit a big black bear,
Where is the big black bear that the big black bug bit?

Betty Bota *(pronounced with a long "o")* brought some butter
But, she said, this butter's bitter.
If I put it in my batter,
it will make my batter bitter.
So she bought some better butter,
and she put it in her batter,
and it made her batter better.

Now give your tongue a good shaking. (It's really fun to have permission to do these kinds of strange things. Blame us for any questions others may raise about propriety ... or your own sanity!)

5. Repeat the following sound combinations:

brrrrrr ...

ta ta ta ta ...

me me me me ...

us us us us ...

la la la la ...

ha ha ha ha ...

bee boy by beau boo ...

dee day die doe do ...

Now do these sounds at different rates and with different pitches, inflections and intonations.

6. Work on breath control. Take an eye dropper, remove the rubber cap, and inhale and exhale deeply and SLOWLY through the little tube. Take as much time as you can with the exhaling. Do this exercise five times a day, every day. In a week or two, your lung capacity will improve.

7. Work on "backing up" your words; have the energy and force come from the throat. Open up and relax your throat. The throat is most relaxed and open during and just after a yawn. The next time you're bored to tears in a meeting, blame us if you *have* to yawn.

8. Be a bear and bellow deeply, clearing your throat. Feel your chords resonate. Get acquainted with the *range* of your voice; it's greater than you think.

9. Take an introduction to one of your upcoming lectures and sing it. (No, we're not trying to embarrass you!) Try moving around and adding gestures. Ham it up and really belt it out. This technique will explode any tendency you might have to use a monotone. After surviving this craziness, adding a few theatrics in class will seem easy. This exercise can also help you overcome any of your own blocks and get psyched for class. (If you're worried about your public image, say it's an exotic Eastern ritual intended to focus intellectual energy! Having said all that, you may still want

to shut the door when you sing your lecture in case there are some around who just won't understand.)

10. Finally, take the plunge and consider joining a choir or auditioning for a play or musical. You can learn a lot and have a great deal of fun. A whole new world of possibilities may open up for you. Along the way you can experiment with ideas and techniques which have helped performers throughout the ages.

Some kind of physical warm ups may also become increasingly important as you get older and find your joints getting stiffer. Throughout the day, and especially right before class, you may find that a few stretching exercises will feel wonderful and help re-energize your entire body. Remember, your own enthusiasm is a very infectious commodity in class.

Exercises for Physical Flexibility and Control

1. Become more aware of your posture. Stand erect, feet shoulder-width apart, knees slightly bent. Keep your head up and your eyes looking out. Try to be *relaxed* and *alert*.

2. Start with your arms stretched out to the sides, parallel to the floor. Rotate your arms from your shoulders in large circles. Now again in small circles. Rotate from the wrists, clockwise and then counter-clockwise. Try rotating your arms in opposite directions. Now try your wrists. This kind of exercise requires a bodily concentration that has wonderful payoffs on stage, especially when small, subtle movements are necessary. You may find similar benefits for your teaching.

3. Now the neck. Move your head in a large circle, first one way and then the other. Feel the tension begin to evaporate. You'll be amazed at the versatility a loose neck can provide for a whole range of characterizations, moods or feelings. Once relaxed, you'll be better prepared for any tension that begins to build. Ask a massage therapist how important a relaxed neck is to the total relaxation of the body. Better yet, treat yourself to a massage. You deserve it!

4. Now bend from the waist. First to the left, left arm by your side, right arm curved above your head and to the left. Shift your weight to the right so that you stretch your left leg. Just hang there. Don't bounce, relax. Now center your weight and slowly bend your upper torso forward, both arms hanging down. With each exhalation you should feel yourself sinking slowly into the floor. Remember, keep your knees slightly bent. Now swing

over to the right with your left arm hooked over your head and your right arm down by your side. Shift your body weight to the left so that your right leg gets a good stretch. Finally, center your weight and bend backwards, arms comfortably at your side. These kinds of stretches help release tensions that build up in your back and spine, in particular, tensions that commonly result from long hours at a desk or hunched over a terminal.

5. Finally, shake your arms and legs. Pretend that you're trying to throw away a hand or a foot.

6. Before the semester begins, and especially if you are assigned to a new room, explore your teaching space. Try out your new and expanded repertoire: shout; use a stage whisper; try making sounds at the top of your vocal range and then at the bottom; how do you sound in the middle of the room, at the back, on either side? Now get physical: jump around in mock frustration, tearing at your hair; run from one side to another to celebrate an imagined superb response from a student; skip wildly to show your childlike exuberance over a delightful solution.

Now visualize yourself performing in the space. See yourself in the various roles you want. Incorporate this visualization into your regular pre-class ritual to reinforce the behaviors you want yourself to develop. (**Note:** Having survived some of these stranger recommendations, adding a little zip or something unusual to class will seem easy. Your inhibitions will have retreated in the face of your new daring do. There is a method to this semi-madness!)

Like the actor, you need to be alert and focused to teach well. Carrying into the classroom concerns which don't belong there—a deadline hanging over your head, the residue from a contentious faculty meeting or some stress at home—can interfere with your concentration. Physical relaxation exercises, such as those described above, can cleanse your mind and body of unwanted distractions.

Some performers also use visualization exercises—for example, putting into an imaginary box all the problems they don't want to bring with them into rehearsal. The contents of the box will still be there later; you can deal with them later, maybe drowning a few in your favorite brew! Likewise, you can put any unwanted voices onto an imaginary tape or compact disk. Turn up the volume so that you hear the voices clearly, then slowly turn it down until you can't hear them at all. When you're ready to work, stash this recording with all those old dusty records in your basement.

Warming Up for Class

Warm-up involves attitude as well as concentration. Here's another exercise:

Get up and walk around the room. As you walk, imagine that with each step you take, your whole body is getting heavier. Your head is growing heavier, your shoulders, your feet, your hips, your arms. With each step, your whole body gets heavier and heavier, until it takes a great effort to move at all, yet you keep moving. (Another Monday morning!)

And now, imagine that with each step you take, your whole body is getting lighter. Lighter with each step, until you reach your normal weight. And you keep walking. (You just got that award!)

And now with each step, you continue to get lighter. Lighter, and still lighter. Your arms become lighter, your head becomes lighter, your hips, your feet, your shoulders. Now your feet are barely skimming the ground, as you become lighter and lighter. (Maybe you did inhale!)

And now, imagine that as you continue walking, you become a little heavier with each step until you reach your normal weight. (Oh oh, you hear a noise outside the door!)

Take a few moments to reflect on what you experienced during the exercise. Which feeling did you prefer — heavier or lighter? Did you experience any change in mood or emotions as you imagined yourself becoming heavy? Light?

Many people who do this sequence report sensations of tiredness, sadness, or depression when they were "heavy." Conversely, "lightness" often stimulates feelings of happiness and freedom. This acting exercise demonstrates in a very basic way the body-mind connection and what actors refer to as the *outside-in* approach to acting.

In the *inside-out* approach, an actor studies a character's motivation and then allows what the character is thinking and feeling to produce the physical characterization "naturally." In the *outside-in* approach, the actor chooses a physical characterization and then allows the physicalization to produce the character's emotional state. For instance, an *outside-in* actor who is playing a depressed character might choose to move in a "heavy" way, while an actor playing a cheerful character might choose a "light" movement pattern. The actor is not just "pretending" to be depressed or cheerful — the movement pattern by itself can stimulate the desired feelings.

Evaluation forms often ask students to comment on their teacher's enthusiasm for the subject matter. Certainly, your sincere interest in the topic at hand communicates itself to students. But the most enthusiastic of us encounter days when we're grumpy and just "not in the mood" for class. An attitude warm-up can help get you in the mood, whether you choose an *inside-out* approach of positive self-talk or an *outside-in* approach of deliberately changing your movement patterns. The point is that you can choose your attitude — if you remember to do so and take the time to warm up. If you choose to move in a more lively and energetic pattern, you should feel more lively and energetic.

Exercises like the ones described above can help you set a more positive physical, mental and emotional tone for yourself. In the midst of your regular routines and pressures, taking time to get ready for class may seem like a luxury you cannot afford. However, if you come to enjoy this kind of preparation, your teaching can really improve. If you feel more energized, your students will undoubtedly respond positively. If you are more focused, your teaching can be more focused. Indeed, these effects can interact; a synergism can develop between you and your students that makes teaching feel more rewarding and your classes more enjoyable.

Chapter 3: The Lecture

Do you want to engage your students during lecture? Do you want to feel more energized, excited, and confident about your teaching? Although the word "lecture" is derived from the Latin word for reading, students today want and need more. With so much fast-paced multimedia available, some students struggle when they're expected to sit and absorb a traditional lecture. Besides, with the advent of desktop publishing, photocopying technologies, and web-based course support programs, you can produce lecture notes for distribution, for placement on reserve, or for perusal on the web. Freed of the requirement to cover merely course content, you can, then, think about your time in class differently.

If you want your students to acquire more than surface learning — to think deeply, for themselves — then you may want to consider alternatives to the traditional lecture. Discovery learning and creativity training, for example, stimulate students to construct meaning for themselves. (Accordingly, we offer in this book separate chapters on these and other approaches that have parallels to the stage.) In this chapter, however, we want to address issues inherent to lecturing.

Why Lecture?

The lecture has been a mainstay in higher education over the centuries, in developing and advanced nations alike. Its advantages are substantial. Quite simply, the lecture allows you to interject the most current thinking, long before definitive findings run the gauntlet of refereed research journals and appear in print. You can pull from a variety of sources and help clarify complex interrelationships. When confusion persists, you can field questions, build on what students do understand, and provide additional examples or alternative explanations. You also can make a topic more relevant by connecting it to current events or hooking your students with controversial ideas.

From the administrative perspective, the lecture represents a flexible structure for scheduling classes and accommodating shifts in enrollments. Once class size reaches into the hundreds, how simple it usually is to put more students into the available seats, regardless of how cramped students may feel as a result. But if the instructional paradigm is about information transmission, then even classroom capacity is no barrier, since the wonders of television and computer networking permit broadcast and access in flexible formats.

Different approaches to instruction can augment what is possible with a lecture format. For example, technology increasingly permits much more in the way of independent and active learning, access to information, and ongoing electronic interactions. Students also can benefit from small-group and cooperative projects, study groups, experiential learning, service-learning, and other activities that encourage critical and creative thinking and promote deeper understanding.

We have to acknowledge, however, the enduring viability of the lecture. Because such close parallels exist between a good performance and an engaging lecture, we will describe a number of ways in which lessons from the stage can help you energize your lectures so that you engage your students and promote learning. In this chapter, we share lessons from the stage that can enhance your preparation, voice, gestures, and teaching materials within the lecture format. We show you how ideas about scripts can help you challenge minds and harness emotions. We describe how training and rehearsal techniques can make performances more believable, and how knowledge about set design and lighting can contribute to performances in subtle but effective ways.

The Challenge to Lecture Well

Despite the lecture's seeming simplicity, you yourself may find it to be a challenging format — especially when:

- Classes are large.
- Some students show up unprepared or unmotivated.
- You look for opportunities for discussion.

- You ask a question and get no response.

- The availability of relevant media is limited.

- There is little support for teaching assistants.

- Some of your students only seem to want to know what will be on the next exam.

- Too many students come late or leave early.

- Chatting among some students interferes with other students sitting nearby.

- Some students are reading the newspaper or sleeping.

- The fear of public speaking shakes your own confidence.

We can assure you that even the best teachers share some of these same fears and frustrations. Rethinking the lecture as a stage and the class as a production can give you many fresh new ideas for addressing these challenges effectively.

In and of itself, public speaking may intimidate you. At the height of the Cold War, public speaking ranked first in a nationwide American poll of "greatest fears," even above nuclear holocaust! Others have put the resulting stress high on lists that include such personal traumas as divorce, loss of employment, and death of loved ones. Even for *extroverts* — people who tend to be energized by interacting with others — a public talk can be a challenge, especially when the group is large or indifferent.

Students create additional tension when they demand simple truths, obsess about grades, or want only *"what's going to be on the next exam"!* As a researcher, you probably find it frustrating to reduce the most tentative understandings of complex matters into self-contained, fifty-minute lectures that make notetaking easy. In this era of fast-paced media images, how can you sustain the attention of your students with just your own descriptions, explanations, and ideas? When film and television productions require so much money, expertise, and equipment, how can you hope to compete on your own? Even if you have a great deal of experience and many insights to share, a strictly-lecture format can prove limiting. Then, of course, you have to deal with the new criticisms of the lecture as too focused on knowledge transmission and too limiting of active and experiential learning opportunities for students.

Lessons from the Stage

A lecturer who stands rooted over a podium and drones on in an uninspired monotone will usually dishearten even the most dedicated listener. In turn, nearly everyone has memories of riveting speakers. Those of us who teach understand that the effective use of posture, voice, gestures, timing, and feeling can be a powerful component of effective instruction. The best teachers in higher education do engage their classes, intellectually and emotionally. They can challenge students to think and rethink, to see new connections and possibilities. Reread what our two public speaking instructors, Greg Dickinson and Eric Aoki, had to say in the "Foreword from the Lectern."

Ken Klopfenstein (Mathematics) is a good example of a gifted lecturer who makes the most of the time he has with students. He is focused and organized, but friendly and flexible. He moves through material efficiently, but with frequent pauses to check on students' understanding and to allow students to think and ask questions. He moves across the front of the classroom, stopping periodically to emphasize key points. What's truly remarkable is the way Ken will build suspense as he works through a particular problem or proof; he then offers the resolution, literally, in the final minute of class. And in linear algebra, mind you!

From a theatre perspective, Ken's performance offers much to applaud and a great model for any instructor in any discipline to emulate. Are these skills born or bred? Both! But whatever your gifts, training, or experiences, you can always learn something from the stage to enhance your preparation, performance, and success as a teacher.

The Teaching Objective as Through-Line

Good lecturing can be a high-wire juggling act. You enter into the hall with certain expectations. You know what you want to cover. But you must be simultaneously aware of the conditions you face on any particular day — the mechanics of getting class started and ended on time, using the board or various pieces of equipment, and picking up on what happened in the previous class session. While doing all of that, you also might want to preview upcoming requirements (e.g., exams, papers, field trips, guest lecturers, demonstrations). What can keep you and your students focused? Your articulation of *learning objectives* — what you hope your students will be able to understand and do by the end of a class period or semester.

Of course, we rarely repeat our lectures. We may update our references or use new examples. Questions and explanations may vary. Few instructors have the time or incentive to polish a particular lecture in ways that parallel how playwrights work and rework to get the language of their scripts just right. But paying attention to certain refinements may produce important dividends for you, your students, and their engagement and learning in your class sessions.

Because plays and movies are so carefully constructed, and because every line, action, and gesture is connected to a central theme, we think study of dramatic structure can help you with your teaching and with student learning. For example, every play and movie has an objective, or *through-line*, that plays out through the characters and the plot. In *Death of a Salesman*, Willy Loman has to confront his own limitations. Ultimately, he kills himself. Shakespeare's Macbeth has to reconcile his own evil after killing his king. In *Field of Dreams*, Shoeless Joe Jackson and his teammates return from the grave to play again after the Kevin Costner character actually builds a ballpark in his Iowa cornfield. Just ask yourself: Would it have been consistent for Thelma and Louise to stop their car and just give up?

Directors and actors trained in the Stanislavski tradition call the unifying element of a script the play's *spine*. Harold Clurman (1972, 27), a major American director, explains that "to begin active direction, a formulation in the simplest terms must be found to state what general action motivates the play, of what fundamental drama or conflict the script's plot and people are the instruments." The director states the spine of the play as an active infinitive verb. For example, Clurman (1972, 28) points out:

> Many things are contained in O'Neill's *Desire Under the Elms*: passion, Oedipal impulses, confessions of unhappiness and hate, guilt feelings, paternal harshness, filial vindictiveness, retribution. But what holds all these ingredients together, what makes a complete meaning, a single specific drama of them all, is the play's spine.

A director will analyze a play in terms of the perceived spine, defining a spine for each character (again, a main action or an objective stated in infinitive verb form) that shows how that character relates to the main action of the play. "Where such a relation is not evident or [is] non-existent," Clurman (1972, 74) points out, "the character performs no function in the play."

Just as a play, film, or novel needs a clear storyline, so does a lecture. Your message should have a clear organizing purpose — a spine. Just as all of the character spines must relate to the play spine, all of the elements of your lecture should help you organize material so as to maximize student learning. Try analyzing one of your lectures as if it were a play script. What is the spine? How does the spine communicate the theme, or the meaning, of the lecture? What are the spines of the various parts of the lecture, and how do they relate to the primary spine? Will students get it?

Such detailed attention to the preparation of a lecture, of course, may require a considerable investment of time. While rewards for research and publication on some campuses may limit the payback from this kind of investment in teaching, there can be considerable benefits here for students and their learning as well as for you in the form of an intrinsic reward for a job well done. In addition, colleagues and administrators invariably appreciate the skillful lecturer who can successfully handle large numbers of students.

Once mastered, these skills transfer easily to conference and other professional presentations you might have to make. Careful attention to your lecture "scripts" also may help you convert lecture notes and presentations into published papers, chapters, or books. You'll want to write about innovations in your own teaching, perhaps where some of these lessons from the stage have made an impact. Ernest Boyer's (1990) groundbreaking report for the Carnegie Commission on Higher Education, *The Professoriate Reconsidered,* makes a very articulate call for an expanded notion of scholarship, one that recognizes the value of scholarship about teaching. Only through encouraging the scholarship of teaching and learning, insisted Boyer, can research universities in particular rebalance their reward systems and encourage higher-quality instruction.

Note, though, the potential danger that lurks when you use your written work as the basis for lectures and then ignore the potential for interaction with students. We offer you the following options to consider:

- As budgets permit, duplicate materials for handouts.

- Alternatively, post materials on your course web site, put them on reserve in the library, include them in a course reader for sale through the bookstore, or make them available for students to copy.

- Try to make more creative use of class time. Here the lecture has distinct advantages over the written script.

From questions and brief discussions to spontaneous digressions, from full-fledged debates to group evaluations of relevant cases, you can often spice up lectures with new and topical material and energize your students with periodic and varied activities. In essence, you can use your written notes as a platform for any number of opportunities to engage students more actively in deeper learning.

Exercises

As we wrote in the Introduction, there is great value in cross-fertilization and incubation for stimulating ideas about creative alternatives. Although the following exercises focus on staged productions, we believe they'll give you some fresh insights into your teaching as well.

1. Analyze a favorite play, film, or television program. Determine what you think the spine might be — what holds it all together, the main action. What is the theme of the piece, and how does the spine point to the theme? See if you can select spines for each of the major characters that relate to the main spine. Watch or read the piece again, noting how the dialogue and actions carry out the spines.

Spine

Learning to recognize spines takes practice. If you have difficulty on your first attempt, try a preliminary step: State the main action of the play in a single sentence (called a *root action*). The root action statement has the following parts:

- A description of the protagonist.

- A description of the main action the protagonist takes during the play.

- A description of the result of that action.

Thus the statement takes the form: "This is a play about a(n) _____ who _____ and thereby _____." Since the spine of a play relates closely to the spine of the protagonist, a clear root action statement will help you discover what action the playwright is imitating in the play — i.e., its spine.

2. Consider your own teaching and reflect on a recent lecture. Was the "spine" clear to your students? the theme? Find a few students and ask

them. How might you apply your knowledge of play construction to improve your future lectures?

Lecture Notes as Script

In addition to the underlying objective or through-line, the notes you prepare for your lecture could resemble scripts in a variety of other ways. Essentially, they organize information and ideas around your central theme in a logical way that is understandable to those who are watching and listening to you. You can include notes about your delivery as well, perhaps in the margins. For example, you can remind yourself to pause at certain points, ask questions or solicit comments, call on particular students, or allow for some silent reflection.

Paradoxically, while instructors in higher education rarely receive formal training in the requirements for effective lecturing, playwrights often go through years of intensive study and practice, a tradition that dates from the very beginnings of Greek theatre and continues on today. Accordingly, we know a lot about successful scriptwriting, and much of it, we believe, can be useful for teachers.

Scholars of drama consider conflict to be the heart of drama. We ourselves may want to eliminate conflict from our personal lives, but without it a play would be boring. Conflicts engage audience interest and generate suspense. How will the conflict be resolved? Who will win, and at what cost? The hero's journey has always been fraught with obstacles, problems, uncertainty, challenges to overcome — real tests of character. It might be useful to think of dramatic conflict on three different levels: conflict between individuals, within a single individual, or between an individual and larger forces (e.g., nature, society, fate). The great plays — those that continue to appeal to generations of audiences — often include all three levels of conflict.

So when you're scripting your lecture, look for opportunities to emphasize the conflicts inherent in the material. Strange or paradoxical phenomena can make for wonderful moments of reflection and questioning. Researchers working in basic mathematics, for example, have long studied what appear to others to be esoteric and koan-like problems. Where will the next discoveries come in chemistry? Physics seems full of oddities, with notions of black holes, quarks, and worm holes, the very nature of the universe pushing against the limits of our earth-bound understanding.

Our own environment has its share of aberrations as well. For example, despite massive amounts of data and the most powerful supercomputers, our ability to predict the weather using conventional approaches continues to be limited. Indeed, chaos theory and hypotheses about nonlinear relationships evolved from these unsolved questions about the weather, for which a small change in temperature could have a dramatic effect on overall weather patterns because of the interplay of many variables.

Look within your own discipline to find ideas that may be counterintuitive or paradoxical. Find and highlight the important questions that remain unanswered.

Ethical issues exist in every discipline, and they offer rich opportunities for addressing more personal conflicts. You can also ask about the "stakes" involved as individual scholars critique existing theories, propose their own, and compete for their place in history. Science, for instance, is full of stories about races between individuals or labs to be the first to announce a particular discovery. The film *And the Band Played On* depicts one such competition as an American and a French lab vie to be the first to discover a viable test for HIV. At the time, the death toll from this mystery disease was ravaging the gay community in particular. Panic and fear mixed with public apathy, ignorance, and resistance in a very deadly brew. Dr. Gallo, an American researcher, is portrayed as sinister in his competitive drive to be the first to find a cure, ignoring the breakthroughs from a French lab and risking the release of unscreened blood supplies that were tainted with the HIV virus. High stakes and high drama!

Managed effectively, conflicts also can help students clarify their own values. In Chapter 6, which explores the developmental case for drama, we describe in great detail how teachers can use dilemmas as catalysts for stimulating growth in moral development among their students. For example, you might explore issues like cheating or plagiarism with a hypothetical case study. You can ask students to judge a particular behavior and then probe their reasoning for their underlying values. "What if" questions can help you identify those conditions that determine the boundaries of student values, when cooperation becomes cheating and paraphrasing becomes plagiarism. Open discussions in class can provide the kind of rich interaction of values and reasoning that stimulates students to reflect and grow while you simultaneously address an issue relevant to your field.

But let's continue our exploration of conflict in the theatre and see what other insights we can glean for you and your fellow teachers. In the fourth century B.C., the philosopher Aristotle argued in his *Poetics* that action is the most significant element of drama, and that playwrights must structure the action of their plays with great care. The play opens with some situation, called the *stasis* or *balance*, which contains the potential for significant action. *Exposition* — background information that is essential to understanding the stasis — gradually unfolds, and the audience senses the instability and the potential for action in the situation.

An *inciting incident* — an event that disrupts the tenuous balance — sets the main action of the play into motion. A *protagonist*, the play's central character, sets out on a course of action in order to achieve a goal. In the course of pursuing his or her goal, the protagonist encounters a series of complications, events, or factors that help or hinder him or her and that build suspense. Most plays contain a *major crisis*, or a *turning point*, when the protagonist must make a choice that will eventually determine the outcome of the play.

Throughout the play, the author creates an *emotional rhythm*, structuring the emotional dynamics so as to build to high points of tension and suspense — *climaxes* — that are usually followed by periods of relative relaxation. The overall rhythm of the play, however, continues a progressive build of emotional involvement to the major emotional climax. The major structural climax then resolves the play's main action in a single moment. The play's resolution delineates the new stasis or balance resulting from the play's action.

The *thematic significance*, or meaning, of a play arises from its action. What action does the playwright choose to represent? What forces are in conflict? What choices do the characters make, especially the protagonist? Why do they make these choices? What happens to them as a result of their choices? What insights about human life can we, the audience, get from the vicarious experience provided by the play?

Not all lectures lend themselves to this kind of design, of course, but the use of drama does have a long and distinguished history as a teaching tool in various disciplines. The Roman poet Horace pointed out that the purpose of drama is not only to entertain but to instruct. Of course, some of the greatest teachers have been great storytellers. Jesus of Nazareth relied much on the *parable*, a type of short story, to communicate his ideas. Plato related the teachings of his mentor Socrates in the form of written dialogues — plays! On campus today — and especially in certain applied disciplines like law, business, or medicine and the health sciences in general — entire courses may evolve from discussions of cases or problems.

By studying the playwright's methods for engaging audience attention and interest, you can enhance your ability to structure your lectures. You can learn to adapt playwriting techniques for building to a climax — to emphasize your major points — and then follow the emotional rhythm of allowing a period of relative relaxation (so that your students can assimilate the new material) before you begin another build. Professors of law and medicine, for example, often use problem- or case-based learning to orient their classes around symptoms or data, raising a series of questions and then moving through the resulting uncertainty and confusion toward some kind of resolution.

Other research on learning can be helpful in structuring your lecture "scripts" or notes, revealing, for example, why the start of a class or the first few minutes of a play or film can be so important. If you're opening is lackluster, your students might disengage early and forget most of the middle portion of your lecture. It is at the beginning of class when students are freshest. Psychologists will say that there is little *proactive* (or prior) *interference* from earlier material. At the end of class, memories are fresher because there is no *retroactive interference* from material that followed. The lecture is over.

As an instructor, you can raise important questions early on and, in the process, increase student interest. You can refer to underlying and core concepts, the conceptual structure that holds information together in some organized fashion. You can keep your objectives on the board or overhead as a reference throughout the class period. You can sprinkle in brief written or discussion activities throughout class as opportunities for students to use these new ideas and consolidate their learning. You can use more concrete examples. In the theatre, during the inciting incident of a play, a major dramatic question forms early for audience members — a question about the outcome of the play. Interest in discovering the answer to this question helps keep an audience attentive to the performance. Read on and see how this could work for you in your classes.

The Case of Oedipus

In *Oedipus the King*, Sophocles presents a stasis in which a plague has been devastating Thebes. In the opening scene, citizens plead with

Oedipus to save the city from the plague. Oedipus replies that he has sent his brother-in-law Creon to ask the oracle for advice. Creon returns with the oracle's message that the plague has occurred to punish the city for harboring the murderer of Laius, the previous king. Creon's announcement (the inciting incident) prompts Oedipus (the protagonist) to set off on a quest to find the murderer of Laius (main action), thus posing the major dramatic question: will Oedipus find the murderer? (Are there central questions you can ask in your lectures that could help hold student interest? Where is the main action? Are there relevant, important, engaging stories for you to tell?)

As the story of Oedipus unfolds, however, we see the major dramatic question evolving, often with each major complication, and reaching new levels of significance. Oedipus first sends for the blind prophet, Tiresias. When Tiresias refuses to help, he and Oedipus quarrel, and Tiresias (in veiled prophetic language) accuses Oedipus himself of the murder. At this point, the major dramatic question changes: Is Oedipus indeed the killer he seeks? Who "sees" things more clearly — the sighted but hot-tempered king or the blind prophet? As the result of Tiresias's accusation, Oedipus jumps to the conclusion that Tiresias and Creon are plotting to overthrow him, and so he threatens to execute them as traitors. (If you open discussion about ethical issues in your own discipline, for example, you can find important "plot points" and questions. Explore these as a playwright might look for dramatic material. What will be engaging — potential grist for stimulating discussions?)

A second major complication occurs when Oedipus's wife, Jocasta, attempting to smooth over the quarrel, tells Oedipus not to trust oracles: the oracle had warned Laius that he would be killed by his own son, but instead the baby was put out on a mountain to die and Laius was murdered by robbers at a place where three roads meet. This revelation starts Oedipus worrying; he suddenly remembers that he once killed an old man at a place where three roads meet. Oedipus sends for the only survivor of the attack, a shepherd who had reported that multiple robbers, not a single assassin, killed Laius. The major dramatic question has again evolved: can oracles be trusted? Will Oedipus prove to be the murderer even though that would contradict the oracle? (In your own discipline, can you find key questions to raise as you build toward conclusions?)

In the meantime, the third major complication arrives in the form of a messenger from Corinth who informs Oedipus that his father, King

Polybus, has died. Oedipus refuses to return to Corinth, however, saying an oracle warned him that he was destined to kill his father and marry his mother; since his mother still lives, he won't risk fulfilling that horrid fate. "No problem," the messenger replies. "She's not really your mother. You were adopted." The messenger reveals that he himself had been given the baby Oedipus by a Theban shepherd. With this complication, the major dramatic question shifts to: who is Oedipus? The simple detective story becomes a search for the nature of human identity. (Telling the human stories in your discipline can add an element of interest that may touch students on a more personal level. What were the twists and turns in the lives of the great thinkers, writers, and activists of your discipline? What lessons can students take from their lives?)

Back to our main story, now. The shepherd arrives. (By one of those quirks of fate common in Greek tragedy, the shepherd who witnessed Laius's murder happens to be the same shepherd who gave the baby to the messenger.) Under pressure, the shepherd finally admits that Oedipus is the son of Laius and Jocasta and his father's murderer — Oedipus has, unwittingly, fulfilled the prophecy. This revelation (the major crisis) leads to another shift in the major dramatic question: what will Oedipus do now that he knows destiny does rule human life? What should be the response of any ethical human being to unbearable self-discovery? (As you think about your own discipline, can you find compelling stories in which there are intriguing twists and turns? What happens to those whose ideas get discredited when paradigms shift?)

Although Jocasta kills herself, Oedipus does not. He blinds himself but remains alive, certain now that his life has some yet-to-be-disclosed purpose (major structural climax). Physically blind, Oedipus now possesses spiritual insight. He does not indulge in blaming the gods for his downfall but instead takes responsibility for his own actions. The resolution of the play shows Oedipus going off into exile to follow where the gods will lead him. (What happens to the tragic figures in your discipline? How has history treated the greats? the wannabes? Are there contributions from some people — women or minorities, for example — that have been ignored?)

Studying the structure of plays shows how playwrights use complications and crises to engage audience interest through stimulating questions, both spoken and unsaid. If you want to sustain student interest throughout your class sessions, if you want to use lectures for more than transmission of information, if you want to make your students think more deeply about the significance of a topic, then you may want to experiment with more of the human stories involved in the evolution of your discipline, with all of their attendant issues and dilemmas.

You can, for instance, structure your lecture around the major questions you want your students to consider. Note that in *Oedipus*, the questions become increasingly more significant as the play progresses. All of the questions work on the simple level of suspense (what will happen?) and thus help sustain audience attention; but they also progressively demand more from the audience intellectually: what is the meaning of what's happening? When you teach, you can refer back to underlying concepts and objectives and key questions, thus helping your students stay more clearly focused on central ideas.

In good drama, the emotions and the intellect work together. As audience members, we engage in the search for meaning after the playwright has drawn us into the story emotionally and we've begun to empathize with the characters; we can put ourselves into Oedipus's shoes and feel with him the horror of having to confront the worst in ourselves, to face the dreadful realization that we have done the very thing we most feared doing. Likewise, our lectures can do more to stimulate emotional identification as well as intellectual inquiry. Relevance has long been associated with motivation, learning, and memory. As Sarason (1999, 51, 48) points out, effective teaching:

> ...[M]eans an effort to achieve a better integration of thinking and feeling. ... When we say that performers seek both to instruct and *move* an audience, we mean that the teacher as performing artist has in some positive way altered the students' conception of the relationship between sense of self and the significance of subject matter — i.e., an increase in competence.

Students will typically invest more energy in searching for answers to questions when they feel, on a personal level, that the material has meaning for them — that the questions raised are important for their own lives.

Writers for the stage and screen learn to craft dialogue and actions that are central to a production's through-line. Everything, every little detail, has a purpose. These writers also incorporate elements to keep the audience engaged, in suspense, laughing, wondering, worrying, thinking.

Writers use surprises, plot twists, or conflicts to add drama and comedy to a production. In a similar way, they focus on the timing of lines, actions and pacing, costuming, lighting, and choreography, all of which can contribute to the ability of individual audience members to engage their thoughts and feelings and "suspend their disbelief."

Across an entire semester, you have only so much time to invest in any one lecture. If you explore a few new possibilities in depth, however, you may learn some things that can have long-lasting benefits. Consider the following ideas:

- Step back and consider the entire lecture as a production with an opening, a clear through-line, a pace that fits the audience and the material, and a build toward a conclusion or climax.

- Consider doing a practice run through the lecture/"script" — a "rehearsal."

- If possible, get someone to videotape the actual lecture. Then analyze the "script" as you saw it "performed," as well as from the perspective of your students.

Exercises

1. Get a copy of a script from a library, a book store, a colleague, or a friend. Read it to get a better appreciation of the careful crafting involved.

2. Rethink a recent lecture and then plan one for the future. Investing some time in crafting one lecture may lead you to some valuable insights that generalize to others.

Hooking Students from the Start

A great deal of research supports the value of student engagement as an important factor in learning (e.g., Ramsden 1992, Eble 1994, McKeachie 2002, Denham and Lieberman 1980, Davis 1993). In his popular book on university teaching, Joseph Lowman (1995) insists that intellectual excitement and rapport are the two most essential factors for engaging college students and prompting their learning. Sarason (1999, 52) emphasizes the obvious: "The way subject matter is taught and experienced by students ensures that students will tune in or turn off." Timpson and Bendel-Simso (1996) describe a number of concepts and choices that instructors in higher education have at their disposal for sustaining student interest — among them discovery and group learning, debates and discussions, demonstrations and role plays, and student-centered and problem-based learning.

While engagement itself is somewhat slippery to identify and measure as a researchable construct, students themselves can certainly tell you whether or not they're absorbed in a particular lecture. They can clearly describe what gets their attention, what sustains it, what allows them to drift off, and what turns them off completely. When asked to describe what has worked and what has not, your fellow teachers also can be remarkably accurate, identifying times when they felt they were losing a class and describing approaches that might have worked to "get the students back."

Plays and movies must have something that grabs the audience member in the first few minutes if they're to have a chance at being successful. Without an effective *hook*, performances may feel long and audiences will likely become restless. Interest must be piqued right away, curiosity whetted. Along with the story and the action, lighting, costuming, and the set combine to augment the impact of the hook. In class, meanwhile, a student's first impressions of you as a teacher can "set the stage" for the rest of the semester. Just as actors "make an entrance," so too can you grab the attention of your class/audience from the very first day.

While audience members may disagree about the exact nature of the hook that worked for them in a particular production, successful films do grab their attention early. Let's look at some specific examples. Whether in the animated version of *Peter Pan* or Steven Spielberg's remake, the kidnaping of the children by Captain Hook sets up the drama to follow. Spielberg also had the opening to *Jurassic Park* shrouded in mystery as workers tried to move a large container with something huge, alive, and very ominous. Remember the accompanying soundtrack? Suddenly, one of the workers is pulled in and, to the sound of screams and chomps, killed and eaten. The hook for *Home Alone* comes when the parents drive to the airport, board their flight, and actually take off before realizing they've forgotten their son. The hook for *Big* occurs when the Tom Hanks character wakes up the morning after his interaction with a strange mechanical genie and discovers that his wish to be big has been granted.

The hook for *ET* happens when the alien spaceship lifts off in a hurry, when pressed by a menacing human search party, and it leaves behind one of its own to cope as best he can. The darkness of that opening night scene — with all of the headlights and flashlights, the urgency in the voices, the foreboding soundtrack, the low shots and quick cuts — creates a sense of impending danger for the viewer. *Gone with the Wind* pulls us in at the very beginning when the roguish Rhett Butler shows a riveting interest in the flighty Scarlett amidst all the brash talk about a "quick victory for the noble South." Remember that scene when they first make eye contact as Scarlett descends the mansion's circular staircase and the camera zooms in on a smiling Clark Gable below, looking up at her?

For teaching, Hunter (1982) describes this hook as *set* — the comments or actions, activities or experiences that pull students into the lesson for the day, engage their emotions, and focus their minds. The classroom as "set" should not be confused with the term "set" that's used for stage and film. As is the case with any audience, students enter your classroom from a variety of prior activities — other classes, home, friends, studies, eating, playing, napping, working, or perhaps just hanging out. Although the degree of anticipation by audience members and students will vary at the outset, your lecture, like the theatrical production, could attempt to capture everyone's interest early on.

Jim Boyd (Philosophy) often has music playing when his Eastern Religions class begins. What a wonderful way to pull students into the material, let them know that class time has begun — Jim often starts the music five to ten minutes before class officially begins — and encourage them to reflect or even meditate a bit about another reality. Note Jim's attempt to create more of a holistic quality to teaching and learning, since meditation is so central to many Eastern religious practices. Boyd can, then, refer back to the music during class as a concrete example of a particular religious or cultural practice.

What can work as a hook in one of your lectures?

- A good question can challenge your students to think, or alert them to connections with events in the news. Something puzzling or complex can stimulate creative alternatives.

- A demonstration at the very outset can raise questions and illustrate principles, which you can then discuss later.

- A brief activity that has students working together on a question or problem can energize everyone at the very beginning of class.

- Some description of the personalities or human drama in the background of your course or discipline can help personalize the course and sustain student interest.

The key is to have your idea of a hook in mind, to be willing to experiment, to look for early engagement, and to assess the impact of what you try.

Exercises

1. Try to identify the hook next time you watch a movie or television drama. Note your level of engagement. The movie industry knows how important the hook is and will add a few carefully edited and fast-paced previews of coming attractions at the end of an episode. These advertisements then serve as mini-hooks of their own. In the last several television seasons, producers have been starting their shows with action, not the traditional theme and credits, to engage viewers before they even identify the show.

2. Now watch another film or play and pay particular attention to the entrances made by the various actors. A key here is to *detach* yourself from the story line and focus solely on the actor's entrance. This *distance* can be important for your own training as you learn how to identify *objectively* what the elements of effective presentations are.

3. Think about some of your past lectures that had good hooks. Try to create a hook or enhance one for an upcoming talk.

The Classroom as Set

Some instructors essentially ignore their classroom spaces. Sure, most have preferences for certain rooms, and nearly everyone who teaches knows about lousy rooms that are too cold or too hot or that have difficult acoustics. Many classrooms contain immovable desks, making small-group assignments nearly impossible. You undoubtedly have your own horror stories about equipment that failed at the worst time; rooms that proved too small or too big; or rooms where projectors created a distracting hum, noise bounced off hard walls, or light streaming in from the windows made it hard to see overheads. Whatever the problems, we carry on as best we can. There's probably not much you can do about your assigned room anyway.

The lesson from the stage that applies here is that the set is integral to the success of a production, so much so that the set designer receives near equal billing to the director and, technically, works for the producer. Every script includes scenic directions, although writers differ in the amount of detail they provide. The set designer, then, works closely with the play's director to create the desired backdrop for the production within the space available and the limitations of budgeted resources.

But back to the classroom. Just what can you do within the limitations of assigned spaces? What helpful lessons can we draw from the stage? Consider the following: Think of the overhead or the board as having more creative possibilities. Bettina Aptheker (Women's Studies) invites students to put relevant announcements on the board before class to save time from the lecture. This makes for a fun backdrop with lots of interesting reading. Some instructors put the day's goals or activities up as a visual reference to help keep everyone focused. Showing a videotape or film can briefly transform your lecture hall into a movie theatre. Music or other sounds can also help re-engage your students. Posters can add color, visuals, and inspiring language. Too many classroom bulletin boards seem only to carry advertisements. You also can change the position of the podium and, thereby, your relationship to students.

In many smaller classrooms, you can move chairs and tables into any number of different configurations. You can also offer demonstrations. You could think of a field trip as a set change. You could use other rooms on occasion, perhaps to take advantage of laboratory equipment or better accommodate small-group activities. When you're telling an anecdote or providing an example, you can use extended descriptions to invoke the imaginations of your students and help set an imaginary stage. Once you reconceptualize your class as a set, you may find any number of ideas to enhance your teaching and student learning.

George Wallace (Natural Resource Management) has a real gift for conceptualizing his teaching "stage" in a very big way — one that often goes far beyond his classroom walls or the campus itself and inevitably impacts student learning. In a course on multicultural education, for example, George had his students conduct a neighborhood walk of a local barrio, talk to residents in the area, and get a personal feel for different people and places. For one course on environmental impact, he has a long and detailed field assignment that requires students to explore a number of local sites. These experiences supplement the students' readings and help form the basis for a rich discussion in class.

Maura Flannery (Biology), a Carnegie Scholar, has as a pedagogical goal helping her students to feel "at home" in a cell — to imagine a cell as a three-dimensional environment. Her strategies include assigning a paper in which students describe transforming their classroom into a cell. The papers show the students' ability to engage in metaphorical thinking, using everyday objects in the room to represent cell structures.

Exercises

1. Recall a lecture you attended in which the use of the room added to the impact of the message. Make a note of what worked for you and why.

2. Rethink one of your lectures for which, in hindsight, you could have done more with the set of your classroom. What can you do in the future to explore this potential?

The Roles You Play

As an instructor, you do much more than lecture: you play a number of different roles with your students. While you may have graduated to a more specialized focus, you might still have the large, introductory course to prepare. As such, you're also part director, producer, set designer, choreographer, costumer, props manager, and, yes, even roadie — someone has to haul all those papers and props around! (Your dean or department secretary won't.)

Let's look at these teaching roles more closely. Before class ever begins, you invariably serve as your own producer, organizing everything from text selection to the placement of readings on reserve at the library, from the preparation of course syllabi to the scheduling of guest speakers. Once class does begin, you then become responsible for a wide range of activities, from clarifying class procedures to ensuring the effective use of overheads, slides, videotapes, and films. As a lecturer, you really are your own master of ceremonies, providing reminders to the class/audience of what has transpired before, announcing upcoming events, introducing the day's topics, fielding questions that arise, moderating discussions, adding final comments at the very end of each session, handling unexpected interruptions, and so on and so on.

Once class is under way, you also serve as your own warm-up act, getting students engaged and helping them focus on the material at hand. As a facilitator of learning, you invariably juggle a mixture of carrots and sticks. As judge and jury for each course, you decide upon the final grade. As mediator, you may have to resolve conflicts that arise, from complaints about grades to squabbles within student project groups. As a surrogate parent, you may be asked about any number of nonacademic issues as well. Sarason (1999, 43) cites Dewey in defining the teacher's role as "one of coaching, managing, and arranging the learning environment."

So what can we offer you from the stage that will help you manage this degree of role complexity? Again, Sarason (1999, 51) compares the teacher to the performer:

> As with any performing artist, the teacher willingly and internally defines a role with characteristics intended to elicit in an audience of students a set of reactions that will move them willingly to persist in the pursuit of new knowledge and skills.

First and foremost, we encourage you to strive for greater awareness of the roles you play. Playwrights, for example, take great care when developing their characters. Producers make sure everything is organized ahead of time. Directors create a unified performance. Your ability to run through these performance roles before teaching can give you a very helpful systematic check.

Let's look at a concrete example. Michael Lipe (Music) is a colleague who's blessed with a wonderful tenor voice. He often takes leading roles in performances on campus. As a relatively short and heavyset fellow, however, he wouldn't seem the likely choice to play a romantic lead. Yet, in one memorable opera production of *Carmen*, he found himself playing opposite a physically stunning soprano, his love interest, who was taller than he and quite thin. While their voices blended beautifully, their differences in size and shape made them initially incongruous, almost unbelievable, as a couple. Yet Lipe exuded such confidence in his role that audiences were quickly won over. His resonant voice and skill as an actor seemed to make the physical differences disappear.

Similarly, you can study the various roles required of you and learn how to develop each of them as needed. As the master of ceremonies, you open the class and help get everyone set for that day's lesson. As public speaker, you must project to the last row and enunciate clearly. As an expert, you come to class knowledgeable and prepared. As a member of your discipline who cares about the subject, you find ways to share that enthusiasm with your students. As a human being who cares about people generally and each of your students as individuals, you convey that sensitivity as well. Like Lipe, you too can be the character you need to be — with sufficient preparation, confidence, and energy.

Additionally, you can make better use of the range of resources that students themselves bring to class. You can do more to assess their understanding and then draw on the students who do "get it" for help in addressing areas of confusion. As a teacher who understands critical thinking, you can create opportunities for your students to engage their minds and emotions fully, and learn for themselves how best to question, analyze, synthesize, and evaluate. As a "coach" who values cooperation, you can develop activities that promote teamwork. As an instructor who cares about the quality of the learning experience, you assess progress on an ongoing basis, solicit feedback, improvise as needed, and experiment with various innovations and ideas for improvements.

Loren Crabtree (History) is a wonderful instructor who successfully blends his expertise as an Asian scholar with a studied commitment to student learning and a caring climate in class. Although stretched to teach a class when he was dean, he nevertheless wanted to try a series of instructional innovations during one particular semester. The best teachers seem ever open to new possibilities. To his more conventional approach of set readings and lecture/discussion, he added a course requirement of a cooperative student presentation. What was new to his role as teacher was the supervision and guidance required to make these projects successful, including the possibility of intervention when one group got derailed, when another was beset by a repeatedly absent member, and when another never really rose to the challenge to do anything other than divide the group's time among the various members for a series of lackluster mini-lectures.

While the instructor must master this range of roles, the playwright constructs a plot with a range of characters in a carefully developed mosaic of actions, motivations, hopes, fears, and responses. The director makes sure it all works on stage. In many ways, you do the same thing as a lecturer. Each role can be "believable" (i.e., effective) in its own right, both in theory and in practice. And as the actor uses study and practice to create a believable role, you too can become more of the character you need to be in each of the roles you must play. For example, the exams you write can match the objectives you state in your syllabus; your enthusiasm for the subject can be reflected in the energy you bring to class; and your concern for students can manifest itself in your willingness to listen to their ideas.

Exercises

1. Think about actors who have played a wide range of roles. Dustin Hoffman and Meryl Streep come to mind for us. Both of these actors have the reputation of working very hard at every new role. For example, it was widely reported that Hoffman spent a great deal of time learning about his autistic character for *Rain Man*. Streep did many of her own stunts in *Wild River*. Study, experimentation, experience, and practice are keys to succeeding in different roles. Now think about the various "hats" you wear as a lecturer. Which are most comfortable? least? Keep a journal of reflections over several class periods. Think about what you might do to improve your performance in your less comfortable roles.

2. Some actors, of course, have been trapped by a certain kind of role. They've become *typecast*. Can Sylvester Stallone do more than Rocky-like films? Was Marilyn Monroe capable of more than her stereotypical "sex goddess" image? Have you been trapped into certain characterizations that limit your use of the lecture? For example, as a self-styled expert, are you uncomfortable with small-group assignments for which you turn control over to your students and the "blind lead the blind"? At times, it might be important for the "blind" to help each other become more independent. At times, your role as "expert" may produce unhealthy dependencies.

The Roles You Could Play

As a lecturer, you bring your training, knowledge, and experiences into your classes. As we've already suggested, why not bring along other "characters" as well — the personalities behind some of that knowledge, the stories that form the backdrop of your field? Science texts, for instance, tend to describe facts and theories in a straightforward manner, with little discussion of the human stories that brought each discovery to light. Why not share more of the thinking and creativity, the frustrations and perseverance, that underlie these discoveries? How did the greats overcome the ignorance of their times, the prevailing paradigms about truth, and strike out in new directions? How did Galileo overcome the "facts" that were taught to him as well as the prohibitions of the church to reconceptualize the relationship of the Earth to the sun?

Surely your students ought to know as much about the *process* of discovery (the thinking and creativity required to discover things) as the discoveries themselves (the *products* of research). It certainly seems that the future will require people to be more creative, more skilled in problem solving and group dynamics, and more able to work as team members with people from different backgrounds and in diverse settings. What is your role in the preparation of future generations? Could your undergraduates participate more in research? How should the curriculum change to accommodate development of creative thinking and collaborative skills?

Actually, role playing one or more characters can *dramatically* enrich any lecture. Imagine the impact of introducing a whole range of characters into a lecture about the "discovery" of the Americas in 1492. What was the perspective of the native? of the soldiers that accompanied Columbus? of the royalty in Spain that bankrolled the exploration? of the missionaries who accompanied later explorations? Such "discoveries" are found across the centuries, on every continent, as groups move and mix, invade, trade, and assimilate.

What advantages might there be in researching such characters before enacting them? First, you can delve into the actual process of discovery and share with your students the actions, motivations, and relationships behind these stories — all of which can be models for thinking and creativity. Second, you can broaden and deepen your own understanding of the field. Third, such efforts can breathe new life into old subjects. If necessary, you and your students can study a new set of characters each year to provide a constant element of freshness for you. Remember: your enthusiasm speaks volumes to students.

The value of role playing may be especially high at this point in history as we hear the canon in literature challenged, as we rethink expert opinion and presumed objectivity, and as we analyze the contextual background of writers and their environments. The flexibility and empathy acquired from assuming a variety of roles may prove helpful when we ourselves seek more diversity in interpretation, and when we ask students to think for themselves and participate more in the *construction* of meaning.

Suzanne Burgoyne has used role playing in theatre history classes — courses that, in theatre departments, are normally considered "academic" rather than "performance" classes. In American Theatre History, for example, students researched their assigned subjects, then presented oral reports to the class — in the character of a significant historical American actor, director, or designer from the period studied. The student presenters wore appropriate costume pieces and brought in relevant photographs and recordings. Following each report, the presenter remained in character to respond to questions from classmates. In World Theatre History II, each student reported on a major theorist of the modern theatre (e.g., Stanislavski, Brecht, Artaud). Following the reports, the students participated in a mock debate — each in the role of his or her theorist. Suzanne found that significant issues about the nature of acting and the role of theatre in society came to life for the students, as each ardently argued his or her theorist's point of view.

Bill Timpson also makes regular use of spontaneous role playing to illustrate particular points, especially when skills are involved and a lecture/discussion can only accomplish so much. At these points, students need to see certain techniques modeled and then have some practice with them. For example, during a presentation on effective communication—which covers reflective listening, "I" messages, and building consensus—one student described a situation in which, as a tutor in a study session, he was constantly in demand to help students solve particular problems they'd just reviewed. On occasion he'd be asked the same question(s) by the same student(s) two or three times. What follows are the alternative responses Bill offered and role played when this issue arose. The responses would allow the tutor to help students think more systematically through their struggles with learning:

- *Tutor:* It seems you're having difficulty with that problem. Can you say why?
- *Tutor:* When we review material and then students come running to me for help right away, I get frustrated because no learning seems to be occurring. Can we discuss this further?
- *Tutor:* When so many students need help after going through similar solutions, I think we need a new plan in this class. Let's use the consensus model to develop something we can all agree to for guiding our study sessions here.

Bill's experiences in a variety of theatre workshops and productions have pushed him toward using more spontaneous role playing as a way to augment traditional lecture/discussion.

Exercises

1. Reflect on the greats in your own field — those who have influenced your own thinking. Consider coming to class as one of these characters or enlisting the help of someone else to play the role. Let your students interact with you as if the character were actually there. Dave Martin (Economics) has extended an approach he developed for his classes into a new book with a catchy title, *Lively Conversations with Dead Economists*, in which he explores various ideas via hypothetical conversations between himself and various economists of the past. It's creative and often fun, and it seems to make an otherwise dry subject come alive, literally and figuratively. J. Willard Hurst (History) has done something similar in using biographies and autobiographies to help personalize the "names" students read in history or law. Again, this technique helps students humanize otherwise distant figures. It also gives students some insight into the reasons behind the writings. Various law faculty are going to courtroom fiction for representation of memorable characters and compelling stories. Student learning begins with engagement, and the human stories behind various events can be effective reference points.

2. Consider the variety of roles you could add through student presentations. Although you may feel inhibited about "acting in public," every class and every campus has students who enjoy this kind of challenge and can do it well. What fun you can have when you open your classes to these sources of creativity and energy. You might also want to contact a colleague who works with actors, on campus or in the community. Recruit some of those actors for role playing in your classes.

Techniques to Enhance Your Roles

It's one thing to recommend that you take advantage of a variety of roles in your teaching, but it's something very different to help you develop and refine those roles. Here, lessons from the stage may be especially helpful. Actors use a variety of approaches to get into their roles. One set of techniques permits them to work from the *inside-out* and draw on their own experiences and feelings for the emotional foundation of their roles on stage. Another technique permits them to work from the *outside-in* and adopt the physical mannerisms, actions, gestures, movements, and facial expressions required for their stage roles.

Inside-Out

Actors can draw upon their own experiences to recreate particular feelings. It can be difficult to feel sad on cue, for example, night after night. Consequently, some performers will "relive" certain events that produced similar feelings in their own lives, using meditation and concentration to recall as much detail as possible. Once those feelings arise again, the actors can then transfer them to the scene on stage. While you may not need any help in feeling tired before class, you may want to try this approach when you need to get up for teaching, when you want to show your enthusiasm, when you need to crank up your energy level to project yourself effectively in a large lecture hall, when deadlines have you distracted, or when problems with a few students have you down.

We know you've had good days and bad, better lectures and some you'd rather forget. Undoubtedly, you're more enthusiastic about some topics and a bit bored with others. Some classes may feel very special to you, just the right chemistry. For such classes you probably feel more focused, clear, responsive, and effective. In some lectures, though, you've probably had to contend with a variety of disturbances — chatter, reading, sleeping, late arrivals, early departures, and the like. An *inside-out* approach may help you draw on the emotions and experiences that accompanied your best teaching in the past so that you can ride through difficult periods and perform more effectively in the present.

Suzanne Burgoyne adds, however, that affective memory techniques can be problematic with actors, dredging up past personal traumas and opening a psychological Pandora's box. She herself has moved away from this sort of invasive technique for actor training, though she fully recognizes that actors do call upon their life experiences when they portray roles. If you're going to use personal memories, Suzanne stresses, focus on the sensory impressions associated with each memory and not on the emotions themselves.

Inside-out approaches also include the actor's analysis of the character's psychology. What does the character want? What strategies does the character employ in pursuing his or her objective? What is the character thinking at this moment in the play? In getting "inside" the role, then, the actor *thinks* in character and actively seeks to attain the character's objective. In other words, the actor imagines himself or herself as the character and behaves *as if* he or she were the character. If the actor is thinking the thoughts of the character, those thoughts will affect how the actor feels, moves, and speaks — and thus the audience's perception of the character.

To use an inside-out approach yourself, then, you need to think about the requirements of the role you want to play. If you want to play a lively, enthusiastic teacher, thinking "I'm tired" or "this class is boring" will interfere with your performance — your body language will reflect your thoughts, and your students will read your body language. If you want to play a passionate, dedicated teacher, then focusing your energy on really achieving your teaching objective can light a fire under you and your students.

Outside-In

Another technique that actors use requires analysis from a more behavioral perspective. Actors choose a way of walking, for instance, or a particular voice for a character, or a gestural pattern. In this approach, the actor begins with the body rather than the psychology of the character. For some performers, the *outside-in* approach seems purely a matter of technical skill. Through manipulating the voice and body, the actor moves the audience by making them believe the character is moved — while feeling nothing at all themselves. However, the outside-in approach also can generate genuine feeling on the part of the actor. An actor who tenses all her muscles in order to play a stressed-out character will soon start feeling stressed out herself. A connection exists between body and mind; thus the outside-in and inside-out approaches are merely different starting points on the way toward a complete characterization.

As an instructor, it's critical for you to think about an important quality like "enthusiasm." For the outside-in approach, you define it in terms of descriptors — what it "looks like" or "sounds like" or how you should "behave." You create the appropriate gestures, movements, expressions, vocal pitch, and timing. Likewise, you can identify the behavioral descriptions you need for other desired qualities in your role as lecturer: for example, the patience you need to listen well when students raise questions, or to wait for them as they formulate their responses; the nimbleness you may want when you facilitate debates and discussions within the lecture format; the concentration you need to sustain focus on a lesson's through-line (learning objectives). How fast should you make your movements and your speech? What about your pitch?

Try behaving in the way you've defined — as "enthusiastic," for instance. See if, just by moving and speaking in an enthusiastic way, you don't find yourself feeling more lively and energized.

Exercises

1. Think about one of your best lectures. Visualize yourself back in the moment. See the room and your students. Hear yourself teach. See yourself lecturing. What did you look like? How did you move and sound? See if the attendant feelings can energize your preparation for an upcoming lecture. Can you recycle some of what worked back then into the *now*?

2. Become aware of your own thought patterns in class. What thoughts are likely to help you achieve your teaching objectives? What thoughts may interfere?

3. Try both approaches — *inside-out* and *outside-in*. Which works best for you? Would a mixture of the two be even better? (Many actors use a combination of approaches.)

4. The goal for using either of these techniques, or both in combination, is to enhance your effectiveness in a *natural* way. Work on finding an appropriate comfort level with each of these approaches.

Pacing

Every good lecture has a certain pace: not so fast as to leave students feeling overwhelmed and weary from notetaking, and not so slow that they drift off. After an introductory *preview,* you could intersperse periods of information-giving with periodic reminders about underlying core concepts, thereby helping your students with the intellectual organization of all they have to assimilate. Ausubel's (1963) groundbreaking research on the *advance organizer* demonstrates the importance of a conceptual framework for supporting student learning and retention. You could also mix in questions (e.g., "How many of you think that...?") with brief discussions (e.g., "Does anyone have a comment on this issue?").

Although you may have a firm grasp of your subject's knowledge base, your students will not. Inevitably, and especially in large introductory settings, some students will not share your enthusiasm for the course material, and a few may even be resistant or downright hostile. Most, however, will respond positively to variety; attention spans have their limitations, even for the best students. For example, you can sprinkle examples and demonstrations throughout a lecture to provide concrete references to the real world, counterweights to more abstract and conceptual material. A conclusion, then, could recap the lecture and re-emphasize essential learning.

Any good script also incorporates a variety of actions and feelings. An audience can absorb only so much tragedy, banter, or suspense during any one stretch. Playwrights change the mood or pace to augment, contrast, or shade certain emotions. Actions on stage can build up in overt or subtle ways toward a climax. So too can you shape a lecture and add examples, demonstrations, and questions to provide variety while moving toward conclusions.

More importantly, alterations in pacing may make a world of difference to students who are struggling. Two different incidents with the same student really brought this issue home to Bill Timpson. In the first instance, Bill called on M, one of his best students, to respond to what another student had said. "I can't answer that," she said. A bit perturbed and thinking that M just wasn't listening, Bill quickly called on another student. The next morning, Bill found a rather angry email message from M noting that she'd just not heard what had been said and wanted it repeated. She went on to complain about the fast pace of class, which, she thought, made discussions brief and superficial. Bill responded on email by apologizing for cutting her off and admitting that the large number of students enrolled (seventy-five) did make him anxious whenever the pace slowed.

A few days later, another incident arose with M. She asked for more information about a course requirement concerning computer applications. When no one else admitted to sharing the same concern, Bill was initially resigned to dealing with M on the issue after class. But he then had the good sense to slow down and ask for those conversant with the Internet to come up to the front and describe their progress with the assignment. Five students came forward, and the resulting discussion was very productive for everyone; it turned out that many other students were also uncertain about the assignment but were unwilling to admit as much. Twenty minutes were lost from Bill's plan for that day, but those twenty minutes proved well worth the shift in plans and change of pace.

As is true in the theatre, a dry and monotonous plodding through even the most brilliantly conceived material can drive off all but the pathologically persistent. Consider putting more of that brilliance onto paper, or on reserve at the library, or on the Web, using more of your class time for the kinds of interactions that can take advantage of the collective talents, creativity, and energy in the room.

At the other end of the continuum is the challenge you inevitably face with material that may be inherently dry, at least on the surface. With such topics, your own energy and enthusiasm can keep an engaging pace to instruction. For example, Irene Vernon (English) teaches a tough course on the law surrounding U.S. relationships with Native Americans. It includes stories of bloody wars and massacres, racist and genocidal thinking, and treaties broken amid official deceit and deception. All of this tortured history is encased within complex legal documents and court opinions, primary sources that are further complicated by racist language and custom. Recognizing the difficulty of the material, Vernon uses her big personality, her booming voice, her natural vivaciousness, and her passionate concern for the material to pull students into active engagement and critical analysis.

Exercises

1. Track the pacing of a favorite movie or play. Note the periods of comic relief. A great thriller is usually more like a roller coaster than a nonstop reign of terror. Periods of calm and unpredictability heighten the fear factor. In the classroom, many instructors use regular reminders about what will be on an upcoming exam to jolt students into paying closer attention. While you should minimize the use of fear in your classes, there are other possibilities worth exploring: your use of pauses or silences; the ways discussions or debates can heat up and animate everyone; or your use of free-writing exercises in class to promote student reflection. Examine one of your recent lectures for pacing. Could you have varied the pace more to heighten students' engagement with the material?

2. Rethink the pacing of an upcoming lecture. For example, can you provide periods of relief from the usual routine — from the presentation of information or the completion of problem sets? Could regular stops for a few questions or comments give you a chance to emphasize certain key

points? Could these stops also allow your students some relief from the intensity of notetaking to think about the ideas and issues you're raising?

Warming Up

This is a bit of a repeat, but we think it's worth repeating: The lecture format can be a very pressured situation, especially as class size increases, and so we think you'll benefit from even a little warm-up. Nothing in teaching comes closer to the requirements for the stage than the lecture. Remember that most performers treat warm-up as a given, often beginning their rehearsal and pre-performance time together with stretches and vocal exercises. Taking a few minutes to warm up for class will help you prepare emotionally and physically, and it will complement your intellectual preparation of the content as well. For a description of some warm-up exercises you can use, be sure to reread Chapter 2.

Movements

Few lectures require extensive movement. Routinely, you enter the classroom and lay out your materials at the front. You may use the board, an overhead, a film, a video, or slides to illustrate key points. You may wander a bit in the front of the classroom. But rarely will you have anything "staged," "blocked," or "choreographed." If you move much at all, you may just pace as you think and talk. Is this approach effective for you? for your students? What else might be possible?

Some teachers have largely abandoned the traditional lecture. Instead, they want something more dynamic and energizing. For example, using a case study approach allows Marty Fettman (pathology) to serve as a facilitator for discussions with classes of one hundred, two hundred, or more. He may move around the lecture hall as different students offer their ideas and others take issue with those ideas. In this way, Marty's students analyze the presenting symptoms and discuss possible remedies. The cases are true to life and require students to act like practicing veterinarians. Marty's forays out from behind the lectern physically shift the focus from his own expertise to a large-group guided discovery process. He challenges his students to think for themselves. Marty's energy, movements, and creativity add life to a professional curriculum often dominated by lecture-based information giving. As a scientist who has flown in space on the shuttle, Marty seems to enjoy the challenge of dynamic and interactive teaching.

Although there's a big tradeoff in the time devoted to content coverage, another popular option for helping you create a more dynamic classroom format involves small-group assignments or student presentations that allow you to get students up, moving, and participating. Apart from the obvious benefit of helping sustain student interest, active learning also can dramatically enhance students' understanding of your material. Developmentalists like Piaget (1952), Bruner (1966), Kohlberg (1981), Gilligan (1982), and Perry (1981, 1999) have long emphasized the power of activity in promoting deeper learning. A new generation of developmentalists like Tharp and Gallimore (1988) and Rogoff (1990) continue to reaffirm the relationship between active learning and the development of critical thinking skills.

Other critics of the traditional information-driven, expert-dominated lecture (e.g., Belenky et al. 1986, Tobias 1990) also call for more participatory learning in higher education, so that women and minority students, in particular, can have more peer support and assistance. Active and cooperative learning within a social context foster success in large and high-demand classes where teachers feel they have to cover a great deal of material.

Historically, the traditional approach to course design and grading has also served a gatekeeping function, often producing an impersonal and competitive environment where norm-referenced assessment (grading on the curve) defines class climate and discourages cooperation. When teachers try to sift through the masses of students to uncover "those few with potential," they inevitably — surprise, surprise — find students much like themselves.

A massive cloning process results, argues Sheila Tobias (1990), one that tends to replicate the values, perspectives, styles, gender, and culture of the teachers, most often older white males. When this occurs, everyone suffers: some students get "weeded" out for the wrong reasons; the disciplines themselves lose out on a rich and diverse talent base; and at the very heart of the research agenda, the cloning process compromises the pursuit of new knowledge, doing more to sustain prevailing paradigms than to support healthy and creative challenges.

We think our lessons from the stage can help you become more aware of the "choreography" that does occur in your classes and that may enhance learning. Every script written for production includes directions for stage movements: who should be where for which lines and actions, and when. Although actors, directors, and choreographers discover the specifics of how to physicalize what is only on paper, writers do sketch out basic movements in the script. Unless improvisation is called for — which is rare — no one wants any surprises on stage.

While spontaneous digressions, questions, and discussions can challenge students' thinking and stimulate their learning, the planned lecture can also benefit from notations about movements or blocking. For example:

- You could give yourself written reminders to get out from behind the lectern when you think you're reading too much from prepared notes and losing students in the process.

- You could remind yourself to move toward a student who asks a question, to get that person's name, and, in this way, help personalize the class more fully. Have students print their first names on sheets of paper, then fold them over to stand up conference style on the front of their desks.

- After giving a small-group assignment, you could make a note to yourself to move quickly around the room to help keep students on task.

- You could indicate when you want to use the overhead projector or where you could stand when slides are showing so as not to block anyone's view.

In *The Teacher Moves: An Analysis of Nonverbal Activity,* Grant and Hennings (1971) report on a variety of studies that affirm the importance of teacher movement in the classroom. In one study, a number of teachers were videotaped and their movements analyzed. A full eighty percent of these movements were deemed relevant to the instructional process, although not in ways you might expect. Over sixty percent involved *conducting* behavior (controlling student participation, getting students' attention). Approximately thirty percent involved *wielding* (moving toward action, picking up assignments, reading). Less than ten percent involved *acting* (emphasizing, illustrating, pantomiming, role playing).

Grant and Hennings go on to make several recommendations for teachers:

- **Eliminate Contradictory Cues.** Too many teachers undercut what they think is exciting when they deliver their lectures in a dry, rigid manner. Students believe what they hear and see. Allow yourself to get animated when appropriate, or reflective when important questions arise, or even confused when a problem gets complex.

- **Increase the Right Kind of Nonverbal Cues.** Teachers dominate much of the allotted classroom time, and nearly all of the time in lectures. Look for opportunities to substitute nonverbal cues for verbal expressions. For example, you can reflect pleasure over a particular response with a facial expression or a hand gesture, thus allowing more space for other students to participate. Felman (2001) describes emphasizing a student's classroom declaration of a paradigm shift with a mock faint, generating applause for the student's transformation.

- **Eliminate Irrelevant Nonverbal Cues.** Given that twenty percent of the teacher's classroom movements are personal and unrelated to instruction, try to minimize irrelevant nonverbal cues. Just think back to your own teachers who were plagued by distracting nervous mannerisms — playing with their hair or beards, constantly adjusting their glasses, blinking excessively, jingling their keys or coins.

Stage directors know that movement draws an audience's attention, so they carefully choreograph all movement on stage. The movement may look spontaneous, but it has been thoroughly planned and rehearsed. In class, you may not want to preplan your gestures, but some basic stage principles about how to use movement for emphasis can prove helpful.

For instance, actors and directors use movement to *point*, or emphasize, significant lines. The principles of pointing involve the relationship between movement and speech. There are four possible ways to use movement with a line of dialogue. One can:

1. Move before the line;

2. Move after the line;

3. Move during the line;

4. Break up the line by saying part of it, moving, then saying the rest.

To illustrate how pointing works, consider the line, "Gwendolyn, will you marry me?" from Oscar Wilde's *The Importance of Being Earnest*.

Let's say the movement the actor will perform is to kneel in front of Gwendolyn. Thus, the actor can:

- Kneel first, then say the line;

- Say the line, then kneel;

- Say the line while kneeling;

- Say part of the line — for instance, "Gwendolyn, will you ..." — then kneel and finish the line — "... marry me?"

Try performing the line yourself, all four ways. Note that:

- Moving before the line emphasizes the line;

- Moving after the line emphasizes the movement;

- Moving during the line de-emphasizes both the line and the movement;

- Movement that breaks up the line emphasizes the part of the line following the movement.

The application of these principles to lecturing is subtle but real: the best place for you to move in relation to a climactic, significant point is probably just before the meaningful statement — or the most important words in that statement. That movement will "point," or draw your students' attention to, the significant statement. The movement doesn't have to be as obvious as pounding on the table. A step, a gesture, or a turn will do the trick. If you've been pacing, a sudden stop can catch the students' interest.

The principles of pointing also make it clear that you should not move during the significant statement — because such movement will distract your audience and de-emphasize the important point you want to make. Good comics instinctively understand timing and pointing; you won't see one move during the punch line of a joke!

Exercises

1. Have someone — a friend, colleague, or student — track your movements during class, noting what happens when and where. What effects do your movements appear to have on student engagement (listening, attentiveness)? Similarly, have someone videotape one of your lectures and get a good look at yourself in action. These kinds of data alone

may suggest areas for improvement. Discussing the results or viewing the tape with others can get you valuable additional opinions.

2. Keep a journal for recording your insights. Jot down your impressions, worries, and hopes before each class and then again immediately after each class is over. Reread your thoughts and reactions to earlier class sessions. What patterns emerge?

3. Once you decide to make a change, either to eliminate distracting movements or add movements as enhancements to your lecture, give yourself several trials. Habits are difficult to break and new ones challenging to implant. Pacing nervously across the front of the class may distract some students. Continuing to talk while you move toward the chalkboard may make you inaudible. You could use a portable microphone to help students hear whatever you do. Moving out from behind the lectern and toward students who ask questions may help re-engage everyone. Your physical proximity to students can affect their motivations. Experiment. Put reminders in your notes.

Here again you can learn a lesson from the stage. Actors know that it's easier to *do* something on stage than to try *not* to do something. For instance, if an actor has fidgety hands, the director will often give him or her something specific to do with them — a character gesture or a stage property to work with. If you discover you have a nervous habit to break, look for a specific, concrete, helpful action you can perform instead of the nervous habit. If you have a tendency to pace aimlessly, for instance, find a way of grounding yourself. While you're learning the new habit, you can write into your lecture script periodic cues to remind yourself to perform the desired behavior.

Solicit ongoing feedback on your progress, perhaps from one or more students who would like to earn some extra credit. Videotaping your class may seem intimidating, but once you get past the initial "shock" of your own appearance — like many professionals, you're probably your own worst critic — this *purely objective* viewpoint can prove helpful. It also will give you a good sense of what your students see. Using both sources of feedback in concert may be ideal.

Voice

Lecturers depend on their voices. Yet few have studied the physiology of the voice or the nuances of speech that can impact their effectiveness in class. Speech scholars, teachers, and coaches, for example, have long known about the benefits of appropriate pauses and timing, of projection and volume, of pitch and inflection, of good articulation and clear enunciation. Most people judge others based in part upon speech. Given your own speech patterns, what do your students think of you? While we cannot expect to do justice to each of these areas within a chapter on lecturing, we can give you enough of an explanation to raise your awareness and get you started.

As we noted earlier, a pause can serve a variety of functions in the theatre: to underscore the conflict of a scene, to hold for a laugh, and most often to allow the audience member to wonder, "What will happen next?" Similar results can come from *pausing* in class. Even without any background as a performer, you can recognize the benefits when time for reflection helps deepen learning.

Anyone who communicates with an audience — whether from the stage or in the classroom — also needs clear articulation and enunciation. This concern may be particularly important for you if you have a regional dialect, a non-English-speaking heritage, or a speaking disability. In these situations, think about consulting with a speech expert on your campus or in your community.

Timing is everything, it's been said. As students in class with a superb lecturer, or as audience members in the presence of great actors, we often admire their "sense of timing." Understanding how rapidly or slowly to deliver a particular line, as well as how long to hold a pause, can help you engage your students or lend power to the actor's performance. In class, changes in pacing can add variety, surprise, and life to your presentation.

Unless you're watching a pantomime or a dance production, however, the "word is the thing," sayeth Shakespeare. Your students *must* be able to hear your voice clearly, even in the very back of a large lecture hall. Use any amplification possible. Even the seasoned performer can tire the trained voice after *projecting* for three hours at a time. Speakers find that two of the most difficult aspects of voice involve *pitch* and *inflection*. Pitch is the quality of vocal sound — the relative highs and lows (i.e., number of vibrations per second), while inflection represents the rise and fall of the voice. *Intonation* is the particular tone.

As students in a lecture hall or as audience members in the theatre, we appreciate teachers and performers who also can add drama and nuances to their lines. For the professional actor, the voice becomes an instrument. In performances of poetic drama, such as Shakespeare, the actor's vocal work can be as varied and melodic as that of a singer. British and French actors are particularly noted for the attention they pay to vocal performance. In France, for instance, people talk about going to "hear" rather than "see" a play. In melodrama and farce, the audience may accept exaggerated vocal expression — the character's squeal of embarrassment or gasp of shock — because of the unrealistic style of the play. In realistic drama, which reflects our everyday lives, we expect actors to give the illusion of speaking naturally and spontaneously.

Students in your classes also expect you to speak naturally — but you, like the actor, can benefit from vocal training to make your voice more expressive. While you may find limited need for using the full range of your voice, changes in *emphasis* can be effective for sustaining student attention and enhancing their understanding. Consider the following suggestions:

- Punctuate key points by increasing the volume of your voice.

- Explore the use of near whispers to express sadness and sensitivity.

- Speed up your talk to reflect your own enthusiasm.

- When you read a passage from a previous era — perhaps out of the history of your discipline — try to capture the right tone.

- Certainly a monotone rings a death knell for any classroom presentation! Avoid it at all cost.

- Seek out a trusted colleague and ask him or her to come to one of your class sessions to assess your monotonal tendencies.

Exercises

1. Experiment with a variety of warm-ups before class, from humming a favorite melody to running up and down your vocal range with "la la la la." You may never have had any formal training or practice, but you still can benefit from some vocal exercises. If nothing else, such exercises can increase your awareness of inflection, pitch, and intonation.

2. Record yourself on audiotape to hear how you sound in class. Then try a videotape to see how well your voice matches what you're doing with your facial expressions, gestures, movements, and props.

Props

Undoubtedly, you make extensive use of props (short for stage *properties*), but you just don't think of them as "props." Anything you use to augment what you say can be considered a prop, including the lectern, chalk, the overhead, slides, videotapes, films, materials for demonstrations, a table, or a chair. You can even include the intellectual "things" you use to supplement your instruction — cases for law or business, problems for medical and health sciences, word and story problems in mathematics. You can improve your use of props by exposing yourself to new ideas, experimenting and receiving feedback, and practicing.

Do you need props for every lecture to be an effective teacher? Not necessarily. Do you remember John Houseman's character — Law professor Kingsley — in the film *Paper Chase*? He rarely used props — only his experience, authority, and commanding presence. Robin Williams's character in *Dead Poets Society* — English teacher John Keating — employed a range of facial expressions, vocal inflections, volume, accents, body movements, postures, and gestures.

Everyone, however, can benefit from thinking about props more consciously. Let us share an example from one of our classes. Piaget (1952) has categorized cognitive development into distinct stages that young people move through as they mature. In addition, Piaget identified certain tasks that serve as markers for movement into more advanced stages. When Bill Timpson lectures about one of these tasks — for example, the conservation of length — his students often struggle to understand that children can think in *qualitatively* different terms. Before age six, it's common for a child to say that a pipe cleaner has gotten shorter when it's been bent in the middle. If you override your own logical thought processes, you yourself can "see" (literally) clearly that the *end points are closer together*. The young child concludes that the entire pipe cleaner has gotten shorter.

In time, children are able to override this visual domination with a more logical conclusion: that is, because nothing was taken away, the pipe cleaner must still be the same length as before. Using a pipe cleaner in class as a prop has helped Bill demonstrate this phenomenon to his own students. Showing a videotape of first- graders struggling with this concept of conservation, some insisting that the pipe cleaner is indeed shorter, then provides the conclusive visual evidence that these university students need. Learning about this phenomenon through lectures or reading alone just isn't as effective.

Lots of other examples come to mind. A physicist brings in a pendulum to demonstrate properties and problems. A sociologist uses large portraits and photographs of the writers he covers in his survey class. Seeing these faces seems to help some students relate better to each writer, to set each within a historical context. A lecturer in music uses a piano to illustrate various concepts. The availability of the piano allows him a certain degree of spontaneity in class — especially valuable when students raise questions.

Surprisingly, many students appreciate even the simplest of props. In the physics class, some students benefit from seeing an idea in action as a supplement to their reading and lecture notes. In the sociology class, many students say that seeing the portraits gives them a historic or visual frame of reference. The images also seem to permit the lecturer to add more personal, biographical, and engaging information to otherwise dry, theoretical material. In the music class, the lecturer enjoys playing and the students respond enthusiastically to live demonstrations.

Working with such props is profoundly important to teachers and learning. We know from so many different sources that appealing to all of the senses has distinct advantages when it comes to teaching and learning. Students do have different sensory strengths and preferences, different learning styles. Using visuals or participatory demonstrations pushes students to engage more than their listening and notetaking skills. Multisensory input can strengthen students' memories, giving them more cues for recall. Active learning can energize everyone.

In class, props can include the most common of items. A text to read from, for example, can become a prop when you hold it up for summary comments. John Finley, a classics professor at Harvard University, was famous for roaming the stage at Sanders Theatre while holding the microphone chord as it trailed behind him, periodically making rather grandiose flips of the chord when he had to change direction. These simple theatrics helped enliven his lectures about Greek and Roman drama. Every campus has its own stories; over the years you yourself have probably seen examples of props that worked famously (as well as those that bombed).

When you use a table at the front of the classroom to sit or lean on, you're using a prop — at least in the tradition of a staged production. An active consciousness of the nature and purpose of the physical objects you use—the props in your class—can help you eliminate distractions, engage your students, and enhance their learning. Some lecturers do seem rooted to their lecterns. Others muffle their words because they talk to the blackboard while they're writing. Some seem addicted to their PowerPoint presentations, slides, or overheads. Others seem wedded to a style of teaching that has them—and their students—writing furiously all class long, often filling and erasing a seemingly endless progression of board panels. While students do stay busy this way, the information could be distributed as handouts or sold as part of course readers, and class time used for activities and interactions that do more to enhance students' understanding and learning.

On stage, the use of any prop is very carefully assessed and orchestrated so that it enhances a scene, action, or character. Playwrights, directors, set designers, and performers know the importance of using props for a specific purpose on stage. The same can be true in class: if you don't use any props at all, you may be missing out on some wonderful instructional allies. But when you fidget with the lectern, you may actually distract some of your students.

What lessons from the stage can help you determine which props might be effective, when, and how? Consider the following suggestions:

- Examine your current use of props, and eliminate those that may be distracting—for example, nervous fidgeting with your notes or chalk. Getting feedback from observers or interviews with students can help you identify these distractions quickly and point you toward possible new behaviors.

- Add props that will enhance your teaching— e.g., a laser pointer, overheads, slides, videotapes or films, or materials that can illustrate or reinforce certain ideas.

- Improve your use of such straightforward props as the board with some forethought, feedback, and experimentation. Your writing may be small and difficult for those in the last row to see; or perhaps you clutter the board and confuse your students; or maybe you could improve your diagrams.

- Experiment with using different-colored chalk or markers so that your students have some visual help with organizing information.

- Think about other kinds of props that could enhance particular topics — a flag when you're discussing national identity or patriotism, articles of clothing as historical references, a pendulum or pulley when you're demonstrating aspects of arcs for physics or math, a vintage instrument when you're telling the story of a particular musician, or actual food items that are introduced as new vocabulary words in a foreign language class. Bill Timpson has made extensive use of outdoor obstacle courses as catalysts for learning about teamwork and risk taking. Climbing up a forty-foot pole and walking across a beam can be a memorable way to help students confront their own fears and develop self-confidence.

Actors love working with props. A particular prop associated with a character can help individualize that character for the audience. Consequently, actors often select character props even if they're not specified in the script. Likewise, you could enhance your classroom "persona" with a judicious choice of props, as the Harvard classics professor we mentioned earlier made the microphone chord his particular trademark. When Suzanne Burgoyne taught in a room that lacked a wall clock, for instance, she brought to class — every day — a foot-high, red and yellow, Big Ben alarm clock, an eccentricity that students enjoyed. Actors also appreciate working with props because "stage business" with the props gives the actors something specific to do, reducing their performance anxiety and the usual accompaniment of fidgety habits.

Two final notes: Whenever you use an animal or a child during a lecture, be prepared to be upstaged. These kinds of distractions can be difficult for an audience member to ignore. Also, even if you can handle mistakes or failures with relative ease, practice with each of your props — especially microphones and audiovisual equipment, particularly when you use a lecture hall for the first time.

Exercises

1. Inventory your classroom needs for chalk, markers, overheads, pointers, slides, computer disks, handouts, and the like. What else is available and how could you learn about it? What else would help? Are you familiar with the equipment? Do other rooms have what you need? Could you get access to them?

2. Review your plans for a future lecture. What props would enhance your talk? What would be interesting for students to see and experience?

Lighting

Like the lecture hall itself, lighting is just there. You learn to deal with it, whatever you have. You may dim the lights for slides or films, or try to counteract the effect of bright sunlight. Lighting can certainly affect what students see on the board or the overhead projector, especially if they're in the back of the room. Yet, teachers typically have little control over the lighting in their classrooms. Minimally, you can always discipline yourself to check with your students about adjustments that might help them. Even though you don't have elaborate lighting equipment, we still believe there are lessons from the stage that you can use to enhance the learning of your students.

Lighting for stage and screen receives a great deal of attention. Most theatres, even amateur ones, enlist the help of someone who's experienced in all aspects of lighting. While written scripts may include some indications, the director and lighting designer are really on their own. Most often, the lighting designer, in consultation with the director, designs a "light plot" and hangs and focuses the lighting instruments, experimenting with different color filters. Considerable time goes into determining and recording the necessary lighting cues. At least one technical rehearsal is devoted to setting lighting levels and cues with the actors on stage.

Stage lighting serves various functions, impacting visibility, emphasis, and mood. The primary function of lighting, of course, is visibility — the audience needs to see the actors' faces. The lighting designer, however, will modify the lighting according to the need for emphasis. The most brightly lit actor draws the most audience attention; observe, for instance, how the follow spot on the lead singer in a musical comedy makes him or her stand out from the chorus.

In theatres today, the darkened auditorium and brightly lit stage direct the focus toward what's happening on stage rather than in the audience. This convention did not become established in the theatre until the nineteenth century; in prior periods of history, audiences were more active, even vocal, shouting out approval or disapproval of the performance, and often coming to the theatre as much to display themselves and interact with their friends as to pay attention to the play. Darkening the auditorium contributed to the transformation of the audience into quiet and passive observers. If you as a teacher rely heavily on dimmed classrooms for slides, films, or videotapes, we suggest you think about the potentially parallel transformation of your students into passive learners.

Creation of mood is the most innovative aspect of lighting design. Common sense shows us how the quality of light affects human emotions. Think, for instance, of how a bright, sunny day can raise everyone's spirits, while dull, overcast skies often have the opposite effect. Lighting designers can manipulate the intensity, direction, and color of stage lighting to create a brooding, malevolent atmosphere for *Macbeth* or a sentimental, romantic mood for a musical comedy love scene.

Given the elaborate equipment that stage designers have at their command, you may see little if any parallel with what you have at your disposal in the classroom. Yet designers in many small theatres achieve impressive effects with few instruments or dimmers but considerable ingenuity. Certainly the principles of visibility and emphasis apply to teaching and learning. For example, spotlights trained on the podium can help keep the focus on the lecturer. A darkened room can augment the impact of slides, film, and television. Some mixture of lighting may serve best for showing overheads. Turn on the lights in the auditorium to encourage questions and discussion — more active involvement from your students.

Creating mood poses a problem in many classrooms. If you have a choice of classrooms, opt for one with plenty of windows and natural lighting, a space where you feel comfortable, alive. Fluorescent lighting has its critics. If you can find a classroom with incandescent lights, grab it! You may not have much choice, but exploring and asking can't hurt. On nice days, consider holding class outside. It's amazing what ingenious and determined faculty members can accomplish, both within and outside the formal rules. Remember that your enthusiasm in class is quite contagious and speaks volumes to students about your interest in the material. Beware if your own enthusiasm is depressed by a "dungeon" of a room.

Knowing what's possible where lighting is concerned may be the biggest challenge for you. While considering what aspects of lighting might impact a presentation, look more carefully at student experience. When Bill Timpson requires presentations in his classes, he often encourages the students to be creative — to think first about learning and then, if appropriate, use lighting as a tool. Given this license, students often light the classroom space in new ways, and their presentations improve accordingly. Your modeling a variety of possibilities can help.

Exercises

1. Take a few minutes to reflect on lectures you've witnessed that have made effective use of lighting to enhance your learning. Conversely, which lectures have been distracting because the lighting was too bright or too dim?

2. Think about an upcoming lecture and what changes you could attempt to make with lighting, no matter how subtle. Use a penlight for focusing attention on slides or overheads. Get to know the lighting options you have in your classroom(s). For example, some rooms allow you to light the board while dimming the lights everywhere else.

3. Get in the habit of checking regularly with your students about the kinds of lighting that help them learn most effectively.

Costumes

Costume design serves important functions in the theatre. Costumes help establish the historical period when a play takes place. Costumes also delineate character, illustrating the social and economic status of each role as well as the individual's personality and tastes. Costume historians argue that all clothing is costume. Clothing provides a means of communicating the "persona" or role a person assumes — the way he or she wants to be perceived by others. Actors discover that merely putting on their costumes helps to transform them into their characters because they feel different in costume. Costumes also affect bearing, posture, and movement. It's hard to play Queen Elizabeth I in jeans!

So what about you? What does costume mean outside the theatre? While we don't espouse the "dress for success" philosophy, we do want to raise your awareness about the choices you have and the potential impact of your clothing on your students and their learning. What you wear may affect how students perceive you. Your clothing can make you the powerful, distant professional or the casual, friendly adult. Everyone notices and smiles when Halloween gives some teachers and students permission to be more playful and dress in costumes, providing relief from the routine of campus life. As you explore the different roles you play in the classroom, think about your own "costuming."

If you're working on changing your role, remember that how you dress can also affect how you feel and behave. A favorite outfit can add some class to the first or last day. Older and more comfortable clothes might make it easier for you to conduct a demonstration or take your students outside on the grass. Students' willingness to join in may also depend on the clothes *they* are wearing, so you should forewarn them of what activities you plan for future class sessions. When working hard in class, Bill Timpson takes off his sport coat or sweater, loosens his tie, or rolls up his sleeves. At the end of the session he often feels a bit like that great soul singer, James Brown — the "hardest working man in show business" — who leaves the stage exhausted, his jacket draped on his shoulders, in a *Cold Sweat* after a charged rendition of *I Feel Good*.

To get more insight into how your clothing impacts your students' learning, look at your student evaluations. Do students see you as distant and intimidating? If so, might a more informal style of clothing help? If you're planning on lecturing about someone from the history of your discipline, see if you can use some clothing from that era to give students a sense of the time and place—a hat or wig, a jacket, accessories, makeup, or even a complete outfit if you can find one. Leigh Ann Wheeler, an assistant professor of History at Bowling Green State University, wore a Victorian costume—complete with corset and bustle—while teaching a class on "Women in the Modern United States" at Rollins College. Observing Leigh Ann's restricted movement and her struggle to get her breath in that corset, her students found the oppression of women embodied in fashion of the period coming to life for them. Now able to imagine how the feminine body felt and moved in the nineteenth century, they were eager to delve into the readings about Victorian women, who at first had seemed far away and perhaps irrelevant to them. Costumes, then, can not only be fun, but also can serve as an important stimulus for learning.

Exercises

1. Take a few minutes and reflect on lecturers you've seen whose clothes or costuming added something, no matter how subtle. Were you ever thrown off by what a lecturer wore?

2. Think about an upcoming lecture and what impact a change in your usual costume could have on it. Try some ideas for laughs. Students appreciate humor. The resulting variety could provide a counterweight to the seriousness and work your course might usually require.

Notes

Most published scripts are designed so that actors, directors, and other stage personnel have plenty of room to make written notes in the margins. These notes become reminders and cues for study and rehearsal. Successful productions are never left to chance, especially when the additional anxiety of performing in front of an audience can block actors' memories and cues — unless they are overlearned. With complete confidence in your command of the material for a particular class, you can concentrate more on reactions from students: who seems alert and who seems confused, who may have a question and who's prepared to respond, who could use a hint and who might be on the verge of an important insight.

The marginal notes a lecturer might use include last-minute updates or comments about current events, ideas about student involvement, responses to questions that arose in previous class sessions, hints about material to be emphasized on the next exam, or announcements about relevant activities on campus. You can make similar use of notes so that you can remember, for example, to:

- Ask specific questions at certain points to probe student thinking and promote more active participation.

- Wait for students who may need a little more time to get their own thoughts together, especially in the very public arena of the classroom.

- Use a visual of some sort — an overhead, a video, or a slide.

- Have students complete a short written response and try to put ideas or solutions into their own words.

- Move to areas of the room you often neglect.

- Poll the entire class on certain issues — e.g., "How many of you believe the best response is _____ ?"

Notes can also help you connect one class session to another. While you've been concentrating on preparing for class, your students, as we mentioned earlier, come from any number of other activities — other classes, chatting with friends, sleeping, eating, even studying! Taking some time at the beginning of each class to remind them of your most recent points and where the day's lecture will go can be very helpful as a warm-up and orientation. You also can make notes about ideas you'd like to apply when the course is offered again—topics you'd approach differently, other examples you'd like to use, or activities that might help resolve the kinds of confusion students experienced this time around.

Exercises

1. Take out some recent lecture notes. Think about what happened in class. What could you have noted that might have helped in the next class period?

2. After the next class session, take a few minutes to reflect on what happened and what you might do differently next time—how you began, what sparked the most interest, where students seemed to lose interest or miss the plot, what you should revisit in future classes, who participated and who did not, and what students learned.

3. Talk to your colleagues and find out who makes notations in the margins of their notes. How do these comments help them?

Impact on Students

In the theatre, a production is not a production until it plays before an audience. While a poor production is quickly forgotten, a good one will engage an audience and a great one is memorable. Unfortunately, there are no guarantees; despite the best of intentions, a good cast of characters, considerable expense, and a lot of hard work, some performances just never catch on with audiences. Hollywood history is full of big-budget, star-studded box office busts. Consider Cimino's *Heaven's Gate*, Dustin Hoffman and Warren Beatty in *Ishtar*, or *Cutthroat Island* with Geena Davis. At last count, Kevin Costner's megabuck *Waterworld* may break even, but $200 million plus?

Just as often there are *sleepers* — productions with low budgets and a cast of unknowns that come out of nowhere to spark a lot of audience interest and make a lot of money. *Pulp Fiction* was produced for a fraction of what it took in. *The Crying Game* surprised everyone, as did *Clueless* and *I Know What You Did Last Summer*. How about the cult classic, *The Rocky Horror Picture Show*, or the black comedy about GM's closing of the Flint, Michigan assembly plant, *Roger and Me?*

The same is true for teaching. Your students can tell you, either directly or through a variety of nonverbal signals, whether or not they're engaged intellectually or emotionally. An experienced lecturer can often *read* a class and make necessary modifications to his or her presentation along the way. You're not tied to your lecture notes as actors are tied to their scripts. Indeed, you have the freedom to improvise and create as you go.

Bill Timpson remembers fondly one of his own professors who would briefly stop her lecture when she noticed any drowsiness. It was a late-afternoon graduate class, and most of those enrolled had already worked a full day. Instead of fighting the problem or giving up and droning on and on, she would just stop and get all of the students on their feet for a few stretching exercises. What a terrific way to re-energize a group! Once back in their seats, Bill remembers, the students were much better able to listen, absorb, and participate actively.

But how do you know what to do? How do you sense the need? You watch. While you lecture, make eye contact. Don't stay buried in your notes. Listen carefully for sounds that indicate restlessness — for coughing or shifting in seats. If you sense your students are beginning to fade and drift off, you then have choices. If your production is bombing, you can change your performance style.

For example, you can stop and take a break of some kind. Or you can alert everyone to hang in there for a bit longer so that you can finish something. You can ask for reactions. You can provoke a discussion with a question or comment. Or you can shift to some other active option for which students must write something in class or join small groups to discuss key points. You might have a simulation ready to move into, or a role play. It might be a good time to practice some skill in class. The fundamental question has to be: what's the use of going on as planned if too many students have disengaged? A number of potential remedies exist, but they all begin with your awareness of the students' degree of intellectual and emotional engagement.

Exercises

1. Try supplementing the more typical end-of-course student evaluations with other forms of feedback. Interview students along the way. Ask your students to take a few minutes periodically to assess particular classes. What worked? What didn't? What could have made the class better?

2. Invite one or more of your colleagues to give you some feedback to balance what you get from your students.

We've suggested a number of lessons from the stage that can enliven both your scripting and performance of lectures. Remember, however, that in theatre, no matter how good the script, a lackluster performance leads to a flop. As Sarason (1999, 133) points out, the same holds true for the classroom:

> Between the script and the audience is a performing artist whose artistry determines to what extent the audience will be stimulated, moved, energized, and responsive, or unmoved, disinterested, bored, disappointed, disillusioned, eager that the occasion should end. No one disputes that in regard to the conventional performing arts; everyone regards that as a glimpse of the obvious. But when it comes to teaching as a performing art, it is another story, the central theme of which is that teachers convey information and demonstrate and supervise the acquisition of skills. ... [A] classroom that recognizes little or not at all the artistry a teacher should have or the fact that each student has an individuality which, if not recognized and nurtured, makes the classroom a frustrating, boring place ... .

We urge you to hone your performing skills, to view your students not just as spectators but as fellow cast members, and to make each lecture a "hit"!

Chapter 4:
Questions, Answers, and Discussions

Do you want lively discussions? Do you want your students to come to class prepared and ready to participate actively — to do their part on the shared journey of teaching and learning? Of course you do. But can your students overcome their timidity and their fear of saying something "dumb," risking criticism from you or looking foolish among their peers? Can those who like to talk in class learn to share center stage, value the opinions of others, and really listen deeply and empathetically? How do you proceed when too few of your students come to class prepared? Do you get charged up by a good question or lively discussion? Does the measured movement through carefully constructed lecture notes leave you flat? Conversely, does the unpredictability of classes where questions fall flat or discussions are dominated by a very few students leave you frustrated?

We think you can have more of what you want from your students and class sessions by attending to a number of lessons from the stage. From your need to shift roles to the importance of *with-it-ness* — your awareness of student/audience reactions and needs — and from a concern for timing and set (mood and environment) to the practice (rehearsal) that your student "actors" will need to carry out their roles, you'll get a fresh perspective and some new insights through the lens of performance. A staged production, with its script and carefully rehearsed organization, may have more direct relevance for a lecture; however, performance does offer important lessons for discussions as well. In this chapter, we'll draw on the performance tradition around *improvisation,* where scenes are set but actions aren't scripted and the outcomes are quite variable.

Some of your students will clearly feel more comfortable with the lecture format, which allows them to play a traditional role and quietly record the organized, expert conclusions you offer. The most pressing concern for these students is typically less about their own independent learning and more about figuring out just what it is you want back on assignments and exams — for that is what will determine who gets what grade and who gets chosen to move on to the next level. As the instructor, what do you do? What options do you have? What lessons from the stage can help you here?

Of course, other students come alive when they have the opportunity to participate more actively in class. They're interested in the course and in learning. They also may have the maturity to articulate their ideas with confidence, and the patience to listen to — and learn from — others. Class participation also can reflect the degree of student preparedness; students who participate most tend to be those who have done their homework and who understand what you're saying. Some of them may even use the opportunity to compete for attention or power. However, after you eliminate the students who haven't completed the reading, too many students may shrink back simply because they lack confidence in themselves or their public speaking skills. As we mentioned earlier, both Tobias (1990) and Belenky and her colleagues (1986) have described the negative effects on many talented students, especially women and minorities, of an isolating and competitive climate in class. What is your role in promoting inclusive discussions, and how can performance skills help you do that?

Many scholars agree about the value of active learning in helping students acquire a deeper understanding of material. Whether in sections, labs, tutorials, or the lecture itself, opportunities to apply key ideas and skills or discuss what was presented in lecture or absorbed through the readings can strengthen students' learning and reveal what they don't understand. Consequently, handling questions effectively or managing productive discussions in class becomes important for you. The tradeoff is inevitably in content coverage. You also must build your own expertise in providing clear explanations and good examples, drawing from a variety of sources, and making connections to issues that are both current and meaningful.

Of course, you may question any suggestion that a curriculum that's already bulging with what "has to be covered" be expanded to include more — i.e., time for questions and discussions. Students are paying their tuition to hear from *you*, aren't they? We won't pretend that your choices are easy ones. Trading a measurable focus on knowledge and product for the more slippery domains of thinking and process can feel dangerous, like sailing into uncharted (and unchartable) waters — perhaps like the difference between canoeing on the calm mountain lake versus surviving a kayak plunge through the whitewater rapids down below. You may well need to rethink some core assumptions you have about teaching, your goals for student learning, and the time and resources you have. In some sense, less (content coverage) may mean more (and deeper) learning.

In truth, whitewater rides can also be quite thrilling, invigorating, and energizing, because they give you a chance to use the skills you've perfected in calmer waters. Try thinking of these "river runs" as if you have the tiller on an oar boat. The ride depends largely on the river (the content and your students), but you do have extensive control over the boat's direction and the timing of your descent through the rapids. Just as actors and directors control the timing and pacing of a production, so too can you keep your discussions slow and smooth or let them rock and roll. Once you develop some skill and confidence with facilitation, you might find it quite stimulating for yourself, engaging for your students, important for the development of critical and creative thinking skills, and...really fun.

Current trends in higher education encourage more opportunities to engage students actively — to challenge them to think more critically and creatively (e.g., Davis 1993; Johnson, Johnson, and Smith 1989; Johnson & Johnson 1994; Lowman 1995; McKeachie 2002; Ramsden 1992; Timpson and Bendel-Simso 1996). Whether you experiment with planned small-group activities or spontaneous large-group exchanges, your teaching repertoire will grow and your understanding of learning—and your students—will deepen. And through it all, you may learn some new roles.

Problems and Challenges

Along with becoming more comfortable with thinking on your feet, you also may need to sharpen certain skills in order to create interactive classrooms effectively. These skills include:

- Formulating good questions.
- Accepting student responses without necessarily agreeing with them.

- Providing additional clarification as needed.
- Challenging students to think critically and more creatively.
- Summarizing and synthesizing what's been said — or not said.
- Encouraging participation while discouraging domination.
- Managing the classroom time you have available.
- Providing closure when needed.
- Focusing on assessment when appropriate.
- Helping everyone stay focused on underlying concepts and goals.

Some instructors ask questions only for rhetorical purposes. These kinds of interjections can certainly have an important place in challenging students to pause and think. However, good questions always have the potential for stimulating deeper student responses and group discussions. You may miss these opportunities by leaping too quickly to rescue a class from ensuing silences. You and your students may have become too comfortable and dependent on what you say as the voice of authority. Quiet in the classroom may feel deadly to the untrained facilitator, but it proves wonderfully effective for sparking new insights.

You also can inhibit student participation when your questions are mostly of the "guess-what's-in-my-mind?" type. In these cases, it's not what students themselves think that matters, but what students think *you* think that counts. Some students won't even rise to this kind of a challenge, perhaps finding it too reminiscent of the approaches teachers used in elementary school. Other students may perceive too much public risk in being wrong.

But there could also be a control issue at play. If you insist on directing the discussion toward some particular conclusion (i.e., convergent thinking), some students may feel uncomfortable suggesting alternative hypotheses. Disagreements may get suppressed. Opportunities for deeper and more meaningful interaction may disappear. Indeed, who wants to hear from others when it is you, the instructor, who ultimately controls the exams and the grades? Perry (1999), for one, would argue that the bigger prize is one of *agency*, for which students learn to lessen their dependency on external sources of authority (you, the text), learn how to evaluate sources on their merits, and, ultimately, become more confident in their own abilities to sort through complex and ambiguous information and arrive at a defensible position while simultaneously staying open to new possibilities.

Along with a need to formulate good questions comes the challenge to acknowledge, clarify, and respond to what students say, and then guide further discussions. Common problems arise when questions from a few vocal and assertive students inhibit other students from participating, or when someone raises an issue that isn't shared by the larger group or is at an angle to the central discussion. Something is also lost when, in your rush to get back *on task* and to *cover* everything you've planned, you miss an opportunity to tap into deeper student beliefs and understandings. Here again, less *teaching* may mean more and deeper *learning*.

Of course, every teacher has had to contend with a variety of students who can disrupt a good discussion — those who are after attention; those who may want power; or those "hurdle jumpers" who only want to know what's "required" and what will be on the next exam, and who consequently care little about the involvement and ideas of their classmates. Rudolph Dreikurs (1968) has some interesting ideas for helping you understand and channel these kinds of motivations into more constructive directions.

Yet, there are other problems as well, barriers that can limit learning to a surface kind of understanding. For example, some students need *time* to formulate their opinions. It's entirely understandable that they let more eager classmates take the initiative. Other students tend to think quite systematically through issues. They may struggle when the discussion bounces all over the place — when there's no attempt to follow a certain line of reasoning to a logical conclusion. Still other students may want to incubate their ideas before hatching anything into the bright and often critical light of a public classroom discussion. Understanding how creativity depends on a period of incubation also can help you and your students develop a useful patience and tolerance for diverse learning needs and preferences.

Even after some students have a response in mind, you may need to provide additional encouragement and opportunities to get them to speak. This problem can intensify, of course, when:

- The class is large.

- You're rushing to cover certain content.

- Some students are more introverted or lack confidence.

- Some students don't have the necessary communication skills.

- The first language of some students is not English.

Certainly some students would just as soon have you do all the work, especially since you're the appointed *expert* and the one who designs the exams and oversees the *grading*. You yourself may reinforce this dependency if you repeatedly grab the spotlight and upstage students' attempts to construct meaning for themselves — i.e., understand the underlying concepts at a deeper level, one that's both correct and congruent with the way they see the world.

Some of your students may be quite complacent about their own learning, enmeshed in what Freire (1970) has termed the *banking* notion of education. In this more traditional but enduring practice, the primary function of teachers is to make "deposits" of information into the minds of the young. During this process, instructors socialize students into a receptive but, Freire argued, fundamentally dysfunctional culture of silence and passivity. Education and learning of a certain type can reinforce student docility. Certainly some students can feel intimidated by open-ended questions requiring deeper analysis, application, synthesis, or assessment, while others become anxious when they're "put on the spot" to come up with specific dates, names, answers, or references. Beyond the importance of full and active participation in discussions generally, we're also committed to the value of critical thinking, the essence of citizenship in a vibrant democracy. We note that Freire himself was exiled from Brazil for years by a ruling military junta that felt threatened by his rejection of educational docility.

In the face of these challenges — engaging students; pulling in students who tend to sit on the sidelines while keeping a check on those who want to dominate; facilitating interactions; promoting listening while challenging students to rethink their positions; getting the pace right; making the most out of pauses; getting a good mix of roles; and more — we think you can learn valuable lessons from the stage. From scripts to characterizations, from sets to timing, performers and playwrights know much about engaging audiences and provoking deeper responses.

Lessons from the Stage

Knowing that you're about to mix it up with students, you could learn more from actors about improvisation—what works and what doesn't. Knowing that many students need some time to digest a question and formulate an opinion, especially when the issues under study are complex and challenging, you could learn from actors how to utilize self-awareness and self-discipline to provide for adequate *wait time*. Knowing that many students find it easier to sit back passively, you also could learn from actors how to shift roles and move from information giving to response facilitation. When concentrating on *through-lines* or *subtext*, the actor keeps clear about the underlying theme—for you, the goals and objectives. Understanding the structure and power of good *scripts*, you could look for ways to add some drama or humor to your own class notes—even subtle touches that might help sustain student interest. In many classes, *timing* and *pacing*—key components for performers that are too often ignored by instructors— an affect the success of discussions.

Other practices from the stage also might come into play. Developing a heightened *stage awareness* can allow you to be more spontaneous in capturing opportunities in class to address concerns, clarify confusion, and deepen student understanding. Your alertness to everything going in class and your ability to simultaneously monitor learning and group dynamics require high levels of concentration. Using a *rehearsal*-like process, you could explore a variety of new approaches, soliciting feedback from students and others and then implementing those ideas that seem most effective.

As an example of what's possible, consider Ed Landesman (Mathematics), an energetic and caring professor who used different kinds of questions to accomplish a variety of objectives. As he would work through a calculus problem on the board, for instance, he would routinely ask for help from students along the way: "What's next? What does that equal?" Students called out responses spontaneously. No hands were raised. There was no spotlight on those responding. It was a lively exchange, more like a conversation with a group that keeps everyone alert and engaged. Landesman used this approach to check student understanding along the way and to prompt sustained attention. At times, he would balance this directive style with more open-ended questions to allow his students to explore their own thinking. Or, he would stop to reflect more deliberately on a particular problem with a student who was stuck. From the observer's standpoint, this all looked like great theatre: engaging, alive yet focused, the pace varying with the content—first fast-paced when Landesman worked problems, but then much slower when he asked "why" and called for more reflective responses.

Although on a very grand scale, the national literacy campaigns that have sprung out of Paulo Freire's (1970) work in Central America, South America, and Africa are additional examples of the value of more active and empowering models of education. In these models, we could see the relevance of performance elements as teachers moved away from information giving and toward facilitated learning. In Cuba, Nicaragua, and Brazil, in particular, poor and illiterate masses literally "bootstrapped" themselves upward through involvement in small, interactive study groups facilitated by volunteers who may have been short on literacy skills themselves but who were long on enthusiasm, commitment, and idealism. A desire to read was built on student stories—for instance, oral descriptions of their own life experiences, concerns, hopes, and dreams—and then transformed slowly, word by word and sentence by sentence, into an understanding of written language (e.g., Timpson 1988). Throughout Freire's work is the imperative that teachers foster engagement through the use of meaningful material, avoid information giving or "banking," and stay committed to a facilitator's role.

In parallel to this work with literacy and empowerment emerged a very original adaptation to the theatre. After the publication of Freire's (1970) classic, *Pedagogy of the Oppressed,* Augusto Boal (1979, 1992, 1995) began to explore its application to the theatre. He later wrote *Theatre of the Oppressed* as well as a number of other provocative works. In these books, he described various ways actors can use the lived experiences of audience members to generate material for the "stage." Every performance would be fresh and meaningful to the audience present. There would be no written scripts to portray; just what the actors could coax from the people in attendance. The struggles, challenges, hopes, and dreams of audience members themselves would become the focus for improvisations. Scenes would be "acted out" by actors (used primarily to jumpstart a scene) and recruits from the audience. Whoever volunteered the issue would get to see other perspectives and possibilities.

Boal's Theatre of the Oppressed can be exciting with a real edge of unpredictability. It's also a profound paradigm shift for performers as theatre traditions are stretched in very new directions. Indeed, this kind of shift parallels what happens when we ask you as an instructor to step beyond traditional pedagogy and do more than just give information or offer new skills—by considering the various benefits that might emerge from exploring what happens on stage.

Staying Focused: Interactions and Through-Lines

Because of the spontaneity associated with questions and the fielding of responses, you may have difficulty remaining focused on your "scripted" goals and objectives. You might be tempted to wander off on a tangent, something you find especially intriguing or that awakens a response from one or more of your students. Questions and discussions can diverge from the central concepts under study and make it difficult for some students to assimilate everything into a coherent, meaningful whole. Of course, there's an important place for the relevant digression or improvisation, but that's a different issue. Here, we want to help you stay focused on a central idea. Ongoing attention to the *through-line* (underlying theme) can work much like Ausubel's (1963) *advance organizer* — a description of the underlying conceptual structure at the start of class that helps students organize and remember the information that follows.

This kind of awareness can help you determine which questions or responses should be addressed outside of class, which could be profitably answered by others in class, and which you could use as catalysts to probe and promote deeper understanding among your students. For example, some students may raise questions about their responses on a particular exam question. Unless enough others have the same concern, you may want to handle the issue during your office hours. Similarly, some students may ask about material that was covered in previous classes or that is clearly presented in the readings. Here, you run some risks. Your responsiveness to students — your willingness to answer any and all questions — may actually serve to discourage those who are keeping up with the material, who complete their readings on time, and who come to class faithfully.

On stage, the through-line helps actors keep their roles clear and focused through the various plot twists and turns. Attention to the through-line forces them to put motivation behind their lines. A successful performance is not one during which every line comes out as written, but rather one during which every line comes across as *believable*.

Let's look at an example from the classroom: the gap between your role as an expert and what your students often need from you as a generalist. Trained in depth, you may find yourself spending a great deal of time in class explaining ideas that are elementary for you. Yet, at conferences and in your own writing, you may be functioning at the very highest levels of sophisticated analysis and complex debate. Can attention to the through-line help you bridge these two worlds? We believe that lessons from the stage can help you in several of these types of areas. For example:

- Figuratively putting on your "generalist's hat" can help you step outside your preferred expert's role and remind yourself of the basics. Bill Timpson has gotten much benefit from his regular tour of duty with undergraduate courses.

- Getting into your "facilitator's role" can help you concentrate more on student learning, where much of the new challenge in teaching on campus lies.

- Reminding yourself of core goals and objectives (the through-line) can help you and your students stay clear about course direction. Try putting your core goals and objectives on the board at the start of each class.

- Developing the kind of *metaconsciousness* that allows actors and public speakers to watch themselves perform can help you better manage your own version of the specialist-generalist gap.

Actors, of course, must become adept at switching in and out of character, and into new and different roles. Knowing the through-line becomes critical in keeping a performance unified. As they develop their characters, actors also get to experiment with different actions or deliveries. After each rehearsal, directors will usually provide notes and invite reactions from the cast about new possibilities for the next rehearsal. This cycle of study and focus, alternating with experimentation and feedback, continues throughout the rehearsal and even the performance period.

When professional actors perform the same role night after night, they must guard against the deadening effects of boredom, of having their roles become lifeless or mechanical. Even the best of plots and through-lines cannot save a stale production. Accordingly, the best actors use each other and audience reactions as feedback for continuous improvement. Typical is the story of one actor who, following the last performance of a two-year run, turned to a fellow actor and said enthusiastically, "I just got a new idea for how to play the opening scene of the third act."

Like the actor, you can learn to channel your energies through study, experimentation, concentration, self-awareness, self-discipline, practice (with set lines and improvisation), and feedback. You too need to keep your performances both focused and fresh. While planning your next class, consider the following ideas:

- Reflect for a bit about your own experiences as a student — what was memorable, effective, and intriguing as well as what was distracting and unfocused.

- Similarly, think about what you could borrow from other contexts — from professional conferences, perhaps.

- Talk to colleagues about their experiences.

- Solicit ideas from your students.

- Stay clear about your through-line (goals and objectives), but try a very different presentation of the material or a different way to organize your instruction.

You could, for instance, experiment with a discovery approach, improvising as you go. You could put some of the material in a self-study format or consider a problem-based or case study approach. You could try role plays or debates, or incorporate student presentations. Admittedly, any change means time and effort on your part. But the benefits for your own renewed energy and increased engagement of your students will likely make your investment more than worthwhile.

Exercises

1. Reflect on a recent period of questions and answers. What was the through-line? Did you stray? If so, how far? Which questions could have been handled more effectively in a different manner? Which responses could have been used as catalysts to improve understanding for the entire group? for changing misconceptions or challenging old beliefs?

2. Take a few moments before your next class to concentrate on your through-line. Highlighting these central concepts and key objectives in your notes can help you remember to stress them during class. Use Ausubel's notion of the *advance organizer* to ensure that you're clear at the

very beginning of class about the conceptual framework holding everything together.

3. Keep a journal for a few weeks and note your reactions to your handling of questions, answers, and the through-line. It doesn't matter what journal format you use; the key is to take the time to reflect and write. Later, you can review what you've written, look for patterns and interrelationships, and add some comments.

4. Because feedback from students is so valuable, recruit one or more students in your class—perhaps a teaching assistant or tutor—to evaluate what happens to the through-line in your class sessions. You could videotape one of your sessions to do the same thing on your own.

Lesson Plans and Scripts

Compared to what's required to get ready to lecture, you may find that formulating questions or anticipating student responses during discussions is comparatively straightforward. In the theatre, actors will use the wide margins in their scripts for personal reminders—cautions, cues about timing, places for emphasis. You can adapt your class notes in a similar way.

Writing the questions you plan to ask into your class "script" also allows you to analyze how each question connects to each lesson's through-line. Many actors will work through each of their lines to explore the underlying subtext of thought and feeling that connects to the through-line and explains motivations. Likewise, you can evaluate the underlying motivation you have for each question. Which questions ask for specific, convergent answers and which are more open-ended and divergent? While the former can help you check students' ongoing attention, the latter are often much better at promoting critical thinking and interactive discussions.

Benjamin Bloom and his colleagues (1956) developed a hierarchy of thinking skills that provides teachers at all levels with a helpful structure for using and evaluating questions:

- At the lowest level of cognitive demand are questions that ask for information — for specific *knowledge*. These questions require relatively straightforward recall.

- The next-higher level of questioning requires *comprehension*; students must demonstrate understanding in their responses.

- Then comes *application*, for which students have to use their knowledge and understanding to solve a particular problem.

- The three highest levels, in ascending order, involve *analysis, synthesis,* and *evaluation.* According to Bloom, students must dissect issues, pull from a variety of resources in formulating their responses, and then judge the soundness of the results.

Having a working knowledge of this hierarchy can allow you to achieve a good mix of cognitive demand in class. For example, some questions at the lower end of Bloom's taxonomy (knowledge, understanding, application) can help you when you're getting a class started, reviewing materials you covered in previous classes, or checking to see that your students are understanding their readings. Ed Landesman (Mathematics) frequently uses these kinds of questions as prompts and probes to keep his introductory calculus classes moving.

Questions at the upper end of Bloom's taxonomy can offer your students more of the intellectual challenge that promotes rethinking and stimulates developmental shifts. Ed Landesman, for example, will periodically focus on a particular student's struggles and use a reflective style to promote deeper learning — e.g., "You're confused about that solution." By planning and teaching with this same hierarchy in mind, you can develop your own ability to exploit opportunities that arise spontaneously — the so-called "teachable moments." For a performance, even the most minor character must be engaged in the action of a particular scene to make it all believable. Otherwise the energy onstage will dissipate and audience members may lose their focus. Unfortunately, too many classrooms look like staged crowd scenes, with a few eager students getting all the lines and lots of "extras" in the background.

To avoid relegating some students to passive "extra" roles, you can use any number of strategies to solicit greater involvement. For instance, you could "prime the learning pump" by having students take a few minutes to write out their own responses in class, perhaps sharing them briefly with their classmates before you open things up for a general class discussion. This approach ensures that everyone has some response and gets to discuss it first in a small group. You could also have your students write out their names and some biographical information on index cards at the start of a course; you can then pull cards at random when you're seeking a response to a question. A word of caution, though: although this approach may promote greater attention and participation, it also may create anxiety among some students.

Engaging Students and Audiences

We know from the work of Belenky and others (1986) that the issue of student participation can have important implications for learning, especially when student diversity comes into play. Women students, in particular, may shrink from participating in discussions that feel competitive and judgmental. These students often prefer small-group interactions as a prelude to a large-group activity. Socialized differently, more of the males may rise to the challenge. After analyzing attrition in large, introductory science classes, Tobias (1990) reported that a number of talented students, including a high proportion of women and minorities, were discouraged by large, impersonal, information-driven classes. They would instead often seek out those disciplines where they could learn in a more supportive, cooperative classroom environment.

Seeing instruction from the perspective of the stage can give you some new insights in this regard, perhaps by helping you become more aware of student reactions or pay more attention to the instructional through-line and learning. You might also think of the rehearsal process as a model for providing ongoing peer support and assistance to your students, both in and out of class.

In turn, restless or rude students can dampen any teacher's enthusiasm, undermining the best of preparations. In response, you may want to " tap dance" faster and faster in class, to entertain the students who don't want to be there. While you could apply the performance skills we're discussing to some kind of "instructional entertainment," that's not our intent. We don't offer quick fixes that avoid a shared responsibility for deeper learning. Instead, we hope you'll come away from this book with some new ideas for engaging students more effectively in class.

Acting companies seek to create an "ensemble" — a performance approach that encourages give and take — as each member of the company works closely with every other member to achieve a common goal: the best possible performance. Certainly actors can be as competitive as anyone else in pursuing their careers. But on stage, cooperation must prevail. Bonding among cast and crew builds during rehearsals and is cemented by the intensity surrounding performances. The resulting intimacy can promote lasting friendships and trust that, in turn, can stimulate creative problem solving.

Current research on effective instruction indicates that an "ensemble" approach also can work in the classroom. For example, many teachers are exploring the use of cooperative small-group activities to enhance student engagement and participation. David and Roger Johnson (1994) have reported extensively on the value of small groups for promoting a more active and mutually supportive context for student learning. Successful small-group work can diminish competitive behavior and promote teamwork among students representing very different backgrounds, interests, needs, and learning styles. You now can draw from a great variety of instructional approaches when you're designing these kinds of assignments (e.g., Timpson and Bendel-Simso 1996). Of course, group learning requires more of your attention, time, and effort. But the benefits of "ensemble" learning typically outweigh the costs.

Exercises

1. Try reformatting your lecture notes or outlines to leave wide margins on both sides. Add notes to yourself about pauses, emphases, and participation reminders. When a class session is over, be sure to make additional notes in the margins for future reference. Check with your students to see if your estimate of their level of engagement matches what they think.

2. As most writers do, you can have someone else review your notes and suggest changes or additions. In particular, analyze the kinds of questions you're asking and your objectives for any discussions you're planning. Watching a videotape of yourself teaching can be similarly instructive.

Hooking Students from the Start

Hooks for stimulating discussion can run the gamut from a challenging question to a provocative statement about a particular issue, from a hint about what will be on an upcoming test to a straightforward appeal for participation, from a riveting demonstration of some principle to a role play about a central character under study. Whatever approach you use, however, you can enhance student learning by paying attention regularly to your underlying goals and objectives (the through-line).

A *role wheel*, as described below, can prove particularly effective in generating discussion. As we pointed out earlier in this book, the conflict inherent in drama helps engage an audience. Role wheels can help your class investigate issues for which there is something to say on both sides of a conflict — for example, tensions over grading policies, ever present ethical issues surrounding cheating or plagiarism, conflicts between animal rights advocates and courses requiring dissection, controversies pitting new theories against the traditional canon, or debates between environmentalists and developers. Your choices for topics are broad indeed.

To set up a role wheel, ask each student to find a partner. The class then forms two concentric circles, so that each student stands facing a partner. Explain that you'll describe a situation the students are to role play with their partners, noting that the students should not try to "act" but put themselves into the situation as you describe it and behave accordingly. You then describe the situation, asking everyone in the inner circle to play "Character A" while the students in the outer circle play "Character B."

For instance, you could describe Character A as an environmentalist picketing a nuclear power plant who attempts to stop and recruit a worker who is entering the facility. You then create a conflict by describing Character B as a worker with a family to support and a lot of unpaid bills left over from six months of unemployment just prior to his getting the job at the plant. (For more examples of role wheel situations, see Chapter 8.)

After describing the situation, you then allow two to three minutes for each role play, monitoring the interaction carefully to sustain student interest. Although the conflict may be unresolved, you can stop the action and have the students switch roles so they can replay the situation from the beginning. After allowing two to three minutes for role reversal, stop again and ask the inner circle to move one person to the right, so that each student stands facing a new partner. You then describe a second situation and repeat the procedure, including the role reversal. You continue to guide the role wheel through a number of situations (two to five seems optimal; after five the students' energy tends to wane), then move directly into discussion.

Processing student experiences in the role wheel exercise can serve as a bridge back into a discussion of the original issue. You can begin by asking questions like these:

- In which of these situations did you find yourself most involved? Why?

- Have you ever been engaged in any conflicts like these?

- What did you experience when you switched roles?

- Were some roles more comfortable for you than others? Why?

- Did any of the situations relate to today's topic for discussion? How?

As "hooks," role wheels have several advantages. First, you can use them with almost any number of students, from small classes to large ones. Second, everyone role plays simultaneously, so all students participate actively. Third, the students are less likely to be stricken with performance anxiety since there's no role play in front of the class and, hence, no "audience." Most importantly, role wheels can help move issues from an abstract level to one that's much more personal and concrete. Students gain a lived sense of how others react to complex and conflicted issues. The role reversal can promote understanding and empathy with other perspectives.

The key to designing an effective role wheel lies in the selection and description of the situations. Obviously the situations must relate to the material under study, illustrating some aspect of a particular topic and then helping your students make connections to their own concerns and values. Actors use a similar process of reflection and values clarification to connect with their characters. It's unlikely, for instance, that an actor playing Oedipus will have any experience with patricide or incest. Actors can, however, search for analogous experiences — occasions when they've realized, belatedly, that their actions have hurt others. The memory of both the pain and the discovery can help them empathize with Oedipus's appalling confrontation with the truth. While role wheel situations may not — indeed should not — tap into such intense trauma, an effective exercise can begin with the students' concerns and then connect to some aspect of the topic at hand. Role wheels generate energetic discussions because students engage with the topic both emotionally and intellectually.

There are other exercises you can use as active "hooks." For instance, Suzanne Burgoyne encountered the "Cyclops" exercise in a human potential workshop and adapted it to introduce discussion of *Oedipus the King* in script analysis and dramatic literature classes. At its core, this exercise involves using the various senses in an active and physical exploration of a topic. After you read how Suzanne has adapted this activity for her own teaching, we'll suggest some possibilities for other disciplines.

Suzanne begins by clearing an open space in the room and explaining to her students that they are all going to play "Cyclops." This creature from Greek mythology has only one eye; students form the monster's single eye by cupping their hands in a circle around their own eyes. Since Cyclops was a grumpy, single-minded monster, Suzanne asks the students to stomp around the room, grumbling and muttering — and growling whenever they bump into another Cyclops.

To enhance the mood, Suzanne also plays a strident selection from Vangelis's "Heaven and Hell" while the student Cyclopses stomp and grumble. Then she stops the action, puts on a "heavenly" cut from the same score, and tells students to close their eyes. Now "blind," the students move through the room slowly, taking care not to bump into others but using their other senses to explore anything with which they come into contact. Concluding the exercise, Suzanne then asks the students to sit down and discuss their experiences:

- What did it feel like to be a Cyclops?

- How did it feel different when you were "blind"?

- What other senses came into play when you couldn't rely on your eyes?

- What did you experience?

- In what ways does this exercise relate to *Oedipus the King*?

Students invariably connect the exercise to the sighted/blind imagery in the play, observing that Oedipus receives many clues to the truth as the play progresses but ignores them because of his Cyclops-like "tunnel vision." When he faces the truth, his whole experience of the world changes. Physically blind, he must now rely on other previously ignored senses and spiritual insights to guide him.

How can this kind of activity be adapted for other classes and different disciplines? To nurture empathy and understanding for people with disabilities, Bill Timpson will have education students "blind" themselves and experience firsthand what it means—physically, emotionally, and intellectually—to depend on other senses. In pairs, students take turns leading each other around the building, exploring their own issues of safety, trust, and risk. On a more symbolic level, students who are "blinded" also get some feel for the challenges faced by researchers who are venturing into the unknown on the frontiers of knowledge. Students can get only so much from discussions or readings. Experiential learning can promote broader and deeper learning as your students wrestle with difficult issues. Give it a chance.

If your classwork requires some trust building or teamwork—for projects, labs, field assignments, cooperative case study analyses, or problem-based learning activities — exercises like these can also "break the ice" and help students bond early on. For example, students can act out various character types who make group work difficult. Exaggerating their characteristics can make for a fun way to illustrate problems that otherwise may be difficult to talk about. Everyone in the group can then keep these character types in mind as they work together throughout the semester.

Exercises like the Cyclops and the role wheel also engage students on a sensory level. Learning styles come into play when individual students demonstrate particular strengths or preferences in one or more of the various modalities—visual, aural, or kinesthetic (touch). Exercises that use more than one format can appeal to a wider variety of students. Hunter (1982) has long been an advocate of using multimodal approaches and "teaching to both sides of the brain." You can explore any number of acting textbooks for these types of ideas and exercises. (See the References with Annotations at the end of this book for our recommendations.)

But what if your great idea for a hook fizzles and flops? We've all had classes when our opening question bombed and we faced a sea of blank stares or some desultory leafing through past notes for a clue or an answer. Faced with a dead audience, the stage actor might experiment with changes in timing, gestures, or expressions. You, however, have greater flexibility. You could try to improvise a new hook on the spot. Perhaps a review of topics from previous class sessions or items in the news can help get your students engaged and focused. A small-group activity might get everyone involved. An in-class writing assignment can also prime the pump. We recommend that you experiment with a variety of approaches for hooking students at the start of class and develop a wide-ranging repertoire of attention getters.

Exercises

1. Watch one of the television talk shows like The Tonight Show with Jay Leno or Oprah Winfrey. Analyze what the hosts do for openings — how they set the stage for the questions and discussions that follow. Their use of hooks should be evident.

2. Analyze a recent period of questions and answers in one of your own class sessions. How effective was the beginning? Did you have any kind of hook? If you did, how could it have been better? If not, what could have worked?

The Classroom as Set

During a lecture, your students must be able to see and hear you. When you move into questions, answers, and discussions, everyone should be able to see and hear everyone else. In fact, participation may vary substantially as a function of "sight lines and acoustics." Straight rows and big rooms can constrain discussions by channeling interactions through you, the instructor, who then acts as gatekeeper. When classes are seated in a circle or around a large table, however, interactions can be more lively and dynamic. Even in rooms where the seats and tables are bolted to the floor, you may be able to adapt your approaches to encourage more interaction and discussion among your students. For example, you can have your students periodically share their ideas with peers seated nearby as a prelude to whole-class discussions.

Those involved with staged performances, film, and television put a great deal of effort into designing and creating just the right set or finding the ideal location. With some imagination and effort, you might be able to reconceptualize your "set" to promote better interactions among your students. To maximize student participation, for instance, you could think of students as "fellow actors" instead of passive audience members. Suddenly the entire room is a set and many more options become possible. Augusto Boal's work (1979, 1992, 1995) attempts to reconceptualize theatre in a very similar way, pulling dilemmas out of the lives of audience members and involving everyone in exploring possible solutions.

Indeed, reconceptualizing students as resources for instruction can open up even more possibilities for helping you enhance and deepen their learning. For example, when you encourage your students to make creative use of the classroom space for their presentations, you can tap their reservoir of ideas. When you use small-group activities in class, you can shift the focus from one large "set" to a decentralized grouping of sets with different casts and crews running in parallel with each other.

Similarly, when you see students as "actors," you can bring them into more active exchanges through debates and case study analyses. More like a town meeting where citizens gather to discuss matters of civic importance, classes that function this way can be very engaging, and can challenge your students to think and rethink what they believe. The ethical, newsworthy, or human issues that exist in every discipline—the stories that surround the movers and shakers—can be a rich source of material.

Whatever you do with the room itself, however, you still need to ground your decisions in course goals and objectives—your "through-line." If you want to nurture critical and creative thinking among your students, you can reconceptualize the class "set" to promote challenging interactions. With this kind of consciousness, you're more likely to seize opportunities to use other spaces that are available, both on and off campus. When asked to contribute in a like manner, your students can (and usually will) respond to the challenge, learn from your lead, and bring their own creative ideas into play. Suddenly the possibilities and limitations of the class "set" become opportunities and challenges for everyone to face.

Exercises

1. Make a list of the most creative uses of class "sets" you've experienced. How did these approaches enhance teaching and learning?

2. What could you try in your own classes? What other physical spaces are available? How could technology help you use "virtual sets" drawn from the Internet? How could you better tap students' ideas, creativity, and energy?

The Roles You Play

When instruction involves questions, answers, and discussions, you'll have to play a variety of roles that are quite different from those required in lecture. In some ways, these roles are more demanding. A degree of spontaneity is required, which can be challenging. Good public speaking skills may not be enough. The increasing diversity of the student population—their differences in background, age, preparation, values, and attitudes—and the increasing concern for critical and creative thinking require you to think on your feet and respond to a variety of questions so that your students can make connections to central course concepts and skills.

For instance, you may need to provide alternative explanations and a variety of examples when students struggle to understand your material. There may be times when you *don't* want to answer directly — when a question can probe, challenge, and spark rethinking. There also may be times when you want to challenge the entire class or call on individuals randomly for their responses.

As you move from formal lecture into discussion, your awareness of the different requirements for each role can help you make the necessary shift. A question-and-answer period, for instance, may mean setting aside your prepared notes so that you can respond more spontaneously. The focus changes from speaking (lecture) to listening (discussion) and empathy as you help the students reflect upon and articulate their own thinking. In a discussion, you also may function as a moderator, ensuring that everyone can hear or that a particular response is understood, perhaps sampling he entire class and making some assessment of the degree of consensus before moving on.

When you want to promote deeper learning in a discussion period, however, you may need to do even more. You might want to put on the counselor's hat, for example, and actively promote (teach, model, require) the language of acceptance, where someone's first response to a comment *reflects* back what he or she has heard and sensed: "So you believe that ... ." You could also help bridge differences by promoting (teaching, modeling, requiring) *empathy*—helping students express their understanding of someone else's experience: "You seem to be (very confident/unsure) about that comment."

When you work in this mode, the pace of class may slow considerably. However, there can be decided benefits as students feel more secure about discussing their ideas and reactions openly. They know their comments will be respected. For example, with topics fraught with potential for conflict and argument—racism and white guilt, the impact of European settlement on native peoples in Australia and the terribly high rates of health problems and unemployment some two hundred years later — Michael Williams (Aboriginal and Torres Strait Islander Studies) routinely used reflective listening and empathic statements to promote a general climate of trust and acceptance in class. While he articulated a core belief in the importance of acceptance as a foundation for building a more tolerant nation now and in the future, he also consistently modeled the necessary communication skills when he taught. The effect of that modeling in class was clearly evident as students found ways to discuss even the most sensitive of issues. Sure, feelings got hurt at times. But Williams used acceptance and empathy to move toward his desired goals of respect, understanding, and appreciation among his students. For him, trusting that the process would work meant staying in character.

There are times when you may want to restrain yourself from answering a question too quickly, but rather stay in character and keep the focus on the student asking the question or the other students in the class. For instance, you might respond, "That's a good question. What do you think? Can anyone else respond?" Your role here would be to challenge your students to think more for themselves. You may not want to provide answers in the most efficient manner possible. You may have to discipline yourself to wait, to look for possible respondents, and perhaps to rephrase a question or offer an additional example or two.

With his curriculum organized around problems (cases requiring students to analyze symptoms and recommend treatments), Michael Aldred (Oral Biology) regularly performed a high-wire act, balancing his role as facilitator of learning with a more traditional role as expert. His goal was to get as much active and focused involvement from his students as possible. Accordingly, he would ask questions and probe. He waited and watched. He cajoled. He encouraged: "Come on, you can do this." He put some students on the spot. Occasionally, he would jump up and take the lead as a last resort. In essence, Aldred was content to walk this tightrope because he was—and still is—convinced that problem-based learning has distinct advantages over traditional teacher-directed instruction in a discipline that prepares professionals for clinical work in the field (primarily dentists in this case).

At times, you may also want to get into character— for example, to answer a question as if you were the person you were discussing. Along with offering some insight into the leaders in your field, this approach also can provide a wonderful model for the ways different people have approached problems generally. Just how would this person have responded to a particular question? What would his or her critics say in reply? If students struggle with a problem, you could also become one of them as you share the various strategies you might consider and the frustrations with which you can empathize. In doing so, you'll contribute to the development of critical and creative thinking among your students.

You may find that your "lecturer" persona actually works against you in your "discussion leader" function, and that a deliberate change of character will help. For example, by taking himself out of the "expert" role, Larry Thornberg has used a form of role play in his veterinary pathology class to stimulate better discussions. Thornberg found that when he asked students to explain a point in class, they clammed up, unwilling to risk sounding stupid by offering an opinion to someone who they thought knew all the answers. In order to combat this perception, Thornberg changed his discussion leader "character." He placed a toy dog on the table and said to his students, "I'm the client. This is my dog. Explain to me what's wrong with the dog and what will happen to it." In essence, Thornberg reversed roles with his students. Instead of "playing" the expert, Thornberg took on the role of client and cast the students in the role of the veterinary experts. This role reversal really empowered the students, opening up discussion. "Discussions go well now," Thornberg says. "I never ask students to explain anything to me. I take myself out of the classroom completely." Practicing veterinarians would undoubtedly applaud.

With the potential for lively discussion and debate, these kinds of problem-based or case study analyses can be great fun and quite challenging. To get a wider diversity of opinion, you can also experiment with having students play different roles. How would a very creative person, or someone who is very deliberate, respond to a particular problem? How about someone from a related discipline? A very different discipline? Role playing can also work when you schedule it as an assignment. That way, your students have the opportunity to research their respective roles, just as actors would do before a production. Because their peers will be in the audience, the performance aspect can push even the most unmotivated student to contribute.

Actors expect to develop new roles for every production. Some roles fit their personalities. Others don't, thus requiring them to "stretch." They then have to study and develop their stage characters, trying different ideas in the process. They solicit feedback, either directly or on videotape.

Rehearsals then allow them to practice repeatedly and refine their roles. Success on stage requires performers to invest in this kind of preparation as a very conscious process.

Exercises

1. Identify the various roles you play in class when you ask questions, respond to student concerns, or facilitate discussions. What are your strengths? What should you build upon? How can you overcome your weaknesses?

2. Recall class sessions or meetings when you yourself were stimulated by questions, answers, or discussions. What "roles" were being played in these situations? How could each role have been even better?

3. Consider your own best and worst instructors. What roles did they play?

4. Think about the roles your best students have played. Were they active in class? Were they well prepared? What skills did they have? How could you help other students play these same roles?

5. Assess your own skill in and comfort with the various roles you have to play in class. Circle "H" (High), "M" (Medium), or "L" (Low) in the space below and note the areas in which you need to develop new competencies:

Skill	Rating	Comfort Needed
Lecturing	H M L	
Questioning	H M L	
Facilitating	H M L	
Motivating participation	H M L	
Listening	H M L	
Directing	H M L	
Encouraging	H M L	
Assessing	H M L	
Training	H M L	

Once you see the potential for improving your students' learning through questions, answers, and discussions, a range of new roles can open up for you. In each case, you can explore the advantages through the actor's keys to success — study, awareness, preparation, exploration and experimentation, solicitation of feedback, and practice/rehearsal. With these strategies in mind, consider the following roles:

Be a Catalyst for Growth

Knowing that learning and development are processes that are internal to each student, accept that you can do only so much from your end. In class, you regularly present new material and ideas. You can also serve as taskmaster, judge, and guide. Students, however, also must play their appointed roles as active, motivated, thinking learners. In truth, perhaps the most important role for you may be as a catalyst for growth, helping your students assess and deepen their own understanding while challenging them to assimilate new information, ideas, and skills. Since active and experiential learning are hallmarks for developmental shifts in thinking, you can look for places to involve your students in stimulating and active ways. (See Chapter 6, which covers development and drama, to learn more about this concept.)

Provide Encouragement and Reinforcement

Knowing that interactive learning is important although difficult for some students, you can also do more to encourage your students to participate actively and productively. In reality, you're applying behavioral principles and offering tangible rewards to shape student responses in this direction. For example, you can thank students for responding. You can celebrate students' efforts to understand and build on the insights they offer. You can refer to their contributions in subsequent discussions. Or you can offer points or a grade for quality classroom participation.

Nurture Creativity

If you believe creativity is important and you want to nurture it in yourself and in your students, then there are several "roles" you can play and encourage. In Chapter 5, which focuses on spontaneity and creativity, we go into some depth on this subject. In general, though, you can look for opportunities to recognize and support divergent thinking (alternative solutions) as opposed to the more traditional focus on convergent ("correct") answers.

Promote Effective Communication Skills

Knowing that success with questions, answers, and discussions rides on the cooperation of everyone in class, you can also increase students' learning by playing the role of a communication skills trainer. Helping your students improve their abilities to listen, empathize, negotiate differences, and resolve conflicts will allow them to learn more from discussions — and in every other aspect of their lives, for that matter. Initially, you may hesitate to give up content coverage for tackling these kinds of process skills. However, if the *quality of the time available* improves — if your students indeed can acquire information through study on their own, allowing you to use class time for *interactions* that enhance and deepen students' learning — then the investment may be a good one.

Keep Track of Time and Task

In many discussions, you lose time and focus when questions lead to diversions that produce little of substance for the class as a whole. When this happens, you can increase your awareness of the interplay among the various factors that impact learning, including time, goals and objectives, engagement, and participation. Some instructors find it useful to write the day's agenda on the board or overhead, including the time allotted for each item. Then you and your students have a constant visual cue that can help keep everyone on track. You're the one who's ultimately responsible for decisions about time and task, of course; but your students can play supporting roles — for example, they can help you and themselves stay on task by pointing out when the discussion has lost its focus.

Obviously you have to provide enough time for discussions, both in terms of quantity and quality. Just as you need a certain discipline to ensure that your students have enough time to respond to your questions, you must also allow enough temporal space for thinking and rethinking to occur. Otherwise, you may only skim the surface and miss important opportunities to mine more of the depths of your discipline and student understanding.

Like the actor, you can develop your "audience awareness" and check to see if everyone heard a question, for example. If necessary, you can then repeat the question. It's also important to keep track of timing — to know how long to stay with certain questions and when to move on. Behind the scenes, the stage manager may be responsible for cuing actors for entrances. At conferences, a moderator may offer cues when a speaker's time is nearly up. Many small groups work better when someone is the timekeeper. If you yourself are having difficulty managing the time you have in discussion sessions — if you get pulled off for too long on various digressions — you might want to explore some kind of cuing mechanism so that everyone is aware of the concern and is encouraged to speak up if a time problem is unfolding. Everyone is then working with their *metacognitive* abilities, thinking about their learning and acting accordingly.

Exercises

1. Recall a class or meeting where there was a particularly effective time period for questions, answers, and discussion. What roles did the instructor, leader, or moderator play?

2. Which of the roles described above could help you? How much of a stretch would it be to expand a particular role or adopt a new one?

Delivery

While your role in a question-and-answer session or general discussion is less "scripted," ideas from the stage can still prove useful. From *timing*, *expressions*, and *gestures* to *movements* and *voice*, performers use various means to enhance their interactions with others on the stage. For a complete discussion of delivery, be sure you read Chapter 3 on lecturing. However, we do have a few specific new points to add here.

Timing

We've already discussed various problems associated with timing and what some possible remedies might be. From your own increased awareness of the role of time in class to more deliberate attempts to increase your own pausing ("wait time") for student responses, you may be able to affect both the quantity and the quality of your students' learning. Some students shrink from the rapid and very public give and take of the typical classroom discussion. Others are inherently reticent, especially when they haven't done the reading!

Expressions

Because of the traditional role of teachers in directing learning at all levels, students tend to pay a good deal of attention to your facial expressions. For a start, you could watch a videotape of yourself teaching and note what students see. One key to improving is to increase your awareness of your own expressions and how those expressions may be affecting your students. Inviting an outside observer to look for particular kinds of expressions could help you accomplish several goals:

- You could get useful feedback about something that's of interest to you.

- You'd have a wonderful opportunity to discuss the issue with the observer after your class session is over.

- You'd improve your own focus on a particular type of expression, thereby increasing your chances of successfully making the changes you desire.

If you want to create a more relaxed and caring mood in class, for example, your own facial reactions could include smiling and showing empathy for student reactions. If you want to appear enthusiastic about your material, your expressions could show some urgency — a desire to get on with what you've planned.

Gestures

When students are responding in one of your classes, you can encourage careful listening by eliminating distracting gestures of your own — e.g., nervous or repetitive mannerisms like playing with a marker or drumming on the lectern. On stage, successful ensemble work can be very demanding. Actors must know their own lines and actions, behave in believable ways, and avoid distractions while others are acting. One cardinal sin among performers is known as upstaging — drawing the audience's focus away from where it rightfully belongs. Likewise, you yourself can become more aware of what's distracting in class and take care not to "upstage" any of your students when the spotlight ought to be on them.

Movement

Be careful of movements that will distract your students from concentrating and learning. For example, pacing across the front of the room while one of your students answers a question can affect the attention of the other students in the class. Stopping to face students who are responding can model the kind of focus you want everyone to have. Beware of being the gatekeeper for all responses, however. You may want to insist that students address their classmates while you observe the reactions of the other students so that you can encourage greater involvement among them.

Your proximity to students might also affect interactions. Try moving toward students who are responding. Doing so can create an intimacy that helps personalize and energize the class. When students experience this direct kind of engagement, more of them may come alive. As Greg Dickinson described in our "Foreword from the Lectern," you can also move away from a speaker and toward a group that has been largely silent, with the goal of awakening their interest. Moving too close, however, may intimidate some students—so use good judgment.

Movements without words can also be useful in a question-and-answer period. Instead of repeating a request for students to speak more loudly, for instance, a simple pantomime of cupping one hand around your ear and straining to hear may get the message across. Instead of asking for responses, look at your students, spread your arms, and beckon responses with your fingers. Ask for help by acting confused, wrinkling your face, and tilting your head with your hands facing upward. Feign ignorance about a particular question by shrugging your shoulders with an "I don't know" expression; then invite others to respond. To get students to finish their remarks, use the stage gesture of a cut across the neck or a "let's wind this up" cranking motion.

Voice

What you say in response to students, and how you say it, can impact the amount and quality of participation you get. From encouragement to expressions of empathy, from participation in a heated debate to some clarification that was needed, your voice can change dramatically in tone, pitch, and volume. Moreover, overusing certain words or phrases— "terrific" or "that's great"—can make you appear too much the cheerleader and less the expert. "OK" or "uh huh" are responses that can also signal that you're listening, but they don't convey any judgment and, therefore, they may encourage a student to continue.

Actors study the voice and routinely exercise their vocal range so that they can have the right qualities for their roles. You can certainly improve your own voice with increased self-awareness and active exploration of the vocal range you have at your disposal. Once again, using videotape, audiotape, or feedback from others about your voice can prove useful.

Props

Props can definitely enhance student engagement and learning in class. If you're discussing the burdens of power for one of Shakespeare's characters, for example, borrowing a crown from the theatre department can add a wonderful visual touch. As students respond, each can try on the crown. As we mentioned earlier in this chapter, Larry Thornberg's "dog" becomes an important focus for student-centered case study discussions in veterinary pathology. When discussing some aspect of molecular structure, a three-dimensional model can be invaluable. In particular, students who are new to a subject may benefit from having these kinds of concrete representations available. Trying to clarify complex ideas or issues with words alone can be difficult in any discipline. As simple as these props might seem to you, they can be memorable for your students.

While facilitating a problem-based learning session (small-group inquiry), Michael Aldred (Oral Biology) once leaped out of his chair and raced down to his office to retrieve a skull when his students seemed stumped about the connectedness of certain musculature with the overall structure of the jaw. These students really needed to see and handle the skull for themselves. Indeed, their future success as practicing dentists will certainly depend on their skill in handling the jaws of real clients.

When the public nature of discussions and the dominance by a few students make it difficult for other students to get the time and space they need to say what they think and feel, there's one especially effective prop you can use: what some Native Americans refer to as a "talking stick." It can be any object a person can easily hold — a small stick, an eraser, a pointer, a book, or the microphone in a large class. There is but one rule: Only the person holding the "talking stick" may speak. That person then decides when to pass the "stick" to someone else.

Using a "talking stick" creates a more deliberate process, and it can certainly change the dynamics of a group discussion. But it can promote better listening as well. No one is allowed to break into a conversation without formal (and physical) permission from the speaker. Those speaking know they'll have the undivided attention of the others in the room. They can take the time they need to formulate their thoughts. Pauses are no longer an open invitation for others to speak. Silences can allow for some reflection. Topics don't have to bounce around like pinballs, ricocheting off the varied reactions of those participating. Holding a brief discussion about the group process can help raise everyone's awareness about the dynamics that make for effective discussion and the choices the students have about ground rules for future sessions, as individuals and as a group.

Exercises

1. Take an inventory of the props you currently use—chalk or marker, pointer, overhead, books, notes, etc. Now make a second list of props that you yourself have seen used during noteworthy classes, where questions, answers, and discussions have been effective. Note the differences between the two lists. What new props could you consider trying? When? How will you know if they're effective?

2. Brainstorm other possible props. Don't limit yourself to what's immediately available. Let yourself dream. Think about the possibilities in various disciplines. What could represent the clash between the environment and development? between local and mass culture? between micro- and macro-economic systems? between intuitive and more deliberate strategies? between old and new paradigms?

3. Now go back and determine which of these props might be useful in one of your own classes, perhaps on a purely experimental basis. Which of the props could you gather and develop over time? Which might take a request for funding from some campus source? Which could become part of a larger external grant request?

Warming Up

Certainly you can identify key questions or issues ahead of time, think through your responses, and anticipate student concerns. Doing so can help you clarify areas you feel are beyond the scope of that day's discussion or even the course itself. Your students will benefit from knowing what, if any, parameters there are on the discussion; where you feel confident leading the students; and what topics would require additional preparation or an invitation for others to join in. By recruiting resource people, you can add wonderful new "characters" and material to your classroom "scenes."

You can also recognize that students, like any audience, may need a warm-up. Questions raised at the outset of class may be met with some silence, avoidance, or resistance. Students may not be sufficiently engaged, aroused, or interested to respond well at first. The issues you raise at the beginning of a class session may work best as a preview of sorts — ideas for students to think and write about, or questions that you can repeat later in the class period.

For their part, performers give a great deal of attention to their audience warm-ups. For example, rock bands and headline comedians routinely use some kind of "opening" act, often well known in its own right. Most plays build up to the inciting incident, when the story really starts. Operas and ballets typically begin with an overture. For a variety of reasons, many films and television shows seem to plunge into their stories almost immediately. Perhaps the modern viewer's tolerance for any delay in the action is shrinking as the MTV-ish approaches of quick-cut editing prevail. What we offer here are a few ideas to get you thinking about the ways you might get your own students started with respect to warm-up.

One possibility is to have your students complete a short writing assignment — just a few sentences or so — on a question you want to address. This activity gives everyone a chance to focus, think, and prepare a response before the discussion begins. You could also have your students discuss their reactions with others in the class, either with partners or within small groups. This strategy is akin to priming their "thinking and talking "pumps" with a topic that can help get everyone more involved. Even students who hesitate to participate at all may feel better prepared and more confident when they can reflect on their responses ahead of time and share them with other students first.

Some language teachers will use music to help "set the stage" and guided imagery to help focus student attention, calming the inevitable nervousness that accompanies classes where frequent and public participation is required. Other teachers will use a review of previous material to set the stage for new learning. Still others will pull material from the news to awaken student interest.

Many people notice the consequences of not warming up only when they don't take enough time to get ready—when they feel rushed, scattered, or unfocused. Athletes can pull muscles—or worse—when they don't warm up adequately. Performers certainly notice when a hasty warm-up affects their concentration on stage. Actors also use warm-ups as part of the ensemble-building process. Just as a physical warm-up helps an actor release extraneous concerns and focus on the task at hand, so too can a short physical warm-up help you engage your students' attention.

Suzanne Burgoyne, for instance, has employed warm-ups in such "academic" theatre classes as dramatic literature and script analysis. Asking the class to stand in a circle, she leads them through a brief routine that includes stretching, "hanging oneself up," massaging each other's shoulders, and "shaking out." Suzanne has found the warm-up routine effective in developing a class atmosphere that is conducive to discussion. Warm-ups get everyone in your class going — especially when you're combating sleepiness in an early-morning session or "postprandial lethargy" in an early-afternoon class!

Some students, though, hesitate to participate no matter what. They may be shy by nature or anxious about speaking in front of a large group. They may worry about sounding "stupid" by asking a "dumb" question. Some come chronically unprepared for class. Others like to think through their ideas carefully, and they rarely find the time or the nerve in class to offer responses or questions of their own. Although a warm-up could help here, these kinds of concerns may require more systematic attention on your part throughout the course.

Exercises

1. Think of activities or events that have required you to warm up. What was the benefit? the risk when you didn't warm up?

2. Make a note on your calendar or in your appointment book to warm up. A few stretching and vocal exercises in your office can help. A short but brisk walk, perhaps on the way to class, can also help. Even if for only five minutes, concentrate on your physical and emotional preparation before class and note the impact on your teaching. What happens if you have to deal with student questions or equipment hassles before class? Does your energy evaporate? Or, early in the semester, when students are

settling in and unsure of just what to expect from you and your course, can your own energy be excessive?

Reactions from Students and Audiences

Audience/class awareness becomes especially important on two levels. At a *micro* level, you have to deal with the individual question that arises and the responses that result. At a *macro* level, you also need to be aware of what the rest of the class is doing. You should keep in mind the *group focus*—how you can pull others into a question from one student in particular. For example, calling for a show of hands can help engage everyone mentally and physically—e.g., "How many of you had that same question?" Or, you can try a spontaneous but brief writing exercise—e.g., "Let me ask each of you to put a few thoughts or feelings down on this question." You could also add a small interactive activity—e.g., "Now I'd like you to turn to a classmate, share what you've written, and see what you have in common."

Problems

We expect our students to behave responsibly in class, and, to a large extent, they do. However, we must remember that the changes they are experiencing in their lives are indeed dramatic. They now have much greater control over their own time, commitments, lifestyles, relationships, and finances. They often make the decision of what campus to attend, what area(s) of study to pursue, what elective courses to take, and when and how to study. Since students and/or their parents ultimately pay for (at least some of) their college education, they begin acting more like paying audience members (motivated "customers").

Indeed, all of these choices and responsibilities inevitably impact what actually happens in class. While most students make the adjustment from high school to college with relative ease, some struggle. Many more students are working these days. There's also a greater mix on campus — of ages, backgrounds, abilities, and motivations. When students are unprepared in lecture, they can easily go unnoticed; small discussion sections, however, can really bog down if one or more students aren't ready to participate. While the back rows in some large lecture classes may become quite "social," students in smaller classes are less likely to chat or sleep.

When you do face problems, try an appeal out of respect for those who *are* trying to listen and learn. Empathizing with those who are tired in your early-morning class can help build trust and open communication. You can always ask disruptive students to stop or leave. Indeed, discussion periods can reveal problems that don't tend to appear when students are busily taking notes and you're controlling the class from the front of the room.

Importantly, some students may need guidance, assistance, and insistence from you to pay attention when their classmates speak. After all, how can student comments ever appear on an exam? You can certainly draw students' attention to good questions and comments and, when appropriate, signal what could appear on a future exam — e.g., "That's a point that could work on a quiz," or, "That gives me an idea for the midterm." At times, you can even remind your students to listen. You could also pull them in with a poll or a short writing and discussion assignment.

It's critical for you to be proactive — to be conscious of the need to keep a group focus as much of the time as possible and to plan for a variety of engaging activities. If you can keep the attention of your students, and if you're successful in building off of their responses and questions, you'll rarely see any serious problems in your classes.

So go for it. Take some chances. Try some discussions in your biggest lectures. Vary the format in your smaller classes. Experiment with role plays and debates. Explore a variety of roles. Raise your awareness of the dynamics involved in a successful discussion. Push on that envelope. Step off into some new, and possibly uncomfortable, directions. Your own learning could energize you and your teaching, connecting you with your students in new ways as you collectively explore new possibilities.

Chapter 5:
Energy, Creativity, and Spontaneity

No matter how much you prepare, you can never predict exactly what will happen in any class session. Of course, you should have your material well organized, carefully sequenced, and sprinkled with relevant examples. But you must always be ready to think on your feet as well. Performers too must develop skills for dealing with the unpredictable; no matter what happens, "the show must go on!" A faculty appointment in higher education requires expertise and often encourages a narrow degree of specialization. Yet the best instructors also possess other qualities that enable them to cope with classroom realities and meet the needs of their students. Of these qualities, *energy*, *creativity*, and *spontaneity* are three of the most important.

In the often hyper-rational arena of academia, mentioning qualities like these may raise eyebrows. Some professors may be skeptical of the value of spontaneity in a culture driven by demands for analysis and proof. One may even hear suspicious murmurs about teachers who receive high ratings, as if they were "pandering" to students—"dumbing down" their course expectations in hopes of getting higher student evaluations, thus transforming teaching awards into "popularity contests."

Some of these same voices might also criticize students, dismissing them as inferior to those "in the good old days," and as having less self-discipline, less motivation, fewer skills, and no preparation for what lies ahead of them because they've been numbed by television, drugs, sex, and rock 'n roll. If these criticisms were accurate, who could blame students for choosing entertainment over substance — for giving lower evaluations to instructors who maintain high expectations? To the contrary, the evidence shows that students are remarkably reliable in assessing the quality of the teaching they receive (e.g., Marsh 1987; Andrew, Timpson, and Nulty 1994.)

When pressed, many of these same critics will admit that instructors should be enthusiastic about their subjects, as well as responsive when students raise questions or discussion begins. When pressed, the critics also will admit that teaching ought to be more than information giving or "prepping" students for exams. Even the best material can get lost in poor delivery. We believe you can stimulate deeper learning among your students if you can get past the minimalist notion of subject coverage — if you can challenge your students to think critically and creatively. When you raise your expectations beyond course coverage, then the instructional value of energy, creativity, and spontaneity becomes clear. Understanding how performers breathe life into written scripts can help you infuse more of these qualities into your teaching.

Improvisation and Spontaneity

The word "improvisation" may strike terror in your heart. What about notes? preparation? expertise? Don't students expect, even demand, an organized presentation? Of course you need to be prepared. But there are times when you need to change direction: When students are disengaged, when your examples just don't work, or when a particular question sparks a lively exchange and you want to go with that flow. Understanding more about the role of spontaneity and experimenting with activities that make you think on your feet can help. While actors too are tied to their scripts, they also can benefit from improvisation when developing their characters, exploring their stage relationships, or attempting to keep their performances fresh.

As Viola Spolin (1983, 3), author of *Improvisation for the Theatre*, points out: "Everyone can act. Everyone can improvise. Anyone who wishes to can play in the theatre and learn to become 'stageworthy.'" Routine performances appear unnatural, disconnected, mechanical, and labored. Training and practice with improvisation, however, can free performers from stereotypical delivery and allow them to act more convincingly — to explore their relationships with others on stage and make their roles more "natural" and believable. Along with explanation of the value of improvisation, Spolin includes numerous exercises. While we offer some ideas for you to try, you may profit from reading her book in its entirety.

For actors, working with improvisation adds fun to otherwise pressured routines. Performers, especially non-professionals, need breaks and periodic reminders about the joys of acting, dancing, and singing. You yourself may benefit from reminders about the joys of teaching. Students will respond positively to your energy and enthusiasm. Just as important, improvisational exercises can help stretch your creative abilities and enhance your flexibility. Even with the best of preparation, you can never anticipate every possibility in class—who will ask what question, which points will need further clarification, or when you'll need additional examples.

When getting a staged production ready, actors often work out their relationships with each other by experimenting with ad-libbed lines, gestures, expressions, and movements. Improvisation allows them to explore a range of situations and possible reactions. Good acting requires much more than delivering lines on cue. It's really about creating believable characters and memorable roles. Missing a cue can be forgiven so long as actors stay in character and the "show goes on." Rarely does the audience even know when the actors have "blown" their lines. The ability to improvise in character has saved many actors and many shows.

Dancers also need energy, creativity, and spontaneity to be able to perform well. Periodic sessions devoted to improvisation can help nurture the creative expressiveness that underlies success on stage. For example, dance teachers will call for ideas and feelings to be created on the spot without words — just movements, postures, gestures, and expressions: "Be a machine. Now, tell a story without words. Be happy, sad, silly, fastidious, cranky, tired." Freed from being required to match music to set moves or synchronize precisely with others, dancers can explore their own ideas. Having this opportunity to express personal feelings through dance can add energy and creative inspiration to the development of the final production.

Are there lessons here for you as a teacher?

Applications in Class

Periodic opportunities for questions or discussions can give you a chance to use your creative and spontaneous skills. You can free yourself from excessive dependency on your notes and engage your students more directly in exploring the material at hand. The resulting shifts in focus and interaction can energize both you and your students.

Sheila Tobias (1990) has been critical of traditional lecture strategies that emphasize information acquisition and competition — in large, introductory science courses in particular. She followed a cohort of "talented dropouts" who started out as science majors but then switched over to other disciplines and went on to be successful. Many of these students were women and/or minorities who reported feeling discouraged, isolated, and unmotivated in the competitive and impersonal science classes. Indeed, most students do better when they can interact, when they get to use their new knowledge and deepen their understanding, and when they have the support and assistance of their peers.

Recognizing this phenomenon, Peggy Delaney (Marine Sciences) has blended a careful organization of content with ongoing sensitivity to students' needs for clarification, assistance, and involvement. She maintains a focused but relaxed pace in her lectures. She comes to each class session with specific goals and objectives in mind, but she then proceeds to teach in a measured, flexible, open manner. Accordingly, students raise questions or add comments at any time. Peggy stops, responds, and then checks to see if there are other reactions before moving on, engaging her students in a series of running conversations. She never seems to hurry and always smiles easily. All questions seem welcomed.

Explaining her approach, Peggy says she wants to avoid what she calls the "firehose" approach to teaching, in which students are "blasted" nonstop with information. In an effort to accommodate the needs of her students, she adjusts her expectations as the class unfolds. She wants her students to think in class, and she tries to channel her enthusiasm into a concern for their learning. Indeed, students have to do more on their own outside of class, but the knowledge and confidence they gain in class allows them to work more independently later. Peggy seems very approachable, and she frequently attracts a large group of students at the end of class who want more from her, creating a crowd scene as the next class tries to move in.

In contrast, Michael Warren (English) uses a more traditional but fast-paced approach to lecturing and schedules regular breaks during class for more spontaneous interchanges with students—questions, comments, discussions. While some students may prefer a slower pace, the breaks allow everyone to catch up and think about the points being made in the lecture. Most students seem to be thoroughly energized by Michael's enthusiasm. His style feels like interval training in track, during which runners alternate back and forth between sprinting and jogging with time for recovery.

When you engage in these kinds of spontaneous interactions, you want to concentrate on picking up important nonverbal signals —which are often subtle—when your students are confused or struggling, bored, anxious about an upcoming exam, or just tired and needing a change of pace. As you reflect on your own teaching and explore various approaches, your own awareness of these signals will grow. For example, you can concentrate on listening more carefully to students' questions and take time in class to explore students' underlying confusion. You can capitalize on issues that excite your students. You can interject creative energy and spontaneity with debates and role plays. Inviting someone to class who has some special expertise can spark new ideas. With you serving as facilitator —fielding questions, summarizing the points made, or posing new possibilities—and watching for student reactions, your guest can be an effective catalyst for deeper learning.

You yourself can help build on what gets said, relating ideas to what has emerged in previous classes or appeared in the readings. You can also play the classic "devil's advocate" role and look for points of controversy or disagreement: "Who can offer an alternative solution or explanation?" You can search back in time or project off into the future: "What was the prevailing paradigm a hundred years ago or a thousand years ago? What will it be a decade from now?" You can probe deeply into particular issues and values and consider how others might respond: "What would the critics say? How would the issue be viewed by scholars in related disciplines?"

Marlene Winell (Human Development) uses improvisation and role playing when teaching students communication skills. Admittedly, the content lends itself easily to such alternative approaches, but her adaptations are still noteworthy. For example, a student once expressed some anxiety about an assignment for which she was supposed to interview another student — someone she didn't know and who was different in some way. "How do you do that?" the student asked in class. "It's hard." Many of her classmates agreed. At that point, Marlene improvised and decided to capture the moment by going right into a role play. (Unaddressed, these fears could have blocked the student's learning and limited the effectiveness of future assignments.) "Pick someone in class and let's try it," Marlene insisted. The student paused, sighed, gulped, then shuffled over to a classmate across the room and mumbled timidly, "I have to do this assignment for class and, like, I need a short interview with someone different. Um, do you think I could interview you for a few minutes maybe?" "Sure," came the quick reply. "Oh, *really*? Wow. OK, thanks!" (Whew ... relief!)

At this point, Marlene asked the student how the interaction felt. "OK, but I was afraid he would say no," the student responded. "All right," Marlene replied, "try it again and this time he'll say no." The two students replayed the scene with the new ending, the fellow begging off politely because he had to get to class. Marlene asked again how the interaction felt to the inquiring student. "Actually, OK. He had a good reason, so I guess I won't die after all. I'll just ask someone else." Marlene then probed further about the cause of the student's initial anxiety. The student suddenly realized that her first reaction was mostly about her own worries about being ridiculed — feelings she really wanted to push through because the assignment was an important one. Other students found this activity a breakthrough for them as well. It quickly became clear that many of them shared the same fears about looking foolish in front of their peers and approaching strangers on campus, especially those who appeared to be "different." Until the underlying feelings were explored and various outcomes considered, many of the students felt blocked.

Here's another example of a discussion format that may have wide applicability. Michael Williams (Aboriginal and Torres Strait Islanders Studies) leads his classes with a similar kind of openness and sensitivity to student needs. For him, such sensitivity becomes especially important in the context of cultural differences: indigenous students in Australia often feel intimidated by the hierarchical, critical, and information-driven nature of many university classes. With the hope of encouraging his students to understand their own thinking and develop their own voices, he encourages an open and accepting climate in class that minimizes judgment and encourages participation.

Michael was once leading a discussion on a traditional Aboriginal story in which a cockatoo gets to speak to a human. For many of us in the room, thinking about the validity of the story was proving to be a dead end. Just what was its "real" significance? What did it really mean to the members of the tribe who had passed it on over the centuries? What did it mean to members of other tribes? After patiently listening to a variety of interpretations, Michael suggested, "Perhaps this issue is really unresolvable and we have to accept that."

The classroom discussion then took an important turn that touched on significant feelings just below the surface. In response to the comments about how different people will find different meaning in a story, a more general discussion ensued about the validity and usefulness of labels. Michael asked: "When thinking about the responses of others, does it make any sense to generalize about the ways in which non-Aboriginal people will interpret this story? what white Europeans will say? Are these categories so big that no sensible conclusions can be reached?" You see, some of the white students in the class were feeling bothered by the labeling that put all of them into one large, amorphous category. But many were nervous about raising the issue directly. Later, it turned out that some of the Aboriginal students had a similar concern. Their perceived differences reflected differences in tribal identity, geographic origin, life experiences, personality, and the like.

Here, Michael was able to make an effective connection with the issues raised in both discussions: that we may have to accept as fundamentally unresolvable these larger questions — the "true" interpretation of the legend and the validity of any generalizations about large groups. Michael's skill in gently focusing the discussion seemed to allow everyone to move to a better understanding while addressing deeply felt concerns.

Michael Aldred (Oral Biology) uses a similar student-centered approach that routinely draws on his energy, creativity, and spontaneity. Michael supports a problem-based method for preparing future dentists, insisting that the traditional lecture doesn't do enough to promote deep understanding. Accordingly, he now lectures as little as possible, relying instead on his ability to raise questions, probe responses, and facilitate discussion. In a rapid-fire style, Michael asks and prompts: "What's going on here? What do you think? Who wants to have a go? C'mon, you can do this. What's the first thing you notice? Look at it. Think. Use your common sense." There is no formal script per se. The focus is on students and their abilities to analyze various cases and explain their conclusions.

Enhancing Creativity

There's a certain looseness to these kinds of improvisations — a looseness that's directly connected to creative expressiveness. You might expect that, by design, any formal "training" in creativity would be somewhat loose and non-prescriptive. Some approaches are indeed freewheeling, but others are quite structured. Viola Spolin (1985), a founder of American improvisational methodology, argues that certain environments and structures promote creative behavior:

- **An Environment that Encourages Personal Freedom.** Our culture, Spolin observes, inhibits creativity because individual feelings of self-worth are regulated by our need for approval from (and fear of the disapproval of) authority figures. For creativity to flower, an environment of trust must be established in which the individual can explore freely without depending on the approval/disapproval dynamic.

- **A Structure that Focuses All Energies on Problem-solving Activities.** Spolin finds a model structure in games, which focus energies upon achieving a specific objective but that also encourage creativity. Games allow individuals to *discover* how they can best reach their goal(s) — there's no one "right" way to proceed. Like a game, an improvisation is not chaos; there are agreed-upon rules for each exercise. Thus, improvisation paradoxically unleashes spontaneity while teaching self-discipline, as participants willingly work within established boundaries and concentrate on solving a problem rather than winning approval. Concentration is the key to problem solving. Spolin emphasizes this relationship by calling the specific objective for each of her theatre games the "point of concentration."

- **A Structure in which Individuals Learn through Experience and Develop Their Awareness of Self, Others, and the Environment.** In fact, Spolin asks us to consider that "what is called talented behavior is simply a greater individual capacity for experiencing" (p. 3). In order to experience the world, we must find the courage to engage it totally and directly—with our senses, intellect, and intuition—instead of routinely accepting definitions handed down to us by authority figures (teachers and experts). "Spontaneity," Spolin insists, "is the moment of personal freedom when we are faced with a reality and see it, explore it, and act accordingly" (p. 4). In the fullest sense of the term, improvisation is experiential education.

Self-awareness

As is true for many people, you might be your own biggest barrier when it comes to innovation. Your own fears and inhibitions and your own perceptions of social norms and taboos may block you. Performers use improvisational exercises and role plays to sharpen their self-awareness and help themselves see their own self-imposed barriers more clearly. As actors walk around in a circle, for instance, a director or choreographer will call out, "Be small. Be big. Be happy. Be dumb. Be disconnected. Be salty. Run. Stumble. Be lazy. Be surreal." The focus is on responding freely to the unusual—on stretching and exploring. It can be lots of fun. After becoming more conscious of their own blocks, the performers can push out and explore new possibilities.

The same is true for instructors. Ken (not his real name), a professor of Earth Sciences, wanted help because of student complaints that his classes were boring, routine, and dry. He had taken Bill Timpson's workshop, "Teaching as Performing," in hopes of getting some new ideas. On end-of-semester evaluations, too many of Ken's students would remark that he didn't seem to care about his material or them. When Bill asked Ken about his response to the evaluations, Ken expressed real frustration, insisting that he truly loved the material, that he always had, and that he found these kinds of comments from students troubling.

The problem seemed to reside primarily in Ken's own sense of a "professorial" self. The image cemented in his head was one of objective expertise, dignified and aloof, rooted behind the lectern. Over time, however, he came to understand the effect this role had on his relationship with students—the distance they felt from him; their experience of his "dignified" demeanor as "remote"; and their perception that his teaching was dry, routine, and uninspired. Gradually, Ken became more aware of the ways he'd been suppressing his own enthusiasm in class. With feedback and encouragement, he began to experiment with a more relaxed and caring presence; he gave himself permission to share more of his own joy and excitement. As you can well imagine, his students responded positively, further reinforcing Ken's desire to change.

Exercises

1. Some language teachers attempt to lower students' anxieties and, thereby, enhance student learning by relaxing their students at the start of

each class. By playing music softly, dimming the lights to show slides, using a quiet voice and a slow cadence, and having students close their eyes while they describe the beauties of the native geography, these teachers promote an increased receptivity to learn (see "Suggestopedia" in Timpson and Tobin 1982). You can try something similar in your own classes, perhaps for a few minutes before an exam, when you're reviewing key concepts, or when you're clarifying what you want from your students.

2. For dancers, *isolations* are exercises that create a heightened physical self-awareness. A choreographer will ask dancers to rotate one shoulder independently of the other or each in opposition to the other, or to move their chests from side to side independently of their hips. Try these techniques. With some exploration and practice, you too can develop a higher degree of bodily awareness. This consciousness can then carry over to the classroom and help you eliminate distracting behaviors. It can also help you add movements and gestures that are more congruent with your words.

3. Augusto Boal (1979, 1992, 1995), author of a number of books on the application of theatre practices for non-actors, likes to begin warm-ups with what he terms *demechanization* exercises, which are intended to break routine (habitual, unthinking) movements and re-engage the senses. With your right hand, trace a perfect circle in the air. Now, put that hand down and, with your left hand, trace a perfect square in the air. Stop that. Now try to do both at the same time. Reverse directions. Notice the concentration required even to attempt both at the same time. Imagine what you'd notice in class if you were this attentive to nonverbal messages — your own and those of your students.

Creative Expression

As an instructor, you have a wonderful opportunity—a license, even a mandate—to create and innovate. If your students become bored and listless, are you able to adjust your plans and do something to re-engage them? If your students come to class unprepared or you find yourself with some extra time before class ends, can you come up with something spontaneously? Unlike an actor, you're not bound by any slavish adherence to your "script." Spontaneous shifts or digressions—questions, personal anecdotes, a role play, an impromptu debate—can renew interest among your students. When student learning is the objective, your goal becomes much more than content coverage and your options (and obligations) increase dramatically.

In the theatre, actors must recreate and re-energize a production every time the curtain goes up. Creative expression is what brings a written script to life. Without that energy and concentration, productions are flat and lifeless. Furthermore, every production crew—whether on a Hollywood film, a big Broadway musical, or a high school production—struggles with limitations of budget and time when trying to create effective sets and costumes. Creativity, then, becomes doubly important for maximizing available resources. For their part, actors will continue to draw on their own creative talents to refine their roles throughout a production's run, making minor adjustments to their delivery, movements, and gestures—all of the subtleties that keep performances sharp, energetic, and believable.

Whenever you go to see a new production of something you've seen before—Shakespeare, a musical, a remake of an old film classic—you have the inevitable tendency to compare one performance against the other. Each theatre artist feels the challenge to add something creative. For instance, every serious Shakespearean actor must think long and hard about the options for delivering Hamlet's famous dilemma: "To be or not to be, that is the question." Just where should the emphasis lie? On "to be"? On "not" or "that" or "the"? On "question"? Multiply this decision by all of the other places that call for artistic interpretation and you quickly see the importance of creativity. Developing a compelling character requires actors to stretch beyond the limits of the known and comfortable.

The same imperative holds true for teaching. Your emphases can help direct student learning. The silences you provide can create spaces for reflection. The activities you design can promote critical and creative thinking. The subtleties you note can help you cue into student struggles and what might prompt new insights. Your enthusiasm can inspire students' commitment. Whatever the discipline, we all share a need to promote creative thinking and expression. The future may indeed belong increasingly to those who can overcome outdated thinking and see new possibilities, cooperate across cultures, and form new alliances.

More concretely, how can we help students respond to the increasing press of technology in the workplace? What can you do in your own courses to encourage the creative use of technology? What new software makes sense? Are there substitutes possible for traditional assignments — perhaps multimedia projects for which students can combine text with graphics, photographs, slides, animation, video, film, and/or sound? Can your students be better linked to you and each other through email discussion groups?

A Whack and a Kick

Along with the exercises described here, we also recommend a variety of books on creativity. For example, Roger von Oech (1983, 1986) has two wonderful and popular books. Written in a very light, readable, and straightforward manner, each book is a good place to begin a more focused study of creativity, teaching, and learning. Along with creativity's applicability to work settings, you might also find it useful on a personal level.

In *A Whack on the Side of the Head* (1983), von Oech discusses the "locks" that confine our minds:

- Insistence on the "right" answer;
- A preoccupation with what is assumed to be logical;
- A conforming impulse to follow the rules;
- The call for practicality;
- The pressure to stay on task;
- The avoidance of ambiguity;
- The fear of making mistakes;
- The prohibitions against play;
- The commandment to be serious;
- The assumption by many that they lack creativity.

Opening these locks, insists von Oech, is something anyone can do.

Exercise

Being aware of the qualities you have that underlie creativity can be a good place to start your study of creativity and its applicability to your teaching. Using your own experiences and understandings, rate yourself on the qualities below. Add comments where appropriate:

Quality	Rating (High/Medium/Low)	Comments
Self-awareness Being able to understand your own strengths and limitations, your needs and goals, your reactions to events around you, etc.	H M L	
Creative thinking Innovating, introducing new possibilities, etc.	H M L	
Being present Concentrating on the task at hand — teaching, learning, questions, responses, the time remaining, the group's needs, etc.	H M L	
Reflecting Thinking and writing about your own experiences, reactions, feelings, concerns, relationships, etc.	H M L	
Spontaneity Feeling free to digress, feeling confident in your own awareness of what's happening and what changes would be helpful, etc.	H M L	
Risk taking Your willingness to take chances, explore new possibilities, learn, etc.	H M L	

1. How have these qualities affected your teaching?

2. How have these qualities impacted your success in facilitating student learning?

Implications for Teaching

In his sequel, *A Kick in the Seat of the Pants* (1986), von Oech describes the four roles that typically comprise the creative process: *explorer, artist, judge,* and *warrior.* Each role represents a set of behaviors and attitudes you can use in your teaching — to explore new approaches, prepare new courses, research new topics, or interact with students — or for personal growth. Because von Oech's roles are not scripted, they have a definite improvisational and creative quality to them.

As an *explorer,* you need courage to venture into uncharted waters and try new approaches. You may need to collect lots of ideas, and be willing to rethink certain assumptions or beliefs. As an explorer, you give yourself permission to break out of ruts, and to analyze and overcome self-imposed fears. You may look inside yourself for new ideas, tapping your own intuition and creativity. Indeed, you may prove to be your own best advisor. Ideally you enjoy — or learn to enjoy — this process of exploration.

Pause for a moment and reflect upon the following:

- What explorations could help you stay energetic and creative as a teacher? For example, is your commitment to course coverage limiting your ability to explore new and more engaging possibilities?
- Is your use of knowledge-based exam questions (multiple-choice, true-false, matching, fill-in-the-blank) emphasizing too much surface learning (memorizing, cramming, regurgitating)?
- Are your current classroom routines just that — habitual and uninspired?

As an *artist,* you can imagine possibilities. You can look at issues or problems from a reverse angle, from a different vantage point, through different lenses. For you as a teacher, you might look at issues or problems from a performer's perspective. Metaphors can help. For example, how might teaching be like conducting an orchestra or directing a film? According to von Oech, an artist learns how to break rules when necessary, how to fool around, and how to let his or her thinking roam and ramble—all of which can help generate fresh insights. Pause and reflect for a moment on the following:

- When are you an *artist* in your teaching?
- What more could you do to be an *artist* in your teaching?
- When do you go more with your own intuition?

Especially when you try some of the more active, performer-based approaches recommended in this book, you may need to shift your definition of "success" from the purely objective and quantifiable (paper-and-pencil exams) to more subjective assessments of deeper learning and creative thinking (observations about the freshness of responses given).

As a *judge,* you need to have a critical eye and an analytical perspective. Countless decisions, big and small, have to be made to achieve success on the stage. In a similar way, you have to make thousands of decisions in your classes to ensure your students learn. Reflect upon the following questions:

- How do you decide exactly what to say and when in your class sessions?
- How do you break bad habits and develop better approaches?
- What readings do you require, and what do you need to say about each?
- How good are you at evaluating student responses and assignments?
- How consistent are you?
- How fair are you?
- How well do your graded assignments match your learning objectives for the class?
- How do you know when a class is going well?
- How do you decide what changes to make in a class?
- What values do you bring to class? expectations? biases?

Finally, as a *warrior,* you must put a plan into practice. Certainly a military analogy has its drawbacks, but the idea of the *warrior* does bring up the connotation of taking action and fighting for what you want. For the stage, rehearsals point everyone involved toward opening night. In your own planning process, you can point toward getting everything organized for the first day of class. Staying with this analogy, you can also think about the "weapons" you can use to attack ignorance and lethargy in class;

your "defenses" against student preoccupation with grades; and the "strategies" and "tactics" you might employ to promote student engagement and deeper learning. Take a moment to think about your own strengths as a teacher/warrior.

Exercise

1. Roger von Oech identifies various "locks" that confine our minds. Evaluate yourself on each of the "locks" below. Reflect on the implications for your teaching:

"Lock"	Rating (High/Medium/Low)	Comments
How important is a "right" answer? Are various solutions possible?	H M L	
How important is logic in your assessment of student learning? Are feelings or intuition permissible in their reasoning?	H M L	
How important are your requirements? Can students suggest alternatives?	H M L	
How important is it for you always to be practical as an instructor? When is the whimsical appropriate?	H M L	
How important is it for you to stay on task constantly? When are digressions useful?	H M L	
How important is it to avoid ambiguity? When does complexity make definitive answers problematic?	H M L	
How important is it for you to be serious? When can you let go, get (appropriately) crazy, and have some fun in class?	H M L	

"Lock"	Rating (High/Medium/Low)	Comments
How important is creativity to you? Where does creativity stand in your hierarchy of course goals?	H M L	

Synectics

Beginning in the early 1960s, William Gordon (1961) attempted to tease out those aspects of creativity that are foundational, generalizable, and trainable. In what he termed *synectics*—from the Greek roots *syn* (to bring together) and *ectics* (diverse elements)—creativity becomes a quality that people from all walks of life could understand and use with practice. Creativity is not some mysterious quality, limited to a very few areas like acting or the other arts. Instead, it's a process and a quality anyone can (and should) apply.

As Alvin Toffler (1974) and other futurists continue to remind us, creativity should become increasingly important, for example, as technology takes over more and more routine tasks. On campus, computers already have proven their value as powerful tools for data analysis, word processing, accessing the Internet, and communicating rapidly both locally and globally. Gordon's (1961) recommendations for anyone interested in nurturing creativity begin with being open to possibilities and the freedom to explore—qualities long valued, in particular, by actors, playwrights, jazz musicians, performance artists, experimental filmmakers, and choreographers among others. Following this line of reasoning, look for evidence of the creativity in your own field:

- Who were the giants and "trailblazers" in the past?
- Who are the free thinkers today?
- Who was/is able to go against the odds, in defiance of conventional wisdom and the prevailing paradigms, and really push a particular field in new directions?
- How did/do these leaders think and function?
- How did/do research and progress proceed?

- What were/are the blocks, blind alleys, false leads, and popular but misguided ventures?

- How might more free, open, and creative thinking advance your field?

Answering these questions for yourself can tap a mother lode of useful examples for you and your students. We think Gordon is right: Creativity is everywhere. You just need to have the right mindset to see its manifestations.

Cultivating the creative can also mean celebrating some aspects of non- or quasi-rational ways of knowing—ways that are more intuitive, perhaps requiring leaps of faith or deriving from sudden insights, musings, or dreams. Most actors certainly use every means available—studied and imagined, analytical and intuited, reflective and impulsive, original and stolen—to make their roles believable and alive. In academia, the history of every discipline is packed with examples where non-, quasi- and hyper-rational processes were all involved (to varying degrees and combinations, and at different points in time) in breakthrough research, creative initiatives, and paradigm shifts. We believe effective instruction also requires a dynamic mix of preparation and spontaneity. Many instructors routinely rely on their intuition to "feel" the need for a change in plans or to gain fresh insights.

Indeed, every class has a unique life of its own, with a special mix of experiences, personalities, abilities, motivations, and expectations. Thinking through all of these variables to plan for a course of study is difficult in the most relaxed of times and often overwhelming in the classroom, where decisions often must be instantaneous — how to say this or that, what information to give with what emphasis, whom to involve and when, how to answer which questions, when to move on, and so on and so forth. The truth is that you must rely upon a variety of means—rational, quasi-rational, and non-rational—to see your *ways* through such complexity. Gordon (1961) asks for more conscious awareness of the creative process as you work through these intricacies.

To cultivate the creative, Gordon recommends regular exercise and *stretching* for your mind and senses. He favors using metaphors to *make what's strange appear more familiar.* When you're introducing a difficult new concept, for instance, you might use concrete metaphors to give students a better foundation for understanding theories and abstractions.

ɪ ʋɪ example, the concept of creativity we're describing here could be likened to the bonding of cast and crew into the cohesive team that's necessary for a polished and successful stage production. Different personalities, talents, motivations, and experiences become connected in an intricate web of overlapping relationships and interdependencies. Just think of your own experiences with groups in which individuals were able to subordinate their differences and capitalize on their collective talents in order to achieve a common end.

Gordon also argues for helping students *make the familiar strange* — for turning ideas or problems upside down and inside-out, and looking at them from different and, hopefully, fresh perspectives. For example, you can look at your classroom as a theatre set. Can you see new possibilities — new arrangements of the seats and desks to encourage different kinds of interactions, or new uses of the wall space to display the results of small-group brainstorming? Can the lighting be changed to spotlight a guest speaker or dim the room when you want quiet reflection?

Finally, Gordon encourages regular *practice*. If you value creativity, then you can promote its use in your teaching and assignments for students. Practice, the repetition of new behaviors, is akin to the rehearsal process that is so central to any staged production. Typically, the more adept performers are in rehearsal, the more open they are to exploration and feedback—and thus the more creative they become. With respect to your own teaching, you can look for places to stretch your thinking about what and how you want your students to learn. Consider taking unique and unusual perspectives, or requiring students to make creative input into class assignments where appropriate.

When Bill Timpson assigns a group presentation in one of his education classes, he often insists that students attempt to add some measure of creativity. Although he deliberately leaves this expectation open-ended, he does give his students several examples of projects that he believes had creative elements. For example, some students have dressed in costumes and used role plays to make a point. Others have invited guest speakers to spice up a discussion. Others have mixed in video clips or music. And still others have had their classmates actively involved as participants. Given this kind of expectation, many students will rise to the challenge and introduce fresh and engaging ideas or activities. Most students enjoy thoroughly the process of dreaming up something new and different, and everyone values the resulting variety in the presentations. This kind of assignment also allows Bill to articulate and emphasize his support for the creative process.

Focusing on the Present

Performers must concentrate on "being present." Practice with improvisation and role plays, for example, can help them hone their abilities to overcome distractions, convert scripted lines into believable dialogue and prescribed blocking into natural movements, and respond effectively to both the expected and the unexpected on stage. To do these things, actors need both independent study and rehearsal to go along with their concentration and energy.

It has taken you years of study and experience to develop your expertise. As is the case with performers, it takes considerable energy and concentration on your part to stay "present" in class. You need spontaneity to respond effectively to students and their questions, along with some creativity to guide students' learning in ways that challenge their faulty assumptions and help them uncover new insights. All of this must happen, of course, as you watch the time you have available and monitor student engagement and reactions.

Gerry Delahunty (Linguistics) tends to move quite quickly through course material, but he pauses regularly to watch for student reactions. He provides that additional measure of wait time that can help students process complex material — and that helps him understand any confusions the students might have while they raise appropriate questions. Gerry uses this focus on the present to guide the challenge he makes to students. One student likened Gerry's class to an hour's worth of intellectual push-ups — high praise indeed!

You can also give students a short stretch break, ask a question or take a poll of student responses, assign a short writing assignment, or have the students discuss their responses briefly with their classmates. In spite of the pressure you'll likely still feel to cover content, you may find that a short and energizing diversion produces dividends for long-term, deeper learning.

Exercises

1. Many people, including teachers and performers, benefit greatly from participating in a variety of meditative practices. Whether it's a man-

tra or yoga, Tai Chi or swimming laps, the repetition of a word or an action can help the mind focus and relax. Given the requirements to orchestrate multiple factors when you're managing instruction and facilitating learning, concentration is vital to you as an instructor. So consider experimenting with the following activities:

- Take some time—perhaps fifteen minutes twice a day—to quiet your mind, focus inward, and achieve a state of relaxed alertness.

- Take a few minutes before and after class to stop working and quiet yourself in a similar manner.

- Use your walks to and from class to clear your mind of distractions.

- Use exercise—jogging, swimming, biking, weightlifting—to achieve a quiet mind.

2. Good communication skills require you to be more present "in the moment." So:

- Practice listening more carefully to what students, colleagues, and friends say to you.

- Practice using reflective statements in which you rephrase what someone has just said and, perhaps, note their feelings.

Concentrate on understanding others before launching into your own stories, explanations, and interpretations. For example, after any exchange you can rate yourself and reflect on your skills as a listener based on the following criteria:

Skill	Rating (High/ Medium/Low)	Comments
How well did you keep the focus on the speaker's issue and keep your own opinions on hold?		
How well did you reflect back the speaker's message?		
How well did you reflect back—observe, sense—the speaker's feelings?		

Ask the person who spoke to you to rate you on these same criteria. Compare your responses with the speaker's responses, and analyze the process as a whole. Then share your ideas and feelings with the speaker.

3. Acting teacher Robert Benedetti (1976, 11) offers the following "here and now" exercise as the second step in his training program for performers:

> Put yourself at rest. … While breathing comfortably, say to yourself sentences describing your immediate awareness. For example, 'Right now I am lying on the floor, I am doing exercise number two, I am making up sentences, what will I do first, my right hand is a little cold,' and so on. Do this as long as you can.

The exercise may sound simple, but most beginning performers find that their minds wander quickly away from the "here and now" and into fantasies of the past and future. With practice, the actor learns to stay in the present moment and to "allow the sentences describing the endless present to fade gradually away, leaving only a restful alertness." As Benedetti points out, "Relaxation and concentration are two aspects of one state of mind and body." After you've tried this particular exercise, record your reactions in a journal. How might this activity help your teaching be more focused on the present?

4. Mirroring exercises form a staple of actor training, both for their effectiveness in developing concentration and for the interpersonal sensitivity they engender. In the basic mirror exercise, two performers stand facing each other. One initiates movement while the other "mirrors" the movement as precisely as possible. The movement may be abstract (e.g., slow sweeps of the hands, turns of the head, bends of the knees) or concrete (e.g., a pantomime of brushing one's teeth). The point is not for the initiators to "fool" their partners with unexpected movements but for both to move simultaneously. Thus, the initiator quickly learns that slow, rhythmic movements are easier for the partner to mirror. Periodically, the acting coach calls out, "Change!" Then, without breaking the flow of the movement, the initiator becomes the mirror and vice versa.

As a second step in the exercise, partners mirror in front of a group and try to fool the audience as to which of them is the initiator and which the mirror – a goal that further heightens their concentration. With practice, the partners become so sensitive to each other that the coach can ask them to move together, each at the same time the initiator and the mirror.

(For specific details on this and other mirror exercises, see Viola Spolin's [1983] *Improvisation for the Theatre*, pages 60 to 62, 66, 75 to 76, 175, and 234 to 235.)

In the classroom, the time you devote to improvisations and role plays also allows for other possibilities. For example, you might experiment when your students are struggling with a particular concept or when maintaining their engagement requires a change. Allow yourself the freedom to fail and, consequently, to learn. Understandably, you may well feel some discomfort at this prospect — some confusion along with some success and some uneasiness about straying too far from your plans. But students are, in general, very understanding, especially when your motivation is to support their learning. With a desire to improve, you can acquire a wonderful license to experiment.

Suggested Exercise

Consider enrolling in an adventure course, a ropes course, an Outward Bound experience, or the like for which experimentation and risk taking are the foci. These programs offer wonderful opportunities for personal development — or for team building and bonding when you complete them with a class or a group of your colleagues.

Reflection

Certain questions are helpful when you change direction and try to interject something new in the classroom:

- Was the experiment worth the time?
- What was gained? lost?
- Would more time help? How about less time?
- Are more guidelines needed?

Some personal reflection about teaching is often helpful, but especially so after you've tried something new. Likewise, it's important for performers to reflect and learn from their explorations: What worked? What didn't? What was fun? What was uncomfortable? Why? What's worth repeating? What needs more development? Where are the blocks and the limitations? How will the audience react?

Exercises

1. Research on classroom effectiveness has identified a factor Kounin (1970) first labeled as *with-it*. This is a quality possessed by teachers who are alert to what's happening in class and can make appropriate decisions on the spot — for example, when their students are confused or disengaged, or when there are enough complaints about an exam to warrant reconsideration of the grading. These kinds of situations require skill in spontaneous decision making. Reflect on the improvisations you yourself have had to make in various classes. What worked, what didn't, and why? What options are worth exploring?

2. Keeping a professional journal can do much to help you develop your self-awareness about energy, creativity, and spontaneity. Excerpts might also prove useful when you're compiling a written description of your efforts at improvement for annual review, promotion, or tenure. Here, we note how journaling can fit into Seldin's (1993) description of possible material for inclusion in a *teaching portfolio*. Consider the following questions for guiding your journal writing:

- How was your energy today for teaching? for other activities? Explain.

- How creative were you feeling today for teaching? for other activities? Explain.

- How spontaneous did you feel today for teaching? for other activities? Explain.

An Introduction to Development, Discovery, and Drama

Learning is orderly and predictable. Knowledge builds in a sequential, stair-step manner. Teaching is about effective delivery. Students should be quiet, attentive, and reflective. Instruction should be systematic and carefully sequenced, much like the scientific method. Maybe! Indeed, some of the best teaching and most profound learning experiences can be spontaneous, inspired, and energized by the challenge of questions left unanswered. Ideas and personalities mix, tumble and, at times, collide in a complex, interactive dance, sometimes ballet-like and at other times more like a mosh pit. New work on chaos theory or the nature of the universe, for example—or any books dealing with the history of science, for that matter —remind us all of the tentativeness of human knowledge and the uncertainty associated with the very search for understanding. Recurring debates about human development and intelligence further frame our general lack of knowledge within a context of what we don't even know about ourselves as a species.

In these next two chapters we want to connect the benefits of performance training with two major lines of research on student learning and instruction. We contend that ideas drawn from the performing arts can also enhance the intellectual and emotional development of students as well as their abilities to address problems and discover solutions. We will make two cases in these chapters: one for turmoil, conflict and "drama" as developmental catalysts for intellectual and emotional growth: and the second for discovery as a "dramatic" way to capture what is exciting and revolutionary in every discipline. We will describe ways in which performance ideas can help you challenge students to clarify their values, broaden their thinking, and deepen their understanding—as well as help you use the great discoveries of your disciplines to engage and inspire.

Chapter 6:
The Developmental Case for Drama

A large and growing body of work describes the variety of stages through which students pass on their way toward more independent and sophisticated systems of thought. Along with the benefits which the stage offers for engaging and energizing students, you can also use drama to capitalize on anomalies, incongruencies, tensions, disagreements and differences as catalysts for inspiring lasting change on a more personal level. The drama inherent in debates, for example, can help spark individual growth, challenging students to rethink their assumptions and to develop more sophisticated methods of analysis and problem solving.

Background

As children, we begin our life's journey by thinking in concrete and egocentric ways; as we mature, we gradually develop a greater ability to handle abstractions and logic, to mediate our thinking with symbols (language, mathematics). When we are very young, we learn about the world primarily through our senses, through touch and taste, sight and sound. As adults, we become less dependent on direct experience and better able to learn through reading, discussion, thinking and imagining. Jean Piaget (1952) and Jerome Bruner (1966) have contributed to our understanding of these processes, reminding us of the importance of hands-on learning in which we help students make sense of the world as *they* experience it, what fits with their understanding at a particular point in time, i.e., *experiential* and *constructivist* learning.

On an emotional level a similar developmental process is at play. Dan Goleman's (1994) ideas about *emotional intelligence* make a strong argument for greater attention to the feelings, attitudes, motivations and re-actions which accompany—and he argues largely determine—the impact of our actions in the world. For what is lost from our talents and insights, our intelligence and knowledge, when we struggle to navigate our own emotions, our frustrations and anger, neediness and desires? Gardner (1983, 1999a, 1999b) goes a step further, critiquing our traditional notions of intelligence (e.g., memory, reasoning) and making a case for *multiple intelligences*. Like Goleman, he calls for more attention to the emotional skills and understanding which underlie our self-awareness *(intrapersonal intelligence)* and effectiveness with others *(interpersonal intelligence).*

On a moral level, we can find similar ideas about a developmental progression. Lawrence Kohlberg (1981) offered a model that has proven useful for teachers at all levels for understanding the thinking of their students. When young, for example, we usually think in terms of obedience and duty, fear and punishment, but over time we develop more concern for our relationships with others and more principled reasoning based on ideas about the collective, social good and what we believe is right. As we develop as individuals, Kohlberg insisted, we do learn to think and feel in qualitatively different ways. Carol Gilligan (1982), in turn, has noted the priority which females, in particular, give to relationships.

While the changes that evolve during childhood are profound, the changes that occur during the years when young people typically enroll in higher education may be less obvious but equally dramatic. Although initially captive to narrow and dualistic thinking (yes-no, right-wrong), students move toward a greater ability to understand the differing perspectives of others (i.e., the range of opinions possible on various issues) and, then, by the time they graduate, to handle greater degrees of complexity and ambiguity (Perry, 1999). In all of these journeys, drama as we are defining it can be a powerful catalyst as instructors attempt to challenge the ways in which students think, and provide guidance as students develop new skills and understanding.

Conflicts on Stage

In the theater, actors look for conflict to heighten audience engagement and sharpen the focus on core issues. In the classroom, the drama of discussion and open exchange of ideas often has the feel of conflict. Prepare your students to see the importance of developmental growth of conflict. As Shurtleff (1978, 43) insists,

> Conflict is what creates drama. Plays are not written about our everyday lives or the moments of peace and placidity but about the extraordinary, the unusual, the climaxes. I am always surprised at how actors try to iron out the conflict that may lurk below the surface of a scene, flattening it instead of heightening it. Perhaps we are taught so thoroughly in our everyday lives to avoid trouble that actors don't realize that they must go looking for it. The more conflict that they find, the more interesting the performance of the play.

Drama has its own roots in tragedy, where heroes battle others, the fates or their own limitations. The odds to overcome seem overwhelming. Think of Judy Garland's character in *The Wizard of Oz* or Robert Redford and Dustin Hoffman as investigative journalists in *All the President's Men*, Robin Williams and Jeff Bridges in *The Fisher King*, Jimmy Stewart as George Bailey in *It's a Wonderful Life*, or Vivian Leigh as Scarlett O'Hara in *Gone with the Wind*, Will Smith as Ali or Tom Hanks in *Saving Private Ryan*, Russell Crowe as Nobel laureate John Nash in *A Beautiful Mind*. Every serious film has its protagonist and antagonist, its share of dangers faced, challenges overcome and lessons learned.

Classroom Climate

First and foremost, a climate of *acceptance* and *trust* must be created to enable students to respond to your efforts to increase engagement, to open up and share honestly their ideas and doubts, their efforts to understand the material. If students are to volunteer more in class even when it may be "cool" to be aloof and disengaged, if you want them to take more risks and feel free to disagree and debate, then you must provide *encouragement, rewards* and *psychological safety*.

An underlying developmental journey moves students from a preoccupation with their peer group toward greater independence — intellectually and emotionally. A similar journey takes young people from fear of the unknown and outright prejudice toward understanding, tolerance of differences, and appreciation for the strengths contained in human diversity. For example, noted ethnohistorian Ron Takaki (1993) wants students to develop greater empathy for others by seeing history through the "different mirrors" which reflect the experiences of various immigrant groups in the U.S. Duane Campbell (1996) goes even further by insisting that understanding of diversity and development of communication skills needed to bridge differences, comprises the foundation for citizenship in a democracy and that they can—and should—be taught in the classroom. As an instructor, your understanding of the potential role which drama can play in attending to differences and building bridges becomes important.

For example, peer pressure can be a powerful deterrent to student participation, motivation, learning and personal change. Particular ideas or behaviors may be unpopular, "politically incorrect" to whichever group is in the majority. However, if you attempt to inject more dramatic conflict in class, you can insist that students practice acceptance and understanding. If need be, you can play the devil's advocate, portraying a particular point of view to help surface minority or unpopular views. In this way, you can help students better understand other perspectives, and approach new or different ideas with greater tolerance.

As in the theater, you have a tightrope to walk when certain views tap into deep feelings or destructive prejudices, when, for example, going to war often means demonizing the enemy and can make any concern for them seem unpatriotic. You must be aware of individual sensibilities and public mores whenever you entertain the controversial. However, knowing the place for tension and conflict in promoting the development of critical and creative thinking will help you to decide what approach to use.

Here is another example of a constructive classroom process which regularly surfaces differences of opinion. Bill Timpson has facilitated numerous sessions for faculty who want student input about a course early in the semester while there is still time to make improvements. At the instructor's request, Bill comes into class to ask students for their appreciations, concerns and recommendations. Some real drama often ensues as students make public statements, both positive and negative, about the course, the teacher, the readings, assignments, etc. At times there are disagreements. However, asking students to reflect on their experiences using this kind of a structured process has proven useful for instructors who want an early indication of student reactions. Soliciting feedback also tends to provide a boost in morale; students appreciate being consulted.

You can certainly do something similar for your own classes. You can invite someone in to facilitate feedback and then leave class to encourage an open discussion. However, you can also solicit feedback face to face.

Indeed, Timpson commonly stops his own classes about a third of the way into a semester, often after the first exam, and reserves thirty minutes or so to ask directly for student feedback. What then happens has real drama as students play out new and empowering roles for them, discussing and debating suggestions for course improvements.

Promoting Engagement

We also want to re-emphasize the value of student engagement as a foundation for intellectual and emotional transformation. Armed with new ideas and skills from the performing arts, you can become a more effective catalyst for student development and deeper learning, provoking when students are passive, facilitating discussions and debates, creating role plays, etc.

One strategy is to make effective classroom use of the notion of *group focus.* A staged production will rarely succeed if only a few members of the audience are *hooked.* Being more conscious of your students as a group can help you keep an entire class engaged, for example, by turning questions or comments from a few into forums for others to participate. You can also take a moment here and there to poll the entire class, e.g., "How many of you agree with that?" These kinds of directions can help pull students out of a receiving mode and into one which requires more active construction of a response.

Cross and Steadman (1996) propose a "one minute paper" as a quick way to assess student understanding. Take a few minutes at the end of class to ask students to respond in writing to two questions: What's the most important thing you learned today? What questions do you still have? Reviewing these papers can give you instant feedback regarding which of your points are getting across—and which aren't. Writing the paper can also stimulate student reflection on their own learning and engage them in the class process, especially if, at the beginning of the next class, you respond to common questions that emerged in the papers.

As another way to promote greater student engagement, some instructors ask students to assist them in developing exam questions. In some of her classes, Suzanne Burgoyne uses the review days prior to the exam to have students bring questions they think should be included on the test. In small groups, then, her students discuss and refine their questions. Later each group presents what they believe to be the most significant questions to the whole class. The students' choice of questions provides feedback to Burgoyne regarding what they consider important in the course material, what analytical skills they think they should have developed at this point in the class, etc. Suzanne finds that most students take this process seriously; many of their questions are ones she would have asked, but others stimulate useful insights for her as well as for the class as a whole. Students also recognize that she values their contribution to the learning experience when they see their own questions appear on the actual exam.

In the theater, cast members typically have a great deal of input into decisions both big and small as a production develops through the rehearsal process. However, while shows invariably revolve around provocative or inherently engaging issues, courses must address foundational — and perhaps dry — curricula. Having students participate more in decisions about assessment may increase their motivation to learn.

Diversity

Mixing a focus on drama with a developmental look at students and learning can also allow you to do more with the diversity in your classes. On stage or screen, differences among characters can produce obstacles and tensions, adding believability and spice to the plot as it unfolds. Accepting the place of obstacles and tensions in your own classes can help you reframe problems into potential catalysts for student growth and deeper learning.

For instance, differences of opinion about a topic or solution can be extended into a discussion or full debate. You can probe student thinking using lots of "what if" questions. You can refrain from pronouncements of what's right or wrong and let the uncertainty motivate students to dig deeper and think for themselves. For developmentalists, exploring student errors can be a much more effective entrée into learning problems and their resolution than the more conventional focus on correct answers.

Effective Communication

Your skill with communication becomes very important for capitalizing on the potential for classroom drama. Using *reflective listening, acceptance, and empathy*, you can help students reflect and think more for themselves. When assigning collaborative work on a project or problem set, you can help students improve their communication skills. When they interact with others to test their ideas, they can sharpen their thinking and deepen their understanding. The conflict or drama arises from those interactions when students have to listen and explain within the same conversation, when they attempt to understand and persuade, when they are forced to reassess their own positions.

Accordingly, you can promote this deeper learning by teaching and practicing the fundamentals of good communication. You can start with *reflective listening* where students learn to focus on others, on helping those speaking clarify their intent. Instead of your own quick answer to a question, you can challenge students to think more deeply by repeating back their concern and asking for their ideas. "Wow, that's an interesting question. What do you think? Does anyone else want to comment?"

On stage, actors typically spend a great deal of time and effort studying their characters and why they might think a certain way, what motivates them. When students can extend this same kind of interest to their classmates, they deepen their own understanding of the material and improve the chances of a successful group result. Reflective listening is a necessary skill.

It can be just as important to teach and practice *empathy* and *acceptance*. These qualities are essential when actors strive to make their characters believable; they are equally vital when students work on cooperative projects or in groups. Here you focus attention on understanding the feelings of others and respecting their experiences whether or not there is any basic agreement. You can help students to reflect on how it must feel *to walk in someone else's shoes.* The focus in class then shifts away from a sole pursuit of the right answer toward greater interest in the development of critical and creative thinking skills and deeper learning.

Another mechanism that can promote better communication is the requirement for *consensus.* Whenever you ask students to *try* to get agreement on a particular conclusion, you force them to listen more deeply to each other. Everyone must participate and express a preference. If differences emerge, they will have to spend some time and effort looking for a shift in thinking or negotiating some common ground.

Used together, these four components of effective communications —reflective listening, acceptance, empathy and consensus—can help break down resistances, convert differences into stimulating exchanges, resolve conflicts, negotiate compromises and open students up to new ideas, viewpoints and possibilities. These skills can be useful across the various disciplines, especially with the increasing interest in group work and teams as alternatives to traditional lecturing.

For example, we now know a great deal about the benefits of study groups for students, especially in those large, demanding introductory science courses where a great amount of information must be mastered. Some instructors help students form study groups where these communication skills become important for their academic success. For a first year seminar intended to help students make a successful transition to college, Bill Timpson has required students to apply their understanding of learning, communication and group work by creating a viable study group for themselves. Most students value this opportunity and quickly see the benefits for their learning and their grades. The challenges of a big campus become smaller and more manageable when a group comes together in this way. New friendships often develop. Bill has also encouraged groups which have formed around a presentation for class to meet outside of class to prepare and rehearse.

Admittedly, concentrating on communication skills will take some time, but the payoff can be worth it in the long run as students then function at higher (more skillful) and deeper (more thoughtful) levels, eventually giving you higher quality instructional time. Moving in this direction can also give you opportunities for interjecting new dramatic possibilities into your teaching. For example, students could productively role play any number of situations relevant to the organization and success of your class:

- A group project that breaks down when one member of the group is unmotivated;

- A class discussion that goes nowhere because one person is dominating;

- A situation in which some students are fearful of comments that could be labeled "politically incorrect;"

- A class session in which several students want to contest their exam grades.

Attending to these kinds of issues can help you promote greater understanding as well as resolve conflicts in the class as a whole or among students working in smaller groups. The possibilities are infinite. As mentioned, you can even enlist students in a kind of classroom meeting where you make a collective effort to improve the course before the end of the semester. With good communication skills, you and your students can explore problem areas in an open and constructive manner and, then, proceed to consider new possibilities.

Active Learning

By wedding some feel for the dramatic with a developmental orientation you can also make much more use of active student learning. Within a performance paradigm, for example, you can see your students either as part of an audience or as members of the cast and crew, each playing a vital role. When you see them as audience members, you want them to be engaged intellectually and emotionally. When you see them as members of cast or crew, you want them to take a much more active role in the construction of the performance itself. We agree with the developmentalists who insist that it may be more in the cauldron of activity — thinking, practicing, solving, applying, creating, producing — where students can best make course material meaningful and understandable for themselves. This can happen in any number of ways. You can:

- Design active experimentation into a laboratory assignment;
- Require a group project for class;
- Make time for discussions and debates;
- Stop a lecture and have students discuss an answer in pairs before moving on;
- Arrange for field experiences like internships and practica;
- Organize tutoring or cooperative study experiences.

As with the development of communication skills, the possibilities for active learning are endless.

The classroom drama here means a switch for students from a purely receptive mode to one where they must actively participate and *construct meaning for themselves.* For instance, they may have to overcome their own inhibitions or fears to interact with others or help with a presentation. They may have to confront an external reference (e.g., you, some other expert, the text, a video) and argue for their own interpretation. This kind of "drama" can have a profound impact on learning, transforming instruction and affecting students on a deep and personal level.

For another example, we note that the latest paradigm shift in science and mathematics education, in particular, involves an effort to operationalize inquiry and induction, to reinvent the instructional process with students active in *constructing* their own knowledge. The following list may help you remember the key concepts:

- Engage students;
- Explore new content and processes;
- Explain the underlying concepts or processes;
- Extend or enrich understanding as time permits;
- Evaluate progress made.

When we refer to *constructivism,* we mean knowledge (understanding, concepts) which students connect to their own experiences. As Davis et al (1990), Yager (1991) and others suggest, constructivist teaching and learning involves complex interactions, open conversations, discussions and debates where ideas are confronted, data re-examined and various possibilities considered. Memory strengthens when ideas become more personally meaningful. Problem- and case-based learning begin with close attention to the details. Hypotheses emerge through conversation, reflection, trial and error. Ideas are tested. Conclusions are suggested, evaluated, refined and re-evaluated.

Again, we find the performance tradition steeped in related skills and strategies. Playwrights and directors rarely confront an audience directly with moral conclusions. From a developmental perspective, it's invariably more effective to challenge people with dilemmas and let them rethink their own positions. For *Twilight: Los Angeles 1992,* a powerful and provocative play about the Rodney King beating, trial and the riots which erupted thereafter, playwright and actress Anna Deveare Smith interviewed a wide range of people close to those events—a gang leader, a former police commissioner, a jury member, a realtor from Beverly Hills, a community organizer, the Editor of the LA Times, then Senator Bill Bradley, fifty in all—and created a script. Using the words of these people, she brought each character to life through a series of monologues and conversations, addressing the audience directly as well as the other characters. Weaving a complex tapestry of perspectives, reactions and values, Smith offers no simple solutions for her audiences, only complex and troubling realities.

Set during the years surrounding the break-up of the Soviet Union, Tony Kushner's play, *Slavs,* paints a similarly complex picture of reality, juxtaposing the idealism of the socialists, the "cultural genius of the Slavic people," with the environmental devastation epitomized by the nuclear accident at Chernobyl. As with Smith's work, *Slavs* ends without any easy resolution, but a challenge to the audience—the actors literally turn from the action on stage to look at the audience—in the form of Lenin's famous question, "What is to be done?" Once again, we note the parallels to Perry's (1999) widely cited work on the cognitive development of college-aged students, where thinking moves from a dualistic orientation toward right and wrong in the earliest stage to a greater ability to understand different perspectives and accept complexity.

The Social Context for Learning

Developmentalists also encourage you to use group learning wherever possible. On stage, the interdependencies of cast and crew provide a rich milieu for creative ideas, support and feedback. In class, lively discussions and small group activities can help students see how their own thinking compares with that of others. Indeed, there is a rich and growing body of literature on cooperative learning (e.g., Johnson & Johnson, 1994). In general, the developmentalists want you to organize a stimulating and challenging environment, and then facilitate engaging student interactions. The classroom drama here is relatively straightforward. Instead of concentrating solely on the delivery of content, you look for opportunities to utilize a more social context—small group activities, games, simulations, role plays, cooperative projects, field trips and the like—to prompt engagement and stimulate learning.

A key to this type of teaching is your attention to the *process* of learning—the skills, attitudes and feelings which students need to make the most of these kinds of experiences. At a skill level, it all begins with good communication. For instance, the Campus Writing Program at the University of Missouri-Columbia encourages teachers of "writing intensive" courses to incorporate peer review of rough drafts of papers into the class structure. Written materials help students focus on specific aspects of the paper: thesis sentence, organization, quality of insights, etc. Just prior to the first in-class peer review session, Suzanne Burgoyne and her teaching assistant use a sample paragraph which has been handed out to the class as the basis for a role play of the oral part of the process, in which the peer reviewer gives feedback to the paper's author.

This particular role-play also includes demonstrations of how *not* to give feedback. In the role of peer reviewer, Suzanne may say: "This is a terrific paper. I wish I could write as well." In the subsequent discussion of each role play, she asks the class, "Was that helpful feedback? Why or why not?" "No," students invariably say, "because it wasn't specific. The reviewer didn't give the author any suggestions on how to improve the paper." As peer reviewer, the TA may say, "You're wrong in your analysis of Hamlet's character. He's really hesitating to kill Claudius because he's not sure the ghost was telling the truth." "Was that helpful feedback?" Burgoyne asks. "No," her students reply, "because there are lots of ways to interpret any play. The reviewer needs to help the writer make a clear case for the writer's interpretation and not impose the reviewer's."

As the role-plays proceed, the teacher and TA show how to give specific feedback in a constructive, encouraging way and how the paper's author can clarify these comments through paraphrasing and questioning. Students find this role-modeling more engaging than any lecture on feedback. They also enjoy the role-reversal of seeing their teacher in the role of student author, accepting feedback and discussing strategies for improving her own writing.

Our Challenge to You

The developmental journey which characterizes the college years may be the most profound across the entire life span. Along with reflecting major life transitions toward greater independence, these years and experiences produce dramatic changes in thinking. At any level—local, regional, national and global—a greater ability to work with ambiguity and complexity may mean the difference in whether humans can live in harmony with each other and without destroying the planet. While higher education may become especially important in the years ahead for providing the intellectual leadership for progress, the performing arts can teach us much about the place for drama in engaging hearts and minds, in imagining new possibilities within a respectful, interactive process.

Chapter 7: Discovery and Drama

As an instructor, your command of the knowledge base in your field is as important as your ability to organize your ideas, communicate complex issues, engage your students, field questions, facilitate discussions, mentor protégés, and all the rest. Students at all levels appreciate both the enthusiasm and clarity you can offer. By helping your students with the interconnections among various ideas and facts, you also help them remember better.

But do you ever say much about the stories of discovery—the processes that produced the underlying knowledge base of your discipline? How did the greats in your field think about the problems they faced and what they didn't know? How did they overcome obstacles, confusion, setbacks, and frustration? How were their ideas incubated and developed, refined or discarded? Therein lie stories that can both engage your students and teach them essential lessons, whatever your discipline.

Given the pressure to cover a lot of material, you may feel compelled to concentrate exclusively on the end products: the "facts" and (supposedly) proven theories. You may feel you have precious little time to address any background stories of discovery. Yet, these dramas can help capture and sustain student interest, providing an important counterweight to the flood of information that often comprises lectures and coursework. These stories also can offer insights into critical and creative thinking, previous and present. Besides … just what is the "half-life" of a degree these days, especially in the sciences or engineering? How soon will some of the information you currently offer prove wanting, replaced by new ideas, language, or paradigms? As technology advances, old ideas seem to wither more quickly under the glare of an ever expanding research community equipped with increasingly powerful technology and instantaneous global communication.

In Charles Dickens's (1854, 47) *Hard Times*, the archetypal austere headmaster, Thomas Gradgrind, describes to a visitor the extreme preoccupation with proven facts that was so characteristic of the nineteenth-century British schoolroom:

> Now, what I want is, Facts. Teach these boys and girls nothing but Facts. Facts alone are wanted in life. Plant nothing else, and root out everything else. You can only form the minds of reasoning animals upon Facts: Nothing else will ever be of any service to them. This is the principle on which I bring up my own children, and this is the principle on which I bring up these children. Stick to Facts, sir!

But that was then and this is now. While Gradgrind is admittedly a caricature, too many instructors seem preoccupied with the "facts" of their own disciplines and the knowledge base they want their students to acquire (especially in introductory courses). Many teachers also want a simple and "objective" assessment system, usually in the form of multiple-choice exam questions. We can understand a narrow emphasis on facts within the hierarchical social structure schools used, in part, to *civilize* children from the poor and working classes, and feed the labor needs of England's booming industrial expansion. However, in today's workplace, technology in particular continues to expand its role, replacing routine labor and demanding far more critical and creative thinking from workers. (We return to this example in Chapter 9, "Scenes for Practice, Fun, and Exploration.") If innovation is the key to the future on all fronts — at work, in the home and community, and on a personal level — then we may need new and different educational paradigms. As Bob Dylan, the poet laureate for those of us who grew up in the 1960s, foretold:

> Come writers and critics
> Who prophesize with your pen
> And keep your eyes wide
> The chance won't come again.
> And don't speak too soon
> For the wheel's still in spin
> And there's no tellin' who
> that it's namin'.
> For the loser now

Will be later to win
For the times they are a-changin'.

We believe there's great potential for using drama in higher education—if you want to go beyond a recitation of the facts. Look for those conflicts, tensions, and stories that will engage your students and challenge them to think.

Scholars bring a lot of knowledge, skill, and baggage to their work: their training; the known information that defined their own years as students; their current theoretical assumptions and life experiences; and their hopes dreams, ambitions, and biases — the stuff that makes them professionals and human beings. Differences of opinion are inevitable, predictable, and part of the rich tapestry of thinking that defines human inquiry and progress. When statistics and events can be interpreted in different ways, do you take full advantage of the diversity of opinion that may exist to engage your students in rich debate and discussion? Or do you shy away from disagreements and conflicts as too "messy" or emotionally charged? We know, for example, many students who felt lost and who struggled to pay attention in the aftermath of the September 11, 2001, terrorist attacks in New York, Washington, and Pennsylvania. While some instructors stopped their regular classes and allowed for comments, questions, and discussions, others carried on with no mention whatsoever of the horrific incidents. Business as usual? Just when is it important to stop and address events in the world outside?

And what of the challenge—the "drama" that occurs when you ask your students to discover solutions on their own? One reason for the remarkable endurance of the lecture format is that it will always be simpler for teachers to give their own explanations than to help their students come up with defensible interpretations of their own. But what do you gain as a teacher when you introduce something strange or puzzling? Think of your own reactions when you first read one of the classic Agatha Christie, Alfred Hitchcock, or Sherlock Holmes mysteries. Are you any good at figuring out *Whodunit?* Were you surprised by the ending in the film *The Usual Suspects?* Hollywood is certainly expert at maintaining suspense. Can you? Are the benefits of increased student engagement and prolonged consideration of a problem—along with the possibility of new insights or discoveries—worth your class time?

At core, discovery is part and parcel of every successful production for stage and screen. In general, stories work best when the writer leaves things unsaid, sparking the imaginations, engaging the minds, and touching the hearts of the people in the audience. For their part, actors, dancers, and vocalists must find what is compelling in their own roles and recreate that magic night after night. Actors often search deeply within themselves to find the experiences that can provide meaning for their characters.

Paradigm Shifts

In the sciences in particular, new research constantly challenges "accepted facts." That's the nature of progress. In the humanities and social sciences, new perspectives and theories challenge the way we think. Certain paradigms gain prominence, but new ones inevitably emerge to rival older, established views (Kuhn 1970). What can you do to prepare your students for the changes that are coming? How can we defend what still seems best about current thinking and practices, question fads, and resist change for change's sake while simultaneously opening up to new possibilities?

Some of these shifts in thinking happen in a relatively orderly fashion, but others occur amidst great uproar. For example, controversy about human evolution began explosively with the publication of Darwin's *The Origin of Species*, and it has continued in one way or another through today's debates about the teaching of creationism. *Survival of the fittest* is a concept that continues to crop up in various guises—as social Darwinism to justify the capitalistic notion of a meritocracy, for example. Check out a copy of the classic film, *Inherit the Wind*, with Frederick March and Spencer Tracy if you want to revisit these issues and arguments. You can hear chilling echoes of old debates reverberating and intimidating teachers still today.

Or, consider the ongoing arguments about the appropriate role of the military during times of peace. Can troops from the United Nations really stem violence where long-standing ethnic hatreds run deep? Knowing what to do about brutal conflicts and savagery in the Middle East, the Balkans, or Africa can try anyone's confidence about the promise of peacekeeping. Does a strong national defense promote peace, or is it more likely that weapons and troops will be used because they're available? Or are both of these ideas true? Does the continued development of advanced weaponry affect the ways countries relate to each other? As the reigning superpower at the start of the twenty-first century, does the mantle of "world cop" fall primarily on America's shoulders? In the wake of the September 11, 2001, terrorist attacks, just how far can America go in "rooting out terrorism around the globe"? And who will pay for it? Honesty and openness seem to raise more questions than answers.

Debates rage in every discipline. In agriculture, for instance, advocates of organic approaches battle their more "scientific" counterparts who prefer the control that's possible through chemical fertilizers and pesticides. Into this debate now come archeologists, who also challenge "modern" ways by helping rural communities in the Andes that want to reclaim unproductive lands. Where malnutrition and hunger are currently widespread, ancient methods, canals, and terraces seem to hold promise for producing lush crops once again in an area long barren. Can paradigms shift backward, reclaiming the future by returning to proven practices from the past? This is great material for engaging drama!

Or, consider the literature about business effectiveness in which Peters, Waterman, and Austin (1984, 1985, 1987) report that they've "rediscovered" some very old truths in the midst of their attention to innovation. They remind modern companies of the necessity to stay "close to the knitting" and concentrate on what they do best; to "care for their customers," and to also innovate and push for new discoveries—which, in terms of their management practices, may indeed be very old ideas about the place for quality and common sense!

Meanwhile, technological advances and computers in particular add to the pressure on old paradigms, automating routine work, increasing access to information, and adding ever new and more powerful tools for data analysis. Teachers at all levels are swept up in this shift. From desktop publishing to computer-mediated learning, from access to the Internet to two-way televised instruction at a distance, instructors in higher education have exciting new options for enhancing their own delivery, engaging their students, and promoting deeper learning among those students. By using the performing paradigm to help incorporate the stories of discovery that form the history of every discipline, you can paint a more memorable picture of the advance of knowledge and the exchange of ideas that underlie each of your courses. As your students move into these fields, they can then draw on these lessons, both as content and process, for examples of what it takes to be a leader in a discipline.

A Place for Curiosity

At its core, discovery is fueled by a human interest in the unknown. Curiosity is one of those qualities everyone possesses from birth, undoubtedly linked to human survival. Yet, some of the loudest critics of schooling —Ivan Ilych, Jonathan Holt, Jonathan Kozol, A.S. Neill, and Howard Gardner—have long decried the complicity of education in the loss of curiosity among students. How can individual interest prevail, they have asked, when control is emphasized over curiosity; when correct form is more important than the substance of underlying thought processes; when socialization to group norms seems more important than individual inventiveness; when learning is prescribed by experts and shaped with grades, praise, and other rewards; and when the use of computer-scored, multiple-choice tests too often emphasizes recall of information, or what Paulo Freire (1970) termed the "banking" notion of education? Behavioral research seems very clear about the damage that's done to individual interests when extrinsic rewards dominate instruction.

In class, you may accomplish much more by teaching less. Consider Joel Primack's story about teaching introductory Physics. Over the years, he has found discovery to be an important mechanism for correcting the myths and misconceptions his students bring to class. He's had little success in attacking these myths directly. When he does, his students only attempt to memorize some new "truth" without really changing their beliefs.

Joel has found that discovery—and computer games in particular —allows his students to experience the world anew and see firsthand that certain beliefs just don't hold up. To illustrate this point, he often uses a demonstration in class that involves motion and a dropped object. Before running across the front of the class and releasing an eraser directly above a wastebasket, he will ask: "Will the eraser: a) land in the wastebasket, b) land on the floor past the basket, or c) land at some other point?" Having polled his class ahead of time, Joel can probe their thinking and then try to undo any misconceptions. (Note his use of variety, movement, performance (demonstration), and audience awareness to teach in this manner.)

Approaches to Discovery

Two powerful engines of the discovery process are *induction* (hypothesis formation) and *deduction* (hypothesis testing). These basic approaches provide a distinction that can give you new possibilities for conveying—and exploring—ideas and information with your students. Each approach has a role in capturing and channeling students' curiosity about resolving unknowns. Each approach also has a role in the development of productions for the stage. And furthermore, each approach has a role in the nurturing of critical thinking for the classroom.

Think of how each of these approaches has been reflected in the various races, debates, and controversies among scientists and scholars in every field: Watson and Crick dueling to be the first to describe the nature of DNA; the critical receptions critics have so often given to new works of art, music, or dance; how Stravinsky was panned when *The Rites of Spring* was first performed; the controversy over cold fusion and what may have been premature claims by scientists in Utah; or the current worldwide pursuit of cures for cancer and AIDS.

The Emotions of Discovery

While you can certainly employ stories, puzzles, and problems that will captivate and challenge your students, you also may need to support your students emotionally as they learn to deal with what is perplexing or unknown. If solutions are difficult or the process is long, students can become frustrated. They may need help to stay enthused and on task. They may need the ongoing support of a small group of peers—a team. And they certainly will need to see discovery valued in your assessment system.

You can often use *empathy* to convey your understanding of students' struggles. You can accept their difficulties as part of the learning process and resist your impulse to run to students' rescue too quickly. You can take a few minutes here and there to share your observations and to listen to student concerns. You can provide guidance, support, and encouragement for navigating inquiry-based assignments—as well as regular reminders about the history of ideas and the potential importance of these kinds of exercises. You also can teach your students about paradigm shifts and what role human emotions have played in advancing—or stifling—new breakthroughs.

Emotions are obviously critical to success on the stage—not only for the actors as they work to create believable characters, but also for cast and crew as they find the necessary energy to bring a large and complex production to life. The challenges of theatrical production can bond a group of strangers into a tight community in a very short time. Part of this process certainly reflects the demands of rehearsal, where long hours are spent in focused study, experimentation, and refinement, intensified by feedback from directors, conductors, and choreographers. Another part of the process reflects the unforgiving demands of a staged performance, for which no amount of sincere effort can *guarantee* audience approval. Finally, it goes without saying that emotions are central to an audience's judgment about artistic success. Whether it's laughter or tears, despair or heroism, audiences always want emotional hooks and surprises to keep them engaged.

Induction

Moving from the most rudimentary hunches and bits of data to a full-blown hypothesis that attempts to provide fundamental understanding is at the heart of much research. Unfortunately, instructors in higher education often neglect to share this history with their students. They give students the facts and conclusions, but they don't describe much of the intervening processes—the false starts and blind alleys, the frustrations, the confusions, and the breakthrough insights. As any good playwright will tell you, this can be the stuff of high drama.

Using the inductive process in class means beginning with raw data or descriptive information. You can then guide your students through a process to group this "stuff" and consider useful labels. Once some tentative agreements have been reached, you can then lead a discussion about the potential interrelationships among these categories. Ultimately, you try to generate hypotheses with generalizable concepts. The drama derives from the active involvement of your students in the construction of meaning. Instead of limiting them to the passive intake of information, you ask them instead to help organize data in ways that make sense to them—to *construct* something meaningful and then test their ideas.

For example, scholars have identified a long list of teacher qualities that students see as effective in helping them learn. When Bill Timpson teaches this material, he often uses an inductive approach to draw ideas from students and generate a list based on their *own* experiences. The drama emerges from the uncertainty of the process. Ultimately, Bill guides the group toward unspecified conclusions, which he can then contrast with the published research on teacher effectiveness. Although this process takes time, Bill likes the way it energizes and empowers his students by grounding their understanding in the context of their own personal experiences.

As is the case with discovery, some students may find induction frustrating and confusing. However, once they see—with your blessing—that the process is important to critical thinking, they can rise to the challenge. You can then use empathy, acceptance, and reflective listening to help the students understand and manage their feelings effectively in support of their own deeper learning.

In coming up with their roles, actors often work inductively, studying the details of a character for clues about motivations and values. John Houseman's portrayal of law professor Kingsley in the film *Paper Chase* offers an interesting study because the script has scenes of a law school lecture hall with examples of inductive inquiry. Here, students are asked—no, required with the ever present threat of classroom humiliation should their memories or reasoning fail—to recite the facts of a particular case when called upon to do so. From this starting point, the principles of law are supposedly affirmed, interrelated, debated and discussed, all within an environment that attempts to model high-pressure, high-stakes courtroom exchanges.

Deduction

"It's elementary, Watson!" proclaimed Sherlock Holmes when pressed to explain his reasoning. Once Holmes had pieced together the disparate threads of evidence and clues for himself and solved the knottiest of crimes, he would connect them all in a staggering display of intellect and *deductive* reasoning. Beginning with the underlying motivation, Holmes would string together the critical events and explain all, down to seemingly irrelevant minutia that were, in fact, essential clues for unraveling some mystery.

Every discipline has its Sherlock Holmes type who knows how to play regularly to students in the collective embodiment of a Watson. You too can add a bit of drama to your presentations, carefully unfolding the details of various lines of research—for example, giving your students insight into all of the factors that affect the discovery process: the clues along the way, the blind alleys, the good luck, the tedious work involved, and the influence of other characters in the plot.

Case Studies and Problem-Based Learning

Using case- and problem-based learning can give you many opportunities to mix discovery with drama. Case studies have been popular in business and law schools for years. Several medical schools have adopted problems as a central organizing focus for their curricula and classroom instruction. One major benefit is the closer connection between what happens in class and what is demanded in the field. The drama of the "real world" can help you better engage and energize your students.

Marty Fettman, for example, makes extensive use of case studies to teach Pathology within a veterinary school, allowing him to begin each class with a real problem. In this way, he uses the class session less for information transmission and more to set the stage for inductive inquiry, describing symptoms and case histories. He challenges his students to consider various solutions and their consequences, just as a practicing veterinarian would. Unlike traditional approaches in which students are expected—often to little or no avail—to complete required readings before class and come prepared to participate, Marty's students come to each new case without any specific prior preparation, equipped only with their experiences, their knowledge to date, and their ability to think. Cases then evolve in a rapid-fire manner, with Marty playing the interrogator: "What would you see under the microscope? Give me another example. Give me the pathway. What about ...? What would be the point of ... ? What would happen if ... ? What are the principal muscles at work here? Did everybody follow that?"

Also popular in business and law schools, where problems are complex and multifaceted, the case study approach puts an emphasis on modeling processes that professionals in the field use to address real issues and problems. Students move from positions as novices who lack the necessary background to positions as active participants who are engaged in high-level analysis and problem resolution. They learn what they need along the way. The *process* of problem solving becomes as important as the knowledge itself.

In Fettman's Pathology class, drama becomes important in several ways:

- In framing a case and its importance through an animal with a particular set of symptoms;

- In surfacing a variety of opinions about the pathology involved and how each problem can be assessed;

- In creating whatever discussion or debate ensues;

- In the ultimate resolution after all of the analysis and research is complete.

The drama here can be very real. You can challenge students to think, analyze, and seek out additional information so that they come to class prepared to present or defend their arguments.

Another teaching example using case studies—but from a different discipline —may help clarify some of the connections between discovery and drama. Wally Bacon (Political Science) frames his International Relations class as an extended role play. He divides the class of forty to sixty freshmen and sophomores into small groups of three or four. Each group represents a "country." Within the "countries," each group member takes on the role of specialist in a particular area: economics, internal security, foreign policy, or intelligence. As G.O.D. (Game Overall Director), Wally manufactures a situation and a context, such as an international conference setting. Each student group must then make decisions regarding how its "country" will interact with the other "countries." The goal for each team is to maximize what its "country" gets out of the negotiations.

One of Wally's instructional objectives is to give his students experience in doing library research and handling information. Here again, the performance aspect of the assignment is what helps motivate the students. They must research their "characters" extensively. They need to learn not only about their own countries (since they can't depart radically from a country's policy as it exists), but also about other countries' positions. Wally requires each group to put out a weekly news bulletin, which may be propagandistic. Other "countries" then have to figure out how accurate the "news" is.

Providing a cooperative learning experience is another objective for Wally's course. Each group has to come up with its own system of making decisions. Collaboratively, they use the information they've found through their texts and own research to develop a strategy or policy profile that will maximize their country's achievements. The process also challenges the students to defend positions orally in class—positions they may disagree with from a personal standpoint.

After this process has run its course, the students engage in a thorough written assessment. Again, they apply the theories they've been learning as they critique themselves and the other teams. To a large extent, Wally depends on the students' assessments to determine grades. Wally's overriding objective (or "spine") for the course is to empower his students to think independently. He believes they learn more through applying theory in the role play than they would by studying pure theory in an ordinary lecture/discussion format.

Augusto Boal's (1979) participatory "Theatre of the Oppressed" (TO) offers engaging techniques for exploring issues dealing with the uses and misuses of power. Applying Paulo Freire's (1970) liberatory "Pedagogy of the Oppressed" concept to theatre, Boal devised an interactive strategy called Forum Theatre in which the audience takes on the role of "spect-actors" and intervenes in the stage action in search of a solution to the problem depicted.

Another TO technique, Image Theatre, has "spect-actors" using each other's bodies to "sculpt" tableaux. After selecting an issue they wish to investigate, participants first create their image of the "real" situation (one in which power is misused). Next, they sculpt an "ideal" image: how they would like the situation to be (participants are empowered). Once the group members come to agreement on the "real" and "ideal" images, they make transitional images, exploring the steps that might be needed to transform the "real" into the "ideal" image.

Like Forum Theatre, Image Theatre can be a powerful active learning tool. As teacher/director, Suzanne Burgoyne first realized its potential while directing a production of David Mamet's *Oleanna* (see "Scenes for Practice, Fun, and Exploration" in Chapter 9). This controversial play deals with the relationship between a condescending male professor and an insecure female student, leading to the student accusing the professor of sexual harassment. Although the original script calls for only two performers, Suzanne decided to cast four professors and four students and have them move in and out of role as the play progressed.

Since *Oleanna* deals with the uses and misuses of power, in one rehearsal Suzanne led the cast in an Image Theatre exploration of the theme: "How do teachers oppress students?" The group eventually agreed upon a "real" image of a traditional classroom, with a male professor at the front of the room haranguing rows of browbeaten students. The "ideal" image created by the cast showed teacher and students joyously engaged in a collaborative active learning project. Finally, the group tried to move from the real image to the ideal, each actor in the tableau making only one move each time the director clapped her hands, thus creating a sequence of slow-motion action. What happened? Amazingly, instead of achieving the ideal image, the students ended up oppressing the teacher—the oppressed becoming the oppressors—which is exactly what occurs in *Oleanna*! The Image Theatre exercise enabled the actors to experience the power dynamic embodied in the script.

Suzanne then proposed sculpting the theme of how students oppress teachers. The cast, composed primarily of undergraduates, protested: "What do you mean, students oppress teachers?!" The students couldn't think of any real-life examples. So Suzanne proceeded to sculpt an image in which a harried professor sits at her desk surrounded by demanding students, all wanting something from her right now. When the group sat down to discuss the exercise, they reported finding it eye opening. "I never realized students had power over teachers," one said. Another added: "It never occurred to me that professors have lots of students demanding help from them all the time. I only thought about *me, my* paper, *my* grade!"

The TO exercise enabled this group of students to discover real-life power dynamics they hadn't previously been aware of. Throughout the rest of the rehearsal period, cast members would come in and report, half-facetiously, "I was oppressed by a teacher today," or, "I saw a student oppressing a professor today!" Since this experience, Suzanne has fruitfully explored the theme of "the oppressive classroom" in Image Theatre sessions with students, middle school teachers, and university faculty.

For more information about Image Theatre, Forum Theatre, and other TO techniques, we recommend Boal's (1992) *Games for Actors and Non-Actors*. Better yet, you can consult the "Pedagogy and Theatre of the Oppressed" web site — www.unomaha.edu/~pto — for schedules of conferences and workshops.

Concluding Thoughts

As we stated in the case we made for drama and development, here again we find the performance paradigm enormously helpful for teachers who want to use inductive and other discovery-based approaches. Considerable research support exists for the heightened levels of student motivation you can generate through inquiry. Connecting your own expertise to some of the performer's skills and practices can definitely enhance your ability to energize and engage your students.

Chapter 8:
Performance Enhancing Exercises

Performers routinely undertake classes and exercises to examine new possibilities, expand their ranges, and hone their skills. Whether actors want to explore some new idea, play with improvisation, perfect certain movements, or develop greater vocal range, *exercises* can prove stimulating, useful, and fun. In this chapter, we offer a variety of activities for you to consider. If you want support and a social context, invite a friend or group of colleagues to join in. Many beginning acting exercises serve dual functions: to help individuals explore various aspects of performance, and to build a supportive group dynamic. Such exercises usually involve the participation of the whole group, with everyone exploring simultaneously; no one is put on the spot to "perform" for the others, except perhaps for a brief moment here or there.

Getting Started

Most performance training takes place in a group setting. Acting involves interacting—with others and/or the environment. If you want to improve your performance skills for teaching, think about forming a support group of like-minded instructors who are willing to devote some time —perhaps each week or each month—to exploring the benefits of performance-based exercises. While you can do some acting exercises on your own, many require at least two participants and an audience. A support group can also offer feedback to group members and—very important— encouragement and assistance as you and perhaps some of your colleagues move into new territory.

Acting teachers devote the first few class periods of any new course to developing an atmosphere where students feel safe and supported by both the teacher and their fellow students. All who participate must believe they can take risks. Success on stage requires vulnerability as actors explore new ways of experiencing and behaving, and as they confront their own inhibitions and fears.

If we as instructors say we want to improve our performance skills, we're really saying we want to change our teaching behavior. While change can be scary, it can also be exhilarating, rewarding, and renewing. One of the reasons why many acting teachers subscribe to Viola Spolin's (1985) "game" approach to training is that games can help make learning fun, encourage participants to overcome their inhibitions, and liberate their creative energies.

The "setting" you choose can support or inhibit the climate for change. It will help for you to have the use of a large, open space, preferably carpeted, with a few chairs and a table to use as "scenery" for various improvisations. The space should be free from potential interruptions; it's hard to feel free to enter into an exercise if you never know when someone unexpected might pop in. Some soundproofing helps as well, protecting you not only from distracting outside noises, but also from worries that any noises you may make might disturb others. "Lighting" also can affect the mood of your group. In contrast to the harshness of fluorescent light, natural or soft, mellow lighting can create a mood that's more conducive to learning—a subtlety often missed by those who design classrooms.

In forming a performance-based support group, you should spend time during your first meetings establishing "ground rules" and developing trust. One way to start would be to have the members of the group share their reasons for wanting to participate, their previous experience with performance work, their fears about acting, and their perceptions of their own strengths and weaknesses as instructors.

We've already mentioned how we ourselves use "trust exercises" in our teaching—activities in which students take turns closing their eyes and falling into the arms of group members, or in which one person leads a blindfolded partner around the room—to underscore students' learning and promote group support for risk taking in class. While we offer a wide range of exercises throughout this book, we also encourage you to explore various acting texts for other ideas.

For instance, the first two chapters of Viola Spolin's (1983) *Improvisation for the Theatre* offer a good introduction to the theory of developing creative behavior, as well as a useful guide to ground rules for a workshop. She emphasizes that performance training is, by nature, experiential learning: We learn by doing, and we learn in the process of doing. Value judgments—our own or those of others—about what we should be doing, learning, or achieving can activate our inhibitions and limit the potential impact of any experience. Using exercises and games can help us open up to new possibilities without disabling preconceptions.

With its orientation toward industrial development, technology, and market forces, Western culture tends to reinforce a kind of competitive thinking. And it puts a premium on winning the approval of customers, investors, governmental leaders, etc. Such dependency on the judgments of others, however, can limit our learning as individuals. For example, there is no single "right" way to play Hamlet; every actor brings something unique to the role. The format for an acting exercise, therefore, involves establishing the "rules of the game," experiencing the activity, and sharing our reactions and learning—as participants and/or as observers.

Approaching the exercises as problems to be solved also helps to keep participants' focus on the activity itself and away from any inhibiting need for approval. Discussing whether a group member found a solution to a problem is easier (and thus less inhibiting) than making a value judgment about whether that person is a "good" or "bad" performer. Nor should we expect to find the "perfect" solution to a performance problem the first time—or even the second or third time—we try an exercise. Like other skills, performance skills develop with practice. As we struggle with a challenging exercise, we can expect periods of frustration to be balanced by the joys of "breakthrough"—moments of insight when the previously incomprehensible becomes crystal clear.

Warm-Ups

Throughout this book, we have argued for the value of warm-ups. Indeed, we've collected a number of warm-up exercises and devoted an entire chapter (Chapter 2) to them. In a workshop setting, warm-ups help participants clear their minds of distractions, limber up their bodies and voices, and build trust with other group members. Stretches, arm swings, head and trunk rotations, humming, singing — whatever works to relieve tension, loosen stiff muscles, and focus energies will serve as a good warm-up activity.

Take turns leading warm-ups. If you feel any anxiety about the public nature of this kind of activity, just remind yourself that you and your group members have granted yourselves artistic license to be weird. Learning to take risks in a supportive environment will have benefits when you later take something new into one of your class sessions. It will help you remember that the ultimate beneficiaries of any improvements you make will be your students.

A warm-up routine also can become a kind of ritual marking a transition from everyday life into a secure space and time for your group's work and play. For example, standing in a circle and massaging each other's shoulders can help everyone relax and focus. Look through the various exercises we recommend for ways to get started. Acting texts offer additional sources for these types of exercises. We particularly recommend Spolin's (1983) *Improvisation for the Theatre* and Augusto Boal's (1992) *Games for Actors and Non-actors*. We like to begin with some general exercises, then move to vocal and physical warm-ups.

To awaken your sense of awareness and spontaneity, we also describe a few theatre games in this chapter. We then suggest a few additional exercises that are more specifically aimed at helping you develop performance skills as a teacher. As you explore these exercises, you might also find some that you can adapt into teaching tools for your classes.

Beginning Exercises and Ground Rules

One group member serves as "guide" for each exercise, explaining the "rules of the game," guiding its playing, and leading the discussion afterward. Guides help create a supportive atmosphere for the group. They encourage everyone to explore. They also keep an eye out for flagging energies or interests so that they can, for example, suggest ending one game and moving on to another. Obviously, experience will help. If you're new to the guide's role, just think of yourself as a volunteer leader who explains the rules, observes the process, and provides feedback when the activity is over. There is no formula. Accordingly, we recommend that, as a guide, you periodically solicit feedback about your role and gather recommendations for improvement.

When debriefing or processing the game, guides encourage the group members to share their experiences, no matter what those experiences may be. Remember: There are no "right" or "wrong" answers. Different people will have different experiences. For instance, when playing games that explore sensory awareness and imagination, you should keep in mind that different people favor different sensory/imaginative modes —visual, aural, or kinesthetic. When asked to imagine something, you may report visual images while someone else reports tactile sensations. People also can have different emotional responses to particular exercises. For example, most people enjoy a relaxation exercise in which they're asked to imagine themselves lying on a beach. But people who don't like heat or who associate beaches with some unpleasant personal experience may react negatively.

One important rule here is the "right of egress"—that is, group members must feel free at any time to withdraw from an exercise if they become physically or emotionally uncomfortable. If a group member chooses to withdraw during a game, the guide should unobtrusively check in with that person to make sure everything is all right. After the exercise, perhaps during processing, some explanation may be offered, but it has to be the individual's choice if the group is to sustain its commitment to trust.

Especially during early sessions, group members may report feeling silly or self-conscious. Some may be unable to stay focused on the exercise —for example, to imagine they're walking through Jello (or whatever a particular exercise requires). During the time set aside for "processing," the guide can encourage group members to share their responses, including negative ones, and to acknowledge that any response is valid if it is what a person experienced. Open and honest communication is essential.

Processing an exercise also can include some discussion about possible implications for teaching. The guide can ask the group members to share their insights. Throughout this book, we've made numerous comparisons between performance on stage and in class. Closing each processing session with a discussion of professional applications keeps the group grounded in its reason for doing this work: to improve their teaching and enhance student learning.

Performance-Based Exercises

In what follows, we describe some exercises that can help you raise your awareness of your skills and point you toward areas for improvement. Try a few of them. Remember, though, that they're like calisthenics: They get you to stretch your creative abilities and explore new possibilities. As a collection of activities, they really have little in common otherwise. Their ultimate value is in helping you improve your teaching. These exercises also should be fun and energizing. Remember that your own enthusiasm "speaks volumes."

Woodchuck

Remember the old tongue twister, "How much wood could a woodchuck chuck if a woodchuck could chuck wood?" To play this game, ask the group to stand in a circle. Each member of the group, in turn, will say one word of the tongue twister. The game puts a few "twists" on the old twister, though: You must divide "woodchuck" into two words, "wood" and "chuck." Conversely, "could a" and "if a" each become single words, "coulda" and "ifa" (shh, don't tell the English prof). Thus, the sentence becomes, "How much wood coulda wood chuck chuck ifa wood chuck could chuck wood?" Explain the changes and have the group repeat the new version two or three times.

Part 1. Start the sentence moving around the circle. Each person should "give" his or her word to the person on his or her right, looking directly into the person's eyes. That person must then "give" the next word in the sentence to the person on his or her right, and so on around the circle. The person who "receives" the last word in the sentence starts over with the first word of the sentence, giving that word to the person on his or her right. As the sentence continues to move around the circle, coach the participants to speed it up and "give" the words as quickly as they can.

Part 2. After the group has become skilled at passing the words, explain Part 2. In this variation, group members "give" the word by pointing at any other member in the circle. That person must then quickly "give" the next word, pointing at someone else, and so on. Again, coach the group to keep the sentence moving as quickly as possible.

Variation 1. In one variation of Part 2, "Shootout at the OK Corral," anyone who says the wrong word or fails to keep the sentence moving at the group's quick pace has been "shot" and drops out of the game. The game continues until there's a winner — the last cowpoke left "alive."

Variation 2. In another variation of Part 2, the players add emotions to the words, responding to the emotional tonality given to the word that was passed by the previous player. For instance, one player might shout angrily, "How!" The second player might respond "much" in a hurt tone. The third might say "wood" in a comforting tone — and so on around the circle. Again, insist that the sentence keep moving quickly.

Processing. What did you experience? What particular "problems" does the exercise pose? Did you solve the problems? If so, how? What skills does the exercise develop? Why do actors need these skills? Why do instructors need them? Could this exercise be a good icebreaker for students, helping them build team spirit for a group activity or project? Does a lively class discussion or debate ever move this fast and really require you to be on your toes?

This simple game promotes *concentration* and *group awareness.* Anyone who stops listening for even a moment will be lost. Actors need intense concentration to stay "in the moment" on stage so that they can create a convincing stage reality. Genuine listening and staying "in the moment" can help you as an instructor, too; you'll be able to respond better to even subtle dynamics in class.

During processing, someone often observes that this kind of exercise helps actors "pick up their cues" and keep the pace of a scene moving. Pace is certainly an issue for instruction as well. For example, expressions of boredom by students may reflect their frustration with a slow and deliberate pace that never varies. Your heightened awareness of pace can make you more alert to changes you might need to make and to the value of offering your students some variety.

This exercise can also develop spontaneity. Several of the variations require the players to make choices. As the pace picks up, the players no longer have time to think rationally about their decisions. Instead, they must respond with their first impulses. Variation 2 forces the players to "read" an emotional tonality and to respond intuitively. Certainly there will be times in class when you need to be more spontaneous, when students are stuck or restless, and when you must use your intuition to come up with a different explanation or an alternative activity.

Adverb Game

Designate one person in the group to be "it." "It" goes out of the room and the other members of the group agree upon an adverb (e.g., "resentfully," "slowly," "frantically," "clumsily"). After returning, "it" asks another member of the group to perform a simple action: walk across the room, greet another group member, or stand on a chair, for instance. The individual must perform the action in the manner of the chosen adverb. "Its" goal is to guess what adverb the group has chosen; the group's goal is to communicate to "it" the chosen adverb through the manner in which they perform the actions.

If "it" cannot guess the adverb from the first performer's action, he or she continues to ask other group members to carry out simple actions until the adverb becomes clear. The group also gives clues through their collective behavior. From the time "it" re-enters the room, everyone in the group portrays the adverb in the way they sit, talk, and carry themselves. After "it" successfully guesses the adverb, the group selects a new "it" and a new adverb and repeats the game.

One important rule: No group member can say the adverb or a variant of the adverb while "it" is in the room.

Processing. What did you experience? What particular problems does the exercise pose? Did you solve the problems? If so, how? What skills does the exercise develop? Why do actors need these skills? Why do instructors need these skills? Do students exhibit nonverbal clues that can give you insights into their reactions? What clues do you give about your interest in your material, your students, and your teaching?

The Adverb Game allows group members to experiment with expressive behavior by performing simple tasks. The group setting enhances trust and reduces performance anxiety. This is a "win/win" type of game, with both "it" and the group focused on the same goal: successful communication through nonverbal means. As members become more skilled at the game, they may choose more difficult adverbs to enact.

Foreign language teachers could experiment with the Adverb Game as a tool to add life and energy to vocabulary building. The game can easily be adapted so that "it" gives instructions in the target language and tries to identify an adverb chosen from that language. Any teacher who uses group learning for projects or presentations might find value in this game. It will help students sharpen their awareness of the emotional components underlying team effectiveness.

Rhythmic Sound and Movement

Because most instructors are so dependent on language, exercises that involve movements, gestures, and other kinds of sounds can be challenging. But such activities can help you develop new awareness about the factors that influence communication, teaching, and learning.

Part 1. Form a circle, with one person in the middle. The one in the middle (leader) performs a rhythmic movement accompanied by a sound (no words allowed). The stranger the pattern and the more it involves voice and body, the better. The leader repeats the pattern, and everyone in the circle imitates the pattern of sound and movement as exactly as possible. The leader then changes places with one of the players in the circle, who moves into the center and becomes the new leader. The exercise continues until everyone has had the opportunity to lead.

Part 2. Play this variation the same way as Part 1, except that the leader must perform a rhythmic sound and movement that expresses how he or she is feeling that day.

Part 3. You can also have the group string the various sounds and movements together, repeating each person's contribution as it's introduced and then periodically reviewing each one beginning with the first. Once everyone has introduced something, you can then "pass the action around" by having the participants repeat what someone else has offered. Whoever made the original sound and movement must then repeat someone else's to keep the action moving.

Processing. What did you experience? What particular problems does the exercise pose? Did you solve the problems? If so, how? Was your experience in Part 2 or 3 different from your experience in Part 1? If so, how? What skills does the exercise develop? Why do actors need these skills? Why do instructors need these skills? Could this kind of activity help students develop empathy and sensitivity toward others?

Augusto Boal uses a version of Part 1 in his workshops and stresses the significance of imitating the leader's patterns as exactly as possible. For instance, if a woman leads, the men in the circle must try not to produce a "masculine" version of the pattern. Boal points out that this exercise provides a step toward change, allowing participants to explore their own potentials by trying out very different responses.

What is happening here? What mechanism is at play? In the act of trying to reproduce someone else's way of moving or singing, we begin to undo our own *mechanizations* and raise our consciousness about possible change. When we're responding to the lead of others, we're trying on their ideas. We're stretching, exploring, experimenting, and, ultimately, rethinking our own ways of behaving. We don't do a caricature, because that would lead us to do different things but in our own way. Instead, we try to understand and make an exact copy of the exterior of the person in the middle, in order to gain a better understanding of his or her interior.

Part 2 serves an additional function as well: It requires the leader to focus on his or her immediate feelings and to express those feelings physically and vocally. In processing, players often comment on the cathartic value of the experience. If the day has been upsetting or frustrating, venting those feelings can help a player let go of them and focus on the present. For this reason, your group might want to incorporate this exercise into its warm-up ritual. As a warm-up, it also provides a quick means of "checking in" on everybody's mood at the beginning of the session.

Space Walk

Part 1. The guide asks the group to begin walking through the space in the room, explaining that he or she will give instructions as the exercise proceeds and emphasizing that this is a personal exploration, not an interactive game. The guide first asks the group members to explore the space they're moving through as if it were a new substance: How does it feel to walk through this space? Then the guide explains that he or she will call out different substances—warm water, gritty mud, cobwebs, cotton candy, orange Jello, champagne ... anything weird or wonderful—and ask the group members to imagine that they're moving through each. The guide tells the players, "Imagine that all of the space in the room has transformed into the new substance—but all of you can still breathe!" Finally, the guide instructs the players to return to reality and explore the space in the room as it is, and to think about how moving through the real space contrasts with moving through the other substances.

Processing. What did you experience? What particular problems does the exercise pose? Did you solve the problems? If so, how? Were some substances easier to imagine than others? Why? What skills does the exercise develop? Why do actors need these skills? Why do instructors need these skills? In other chapters, we've noted the disjunction that may occur between your message and your gestures—your nonverbal expressions and your movements in class. We discussed, for example, how being rigidly rooted to the lectern can undermine your enthusiasm and your students' engagement. Can this exercise help you build your self-awareness?

Part 1 of the exercise deals with sensory awareness and imagination. Players often report difficulty with imagining themselves moving through unusual substances. After all, when do we ever walk through Jello? As we describe in Chapter 5, however, imaginative abilities are like other skills in that you can develop them with practice. To counteract the deadening effects of routine in your teaching—large classes, set curricula, the need to cover the basics, inflexible schedules, lousy room assignments, the scarcity of rewards—you could develop more creative approaches that will energize both you and your students. In her book on improvisation, Viola Spolin (1983) devotes considerable time to describing imagination and sensory awareness exercises.

Part 2. This activity may be more challenging for new guides, but the benefits for the players can make it worthwhile. Divide the group in half. One half will perform the exercise while the other half observes. The guide again asks the players to walk through the space in the room, and he or she calls out additional instructions as the activity unfolds. But as the action unfolds, the guide and the other observers examine the players closely, noting the parts of the body where individuals seem to carry most of their tension. During the ensuing exercise, the guide can try to emphasize those parts of the body.

First, the guide coaches the players to allow the space to support them: "Let this space support your head, your shoulders, your forehead, your knees." The guide continues to remind the players that space supports them as they move. The guide then announces that space *no longer* supports the players; they must do something or they will fly into a million, billion pieces: "Grab your shoulders! Hold onto your eyeballs, your chin, your neck, your fingers!" Then the guide returns the activity to the way it began and tells the players that space is supporting them again. The guide continues to alternate between space support and lack of support until the participants clearly experience the difference between the two. You can then repeat the exercise, with the observers becoming the players and the first group of players becoming the new observers.

Processing. Ask the players what they experienced when space supported them. What was the difference when they had to support themselves? As always, discuss how the exercise applies to performance work for the actor and to teaching for the instructor. For example, how does your teaching space support you — physically, intellectually, emotionally? How does it limit you? Have you given yourself permission to explore what could be possible, or do you let your preconceptions narrow your options? Does the design of the lecture hall inhibit you from walking up and down the aisles to facilitate discussions? Can you reframe the traditional classroom "hierarchical barrier" (i.e., instructor at the front and students in their seats) to incorporate more student presentations? What other alternatives are possible? Can you go outside? Are field trips possible?

Spolin (1983, 82) observes that this exercise can help participants become aware of which parts of their own bodies they habitually hold rigid. She notes: "One student who customarily had a tight expression on his face that gave him what might be called a 'mean' look first became aware of his rigidity through this exercise." Acting requires performers to study themselves so that they become aware of their personal habits. In order to transform themselves into characters other than themselves, actors must identify their own habits and patterns so that they can change them as needed. Likewise, instructors who want to improve their performance in class and enhance student learning need to confront their own personal patterns and make choices about which to keep and which to change.

Part 3. The guide again divides the group into players and observers, and asks the players to walk through the space in the room. This time, though, when the guide calls out different parts of the body, the players must imagine that part as the "center" that initiates movement. Players may find it helpful to think about a string attached to that part of the body, pulling them through the space. The guide may call out, "Nose, left shoulder, right knee, chin, pelvis, right ear, left big toe, belly button," and so on, each time giving players sufficient time to experience the new "center." The guide then tells the players to move "normally" through space. As they do so, the guide coaches them to try to identify what their own habitual center of movement is. The exercise is then repeated, with the players becoming the observers and the observers becoming the players.

Processing. Ask the players how they experienced the different centers. Ask the observers what the players looked like when they were moving — for example, when they were being pulled by the nose. Were the players able to identify their own habitual centers? If not, you could assign everyone a partner and ask the partners to observe each other's movements and help identify their respective centers. Next, consider the implications for teaching: are there times when you could change your own posture or movements to emphasize a point or show empathy—for example, when students are anxious about an upcoming exam, forgetful about assignments, or struggling with a problem?

One "outside-in" approach to developing a character involves selecting an appropriate center for the character and developing a posture and movement pattern based on that center. An obvious choice of center for a gossipy, inquisitive character, for example, might be the nose! In *The Actor at Work*, Robert Benedetti (1976, 79) argues that there are "five primary character centers that, by bodily logic and by cultural tradition, are each associated with a different sort of person." He encourages acting students to study these character types so that they can make good choices about where to place their characters' centers.

To make choices about character centers, however, actors must work to develop a "neutral" postural alignment and to strengthen their sense of how energy and movement flow from their own personal center. This "centering" work enhances the actor's "stage presence." Stage presence, or "charisma," can also be a useful attribute for you as an instructor.

Energy Center

The guide coaches the players through all parts of the exercise, allowing sufficient time to explore each activity before explaining the next. (**Note:** There should be no verbal interaction during this exercise.)

Part 1. Finding Center. Begin with the "Hanging Yourself Up" exercise we described in Chapter 2. Then explore your center in the following stages:

- Move either foot out to the side about two feet; rock from foot to foot, feeling your center of gravity moving from side to side. Gradually come to rest on center, just like a pendulum comes to a stop.

- Move either foot forward about two feet; find your center with front-to-back motions the same way.

- Move your center around rotationally, exploring the limits of various stances. Feel the weight of your body flowing into the ground out of your center and through your legs. Feel "rooted," as if your weight were a root reaching into the ground beneath you.

- Bring your feet together and explore the center.

- Imagine a cord entering the top of your head and attached to your center. "Lift" yourself upward in small jumps by "tugging" on this "cord."

- Jump to a specific place by lifting the center and then putting it down at your destination. You land perfectly centered, stable and without jiggling, but lightly. At no time in your jump do you lose your center.

- Walk to a specific place by lifting the center up through the top of your head, holding it up while you walk, and setting it down at your destination.

Part 2. The Energy Center. The guide gives the following instructions.

- Hang yourself up once again. Stand with your legs comfortably apart, knees slightly flexed (not locked). Find your center.

- Focus on your breathing. Breathe deeply, comfortably, and naturally. Imagine an energy center in the middle of your body. You may visualize this center however you wish. You might imagine it as a little glowing sun. Imagine that with each breath you take, you bring energy in from the outside world and store it in your center, which then glows more brightly. Continue to breathe deeply, storing energy in your center and enjoying the glowing warmth in the center of your body.

- As you continue to breathe, imagine that energy is flowing from your center down through your legs, through your ankles and feet, and making contact with the earth. Don't worry if you don't "really" feel the energy flowing in this exercise. Imagine you do; imagine what it would be like to feel the flow of energy. Feel and enjoy the flow of energy from your center, down through your legs and your feet, grounding you.

- Now imagine energy flowing from your center up through your chest, into your shoulders, down through your arms, into your hands, out the palms of your hands and your fingertips, and finally making contact with the air. Enjoy the feeling of energy flowing through your upper body and arms. You may even feel a slight tingle in your fingers as the energy flows through them.

- Again, imagine energy flowing from your center up through your chest. This time, the energy continues up your neck, into your head, flowing out your eyes and the top of your head, and eventually making contact with the air.

- As you continue to breathe, deeply and easily, you store more energy in your center, which glows brighter and brighter. And this energy continues to flow—down your legs, through your feet, and into the earth ... up through your chest, down your arms, out your hands and fingertips ... up through your chest, through your neck, into your head, out your eyes, and out the top of your head.

Part 3. Attract/Reject. The guide then asks the players to begin moving throughout the room, remaining aware of the energy flowing from their centers and throughout their bodies as they do so. After allowing the players to experience movement with energy flow, the guide calls out, in turn, three different uses for the energy: attract, reject, and neutral. The guide explains that when they hear "attract," the players should use their energy to "attract" or "pull" the other players toward them. (**Note:** Players may feel more comfortable if the guide instructs them that the "attractive" use of energy need not be sexual in nature.)

When the guide calls out "reject," the players must use their energy to "reject" the other players or "push" them away. When the guide calls "neutral," the players remain aware of the energy flow and of the other players, but they neither attract nor reject with their energy. In all three cases, the players should continue to move through the room and to make eye contact with their fellow players as they move past them.

Processing. What did you experience? What particular problems does the exercise pose? Did you solve the problems? If so, how? Did you feel most comfortable using energy to attract, to reject, or in neutral? What skills does the exercise develop? Why do actors need these skills? Why do instructors need these skills? When might your movements add some fun energy to a discussion of the attractions and rejections that occur in nature, with magnets, with sub-atomic particles, with chemicals, with personalities, or with ideas?

Some people seem most comfortable using energy to attract — i.e., to mobilize their resources and lead, or to socialize with others and work in teams. Others can be abrasive, perhaps focusing more on goals and outcomes at all costs, and thus pushing people away with their energy. Certainly there are situations when using "rejective" energy is indeed appropriate, or when you may wish to "hide" with neutral energy, not wanting to draw attention to yourself. You yourself may use energy in these ways without consciously knowing it.

Encourage the group members to pay attention to their use of energy during the following week, especially in class, and to note moments when they become aware of using energy to attract or reject. As your own awareness of energy develops, you may begin to notice more about your students and their energy — for example, how small-group activities can be affected by the push and pull of individual energies. Indeed, this exercise may prove valuable for students themselves to experience if you assign group work.

Since energy flow and stage presence can be heightened through centering and conscious awareness of energy use, group members can incorporate parts of this exercise into their personal pre-class warm-up routines. The participants might also benefit from repeating the exercise at future sessions in order to practice "attracting" and "rejecting" each other.

More Advanced Work

When you feel comfortable with these introductory exercises, you may want to explore others that are more challenging. As you consider these advanced activities, however, monitor your own level of comfort. What, if any, inhibitions do you feel? The more you become aware of these blocks, the more you'll be free to grow in new directions. Above all, have fun. Create. Explore possibilities by yourself and with others. The benefits for your teaching will evolve naturally as your awareness of self and others grows.

Inner Monologue

Actors who work "inside-out" employ a technique called *inner monologue*. In order to experience the power of inner monologue for yourself, try the following exercise with your group:

A sidewalk serves as the setting for the improvisation. Choose two people to play the scene. Starting from opposite sides of the room, each character will walk down an imaginary sidewalk, greet the other character, then continue on his or her way. Each character has one line of dialogue: Character A will speak first and say, "Hello. How are you?" Character B will reply, "I'm fine. How are you?" The performers must say only the lines assigned to them, nothing else.

In order to prepare for this exercise, write on slips of paper a line or two of "inner monologue"—in other words, what one of the characters might be thinking while greeting the other. Examples:

- "I'll never forgive you for what you did to me!"
- "What's happened to you? You look awful!"
- "What have I done to offend you?"
- "No time to talk! I'm late for an important meeting."
- "The last time I saw you, I made a real fool of myself at that party. I hope you don't remember!"
- "I can't believe it! I just won the lottery!"

Put the slips of paper in an envelope and ask each player to draw one before enacting the scene. Instruct each player to think the inner monologue written on the paper while greeting the other character. Ask the rest of the group to observe the scene closely to see if they can identify what each character is thinking.

In the discussion following the scene, ask the observers what the characters might have been thinking and what the actor did to gave that impression. Then have the actors tell the group what thoughts they found on their slips of paper. Thank them for their "performance" and lead a round of applause. Repeat the scene with two more players, who draw new slips of paper out of the envelope. Follow this "performance" with an analysis, as above, and repeat the exercise until everyone has had a chance to "perform."

Processing. What did you experience? As an observer, could you tell what the performers were thinking? If so, how? What skills does the exercise develop? Why do actors need these skills? Why do instructors need these skills? When does your "inner monologue" color your words in class? When does your preoccupation with other work show through? your tiredness? your boredom with the material? your frustration with unprepared, unresponsive, or rude students?

When analyzing the characters' thoughts, observers typically find clues in the players' nonverbal behaviors: movement patterns, gestures, facial expressions, or tones of voice. For instance, someone might conclude that a character was thinking aggressive thoughts because "Paul stood right in Sheila's path and glared at her. His voice seemed low and threatening."

Even when watching non-trained performers, the observers make interpretations that often correspond very closely with the assigned inner monologue. Why? For one thing, as part of our socialization process we humans have learned to "read" nonverbal cues. For another, just thinking certain thoughts can spontaneously influence your nonverbal behavior; you don't consciously have to design a particular behavior pattern. Note that all of the pairs of characters who perform the exercise speak the same words—yet the performed scenes will look very different in terms of the emotional content and the relationships between the characters. Actors know very well that they cannot rely on words alone—the written dialogue of a play—to communicate the emotional dynamics of a scene.

"Inside-out" actors work to discover the "inner monologue" for their characters at every moment during the play. When performing, they actually think the character's thoughts, knowing their voices and bodies will then communicate those thoughts to the audience. Have you ever noticed the panic on the face of an actor who's forgotten his or her lines? The actor doesn't intend to portray terror, but the thought of his or her character has been interrupted by his or her personal inner monologue: "Oh, no! What's my line?"

Students constantly read your nonverbal cues. Reminding yourself of that fact may help you make conscious choices about your inner monologue. You may not be able to see yourself, but you can become more aware of what you're thinking and, thus, what nonverbal messages you may be sending. While lecturing, you may be thinking, "This is a really exciting insight!" or, "I really need to hurry to get through all of this material!" When a student asks a question, if your inner monologue says, "Hey, I covered that last week," then no matter what polite words you may use to respond, the student may pick up on your impatience.

Communication is a two-way street, of course. As we've pointed out elsewhere in this book, actors on stage learn how to "play" an audience, making subtle changes in their performances to adjust to audience feedback. If you can remember to keep checking the nonverbal responses of your students, you can pick up cues when they're interested, confused, or just plain bored. Do you ever notice the glazed look in the eyes of a whole class at the end of a long and complicated explanation?

Objectives

We teachers often talk about *instructional objectives*—what we want learners to be able to do in measurable terms. Selecting objectives and telling students what they are can help you keep your expectations clear and focused. In the theatre, action on stage is intensified when actors have competing objectives—when they want different things. The actors' use of objectives is, thus, somewhat different, but nonetheless useful for you to explore.

For example, performers trained in the Stanislavski system identify their characters' objectives for the play as a whole, for each individual scene, and for each part of a scene during which the objective remains unchanged. Actors will state their objectives as infinitive verb phrases. Why verbs? Because verbs are action words and thus easier to portray.

With your support group, try the following exercise in working with objectives:

> **Setting:** A university professor's office. You need a desk or table and two chairs.
>
> **Characters:** The instructor and one of his or her students.
>
> **Situation:** The student has missed an important exam for the teacher's class.

General Objectives: The student just overslept, but he or she wants to persuade the professor to give him or her a makeup exam. Working with large classes and dealing with frequent appeals from students for exceptions to this and that, this instructor has developed a series of course policies that work well. Not believing the student has a valid reason and of the opinion that the student needs to suffer the consequences, the professor wants to refuse to give a makeup test. Be aware that we're setting up a "win-lose" situation in this first scene. If you find this approach uncomfortable, rest assured that we will give you a chance to work with a "win-win" solution in Part 3.

Part 1. Ask for two volunteers, one to play the student and one to play the professor. The student will enter the instructor's office, and both participants will then improvise the scene. Each participant concentrates on trying to achieve his or her objective. The student will "win" if the teacher agrees to give a makeup exam. The professor will "win" if the student gives up and leaves the office. If the scene goes on for more than three minutes and neither person has "won," stop it and proceed to Part 2.

Part 2. At some point prior to the exercise, write on slips of paper infinitive verbs describing specific tactics that either the student or the professor might use in order to achieve his or her general objective. Put the student tactics in an envelope marked "student" and the teacher tactics in an envelope marked "teacher." Some student tactics might be: "to impress," "to flatter," "to threaten," "to blame," "to beg," "to bargain," or "to charm." Some instructor tactics might be: "to ignore," "to pass the buck," "to justify," "to ridicule," "to psychoanalyze," "to sympathize," or "to apologize."

Repeat the improvisation, using the same actors, the same situation, and the same general objectives. This time, however, ask each actor to draw a tactic out of the appropriate envelope and to concentrate on playing that tactic, using it to accomplish his or her objective. Ask the group members to observe the "improv" closely to see if they can identify which tactics the players are using. Again, if the improv goes on for more than three minutes without either player "winning," stop it, give the players a round of applause, and move to Part 3.

Part 3. Have these same actors try to find a solution that is mutually agreeable—one that accommodates the needs of both parties as well as the course or institutional requirements.

Processing. Ask the observers what tactics each character used. How could they tell? Which scene was most interesting to watch: the first, the second, or the third? Which was the best solution? Ask the actors which scene they found easier to play and why.

In most cases, the audience finds the second of the first two scenes livelier and more interesting. The players, too, usually discover the second version easier to play. The third scene may prove easiest of all, although it is clearly lacking in "dramatic content." Focusing on a specific, clearly stated tactic energizes the actor—he or she has something definite to do. Actors quickly realize that finding something to do on stage also relieves performance anxiety and self-consciousness.

When you as an instructor have clear objectives in mind for a class, you tend to provide appropriate energy, organization, and focus. Watching your own use of time in class may give you clues about your real objectives. For example, if you have a "soft" start to class, you may value a more informal and relaxed climate that promotes easy and open interactions with your students. If you have a more "driven" start, you may have a lot to cover and little time left for unplanned interruptions (including questions, comments, or spontaneous debates).

Repeat Part 2 of the exercise, having each set of players draw new objectives (infinitive verbs) from the envelopes, until everyone has had the opportunity to try the improvisation. Each time, applaud the players and ask the group what objectives the characters played.

Drawing from Boal's work with "Forum Theatre," you could experiment with yet another approach to this scene: Starting with the student as "protagonist" facing a seemingly impossible "antagonist," other members of the group can say "stop" at any point in the scene when they believe they have a new idea. That person then replaces the protagonist and replays the scene. After each scene, you then hold a brief discussion with the group and attempt to analyze what new element was added, what new possibility was suggested. The scene is replayed again and proceeds until someone else has something new to offer. Along the way, you want to keep asking: "Is this scene real?" Throughout the process, Boal insists on excluding "magical" solutions. The scene must stay grounded in a difficult and real context. In the end, everyone has contributed to rethinking and replaying that can provide new possibilities.

Additional processing. Discuss the exercise as a whole. Did the players solve the problem in the first two parts? Was there a point in any of the scenes when one character spontaneously changed tactics? If so, why did this occur? How did the "win-win" scene differ from the "win-lose" scenes? from Boal's approach? Which scene was more real? more desirable?

Actors choose verbs for objectives that: 1) specify precisely the tactic their character employs to get what he or she wants from someone else, and 2) engage the actor's body and imagination. Effective objectives, in other words, stimulate the actor to action. Like the actor, you can also study your "scripts" — your lesson plans — to identify the specific tactics that may be most helpful in achieving your instructional goals for a class session. Like the actor, you may wish to note in your lecture "script" a particular tactic-verb (objective) to "play" for each section of class (actors call these divisions *motivational units*).

In general, tactics that are stimulating for you work best. Actors soon learn that verbs like "to tell," "to inform," "to explain," and "to ask" don't make good objectives—frankly, they prove boring on stage. More charged language, however, can provoke specific actions or emotional involvement by the actor. Verbs such as "to challenge," "to inspire," "to encourage," "to probe," or "to justify" help create more energetic performances. There is certainly a time and a place for charged and uncharged language in and out of class. Being aware of these dynamics can provide some new breadth to your teaching repertoire—some energizing new choices. For example, in Chapters 6 and 7 we described approaches that require a very different role from the instructor who is used to lecturing—very different goals and objectives indeed.

Of course, a tactic you've planned may not work. In any interaction, both parties have tactics they're using to accomplish their objectives. As was the case in the improvised teacher/student conflict, when one tactic meets another that is incompatible, one or both parties must adjust. It's difficult to continue "to charm" if the other person's tactic is "to humiliate." As we've suggested elsewhere in this book, when you're alert to it, you can "read" student feedback — whether verbal or nonverbal — and switch tactics when necessary.

Gibberish

Viola Spolin uses gibberish exercises extensively in her improvisational training program for actors. Speaking in gibberish requires the performer to substitute "shaped sounds for recognizable words." The performer talks in nonsense syllables and, in effect, creates a new language. "Open the door" may become, for instance, "Oo gla gla!" or, "Shripti seeps!"—depending on who gives the command. As Spolin (1983, 120) explains:

> Gibberish is a vocal utterance accompanying an action, not the translation of an English phrase. The meaning of a sound in gibberish should not be understood unless the actor conveys it by his action, expressions, or tone of voice.

Working with gibberish enhances the actor's facility with nonverbal expression. Spolin (1983, 120) points out that "gibberish develops the expressive physical language vital to stage life, by removing the dependency on words alone to express meaning."

As an instructor seeking to develop expressive qualities, you too may benefit from gibberish exercises. It is, in essence, a consciousness-raising activity. Most teachers dominate the talk time available in class. If you lecture, you may see that as your responsibility. However, you have to ask yourself a key question: How much "space" could be opened in class—for reflection, interaction, discussion, and a deeper kind of learning—if you were to make more use of nonverbal communications?

Try the following series of gibberish improvs with your support group. (A word of encouragement may be necessary here. As an instructor, you're undoubtedly quite comfortable speaking in front of groups. Indeed, you may well enjoy the spotlight and the challenge. Undertaking an exercise that takes away your language, your traditional source of communication, can be unsettling. Trust us: Getting past these natural anxieties and creating a new language can raise your awareness about a range of nonverbal factors that affect communication. Besides, it can be great fun. And if you can do these exercises, you can do anything! Go for it!)

Part 1. Start by practicing simple commands in gibberish. Take turns asking someone to stand up, sit down, open a window, sing a scale, etc.—in gibberish. Accompany each command with a gesture. Continue communicating until the person understands the command and performs the desired action.

Part 2. Select two players at random and ask them to go "on stage," without prior planning. Each player in turn tells the other in gibberish about something that has happened to him or her while the rest of the group observes.

Processing. After the exercise, ask the first player what the second player said. Ask the second player what the first player said. Ask the audience what was communicated to them by each of the players. Did the players solve the problem of communicating with gibberish?

Part 3. Ask each player, in turn, to go "on stage" and sell or demonstrate something to the audience in gibberish. The player is to "pitch" a product to the audience, making direct eye contact with them.

Processing. Again, ask the audience to describe what the performer communicated to them. Did the performer make genuine contact with the audience? Did the performer solve the problem?

Part 4. Select two teams of two players each. One member of each team plays the "ambassador" and one the "translator." Both members of a single team speak the same gibberish language; give them a few minutes to work together to develop their shared "language." (**Note:** They should not attempt to come up with "definitions" for particular sounds; rather, they should simply create a particular kind of sound "language." For instance, one language might be very sibilant or hissing, another very guttural from back in the throat.)

Then give the teams a particular conflict situation to improvise. For instance, the two ambassadors might be meeting to try to negotiate a peace treaty, solve a border dispute, or reach a trade agreement. Each ambassador will speak to a translator only in the agreed-upon gibberish language (the ambassadors, supposedly, do not understand English). The translators will speak to each other in English. Each translator must translate the other ambassador's demands (as expressed by that ambassador's translator) into gibberish and then translate into English—as accurately as possible—whatever his or her ambassador replies. After the ambassadors reach an agreement (or declare war!), discuss the exercise.

Processing. Ask each ambassador about the accuracy of the translations. Ask each translator how fully his or her ambassador communicated. Ask the audience members what each player communicated to them. Did the players solve the problem?

When performers first start working with gibberish, they tend to communicate with elaborate, detailed pantomimes, trying to substitute illustrative gestures for the words they normally rely on. As actors become more "fluent" in gibberish, however, their responses become more organic —and more subtle.

Gibberish work intensifies the actor's focus on communication and awareness of nuances. The performer must really concentrate on listening, observing, and opening himself or herself to others in order to communicate successfully with gibberish.

Because this exercise requires intense and direct connection with other people, the person who habitually relies solely on words to communicate often resists. Relying too much on words to communicate, however, can get in the way of genuine communication. Spolin (1983, 121) quotes one student who found gibberish difficult and anxiety producing: "You are on your own when you speak gibberish!" the student complained. "[W]hen you use words, people know the words you are saying. So you don't have to do anything yourself."

Do we instructors rely too much on our words to do all the work?

Part 5. After all of you have become comfortable with gibberish, ask each participant to present a section of an actual lecture—in gibberish. As usual, ask the audience members what each player is communicating to them. Then have each player repeat the same section of the lecture in English.

Processing. Again, ask the audience members what they understood from the gibberish lecture. What was different when the speaker used English? Which approach was more interesting? more energetic? In which version did the lecturer concentrate more on communicating with the audience members? Did any of the gestures, intonations, etc. "carry over" from the gibberish version to the English version?

Role Wheel

In Chapter 4, we introduced the *role wheel* as a "hook" to stimulate class discussion. We suggest that you and your group experiment with role wheels. If you need to, review our description of the concept in Chapter 4.

Working in pairs, each person plays one role for two to three minutes and then switches roles. For the next situation, move along the "wheel" and pick another partner.

Situation 1. *Character A: Student.* You've received your most recent semester grades, and your grade point average (GPA) has fallen below that needed to maintain your scholarship. Losing the scholarship will cause financial hardship for you. So you ask the instructor of a class in which you received a C if there's any way you can boost your grade.

Character B: Teacher. The administration has complained about grade inflation and about the large number of grade changes professors have been making in recent years. (**Note:** The person playing the teacher should establish the nature of the class.)

Situation 2. *Character A: Teacher.* A student in one of your introductory courses shows exceptional promise for your field. You talk to the student and encourage him or her to become a major. (**Note:** The person playing the teacher should establish the class and the field.)

Character B: Student. This is your favorite class, and you find yourself fascinated by the subject. However, you and your parents have planned for you to pursue a different professional career, one you consider more lucrative.

Situation 3. *Character A: Teacher.* You've been teaching for a number of years. When you started, you loved teaching. But now you're feeling burned out and resentful of the long hours and the low pay. You've been offered a job outside of academia that offers a substantially better salary, and you're considering taking it.

Character B: Student. This particular teacher has been your mentor. You think he or she is a wonderful teacher. You hear he or she has been thinking about giving up teaching, and you don't want him or her to leave. So you approach him or her.

Situation 4. *Character A: Teacher.* You've been attending workshops on using active, experiential, and collaborative learning techniques, and you're excited with the changes you've made in your class. You think your new approach will stimulate more in-depth student learning.

Character B: Student. You're taking a class from Character A and you find the class confusing. You just want traditional lectures, and to find out what's going to be on the exams so that you can get good grades on them. You come to see Character A during office hours.

Processing, Part 1. In which of the situations were you most engaged? Why? Have you had an experience similar to any of those in the role wheel? How did you handle them? What did you learn from the role reversal? Did everyone handle the situation the same way? What issues did the role wheel raise? How do you feel about these issues?

Processing, Part 2. After processing the role wheel experience, discuss the role wheel as an exercise. Were the instructions clear? Could the description of the situations be improved? If so, how? Did you have enough time in each situation? too much? What was the value of the role reversal? Did the role wheel stimulate significant discussion? If so, how? Is this an effective way to surface tough issues and get them aired among friends and colleagues? How could this kind of exercise help your students?

Following the initial experience with the role wheel, each member of the group should design an activity that is suitable for use in class. In subsequent meetings, group members can then take turns leading and processing their role wheels. After this "rehearsal," the group can provide feedback on role wheel design and facilitation before the group member actually tries the role wheel in class.

Summary

We hope you'll explore these unique exercises and the impact they can have on your teaching. We continue to explore possibilities in our own classes and with our colleagues. Let us know what works for you, what doesn't, and what other ideas you might have.

Chapter 9: Scenes for Practice, Fun, and Exploration

We offer you now a variety of writings and references to theatre pieces and films that speak to teaching. Use them for whatever insight you can get ...or, better yet, explore each as a performance piece. Go to your library and read these plays. Try to get copies of the movie scripts. Consider each character. What's believable? What's not? Why? Try your hand at acting out scenes as scripted, or write your own. What connects to your own experiences as an instructor, and your values and beliefs? Use these ideas for your own role plays. Try different interpretations.

Stand and Deliver

A remarkable film and a true story. Jaime Escalante moved from a relatively high-paying job in the high-tech industry to what he thought would be his "calling"—a position teaching computer skills at Garfield High School, a barrio school in East Los Angeles. Bolivian by birth, Escalante did not bring any expectations that Hispanics were inferior as a group; in his home country of Bolivia, brown-skinned people could be seen at every level of society, industry, and government. The role of schools was to give voice to the talent, to inspire and guide, and, most of all, to challenge young people to do the work. "All that is required," he loved to repeat, "is ganas: desire."

What makes the film so intriguing is its authenticity: It was a project for the actor James Olmos when he was in film school, and many of the actors in the film were recruited from the community. When you see the film, look for the ways Escalante stretches beyond the norm. In one scene, he comes to class wearing an apron and a chef's hat, dramatically cutting an apple with a cleaver to create fractions. He was clearly having fun and the students got hooked. He frequently used gestures to create images, references for key concepts he was trying to get across. He had little rhythmic clapping and sound rituals for everyone to mimic as a warm-up.

When Escalante himself visited the campus of Colorado State University, Bill Timpson had him come to a class for prospective teachers. The students were watching the film at the time—and the mannerisms Olmos had captured in the lead role were all there.

Dead Poets Society

Wonderful scenes of high school classrooms—the dull and repetitive Latin class, the threatening math teacher, the demanding science teacher, and then the mercurial Mr. Keating, challenging his students to "seize the day" (*carpe diem*). Whether standing on desktops, having his students rip out a deadly dull analysis of poetry from their texts, or bringing wildly different and creative interpretations to classic plays—reading Hamlet as Marlon Brando's "Godfather" character or as John Wayne—the Robin Williams character calls for a deeper response from students... more that is personally meaningful. "What will your verse be?" he implores.

October Sky

A true story about four boys from a small, poor coal mining town in West Virginia who turned their fascination with rockets in the 1950s into winning a national science competition and college scholarships. Homer Hickman would later work for NASA in its space exploration program— and write *The Rocket Boys*, which then became the basis for the hit movie, *October Sky*. Bound to touch your heartstrings, this film shows the boys finding that one special teacher who feeds their dreams when few others could see past the hard realities and the dangers of the mines.

Higher Learning

John Singleton's dark film about racial tensions among college students that boil over into tragedy when a white supremacist group of skinheads sparks a shooting spree. What resonates for many is a scene in which the professor played by Lawrence Fishburn draws on philosopher John Rousseau to connect apathy with that which corrodes democracy from within. In one confrontational classroom scene, Fishburn empties his lunch bag, blows into it, and then explodes it over a sleeping student. "I am not a baby sitter," he warns. "Do not waste my time. Like anything else in life, you will get out of this course what you put into it."

Music of the Heart

A music teacher played by Meryl Streep defies conventional wisdom and begins a violin class in an inner-city New York elementary school. Despite the growing popularity of her classes and the healthy discipline she requires, budget cuts threaten her program's continuation—until students, community members, and a celebrity violinist join in for a fundraising concert at Carnegie Hall that pulls at everyone's heartstrings.

Mr. Holland's Opus

A frustrated composer takes a "day job" as a high school music teacher, only to find his true calling is with students and their music. His gaudy surprise farewell concert transforms a quiet retirement into a celebration of a life's contribution.

Dangerous Minds

An ex-marine walks into an inner-city "classroom from hell," only to have her hopes to teach blocked by students whose own dreams seem to have been lost through a revolving door of teachers and substitutes who run from their rebelliousness and foul language. Michelle Pfeifer's character must face a similar challenge if the students are to salvage something useful from this class.

Ferris Bueller's Day Off

A classic scene of every student's classroom nightmare, a teacher who drones on and on, "Anyone? Anyone?" only to answer his own feeble attempts at getting some discussion going. Ferris Bueller's own creative, spontaneous energies then play out in his day of hooky from school.

"When I Heard the Learn'd Astronomer ..."

This short poem by Walt Whitman still rings true today, when the inherent curiosities of students collide with the studied analyses of their professors. But many academics undoubtedly began their own careers in a similar manner. Can you empathize with both characters in this poem—the student and the learned astronomer? Remember our discussion about the interface of discovery and drama (Chapter 7)? Could astronomers do more to sustain a student's sense of wonder while also conveying the underlying theories and principles? Was this one of Carl Sagan's gifts? Or do scientists run some risks by teaching the basics to undergraduates or writing simply for the public? Try playing the scene described in Whitman's poem from each perspective. Change some of the words if you need to.

When I Heard the Learn'd Astronomer

When I heard the learn'd astronomer,
When the proofs, the figures, were ranged in columns
    before me,
When I was shown the charts and diagrams, to add,
    divide, and measure them,
When I sitting heard the astronomer where he lectured
    with much applause in the lecture room,
How soon unaccountable I became tired and sick,
Till rising and gliding out I wander'd off by myself,
In the mystical moist night air, and from time to time,
Look'd up in perfect silence at the stars.

All the World's a Stage ...

In Shakespeare's *As You Like It* (Act II, Scene 7), the melancholy jester Jacques delivers his oft-recited description of the seasons of human life. Try this excerpt from different perspectives: a young instructor fresh out of graduate school; a senior administrator who is eagerly anticipating retirement; a naive and underprepared first-year student; a graduating senior who's worried about his or her career prospects. How does your reading change with your different characterizations?

All the world's a stage,
And all the men and women merely players.
They have their exits and their entrances;
And one man in his time plays many parts.
His acts begin seven ages. At first the infant,
Mewling and puking in the nurse's arms.
And then the whining schoolboy, with his satchel
And shining morning face, creeping like snail
Unwillingly to school. And then the lover,
Sighing like a furnace, with a woeful ballad

Made to his mistress' eyebrow. Then a soldier,
Full of strange oaths, and bearded like the pard;
Jealous in honour, sudden and quick in quarrel,
Seeking the bubble reputation
Even in the cannon's mouth. And then the justice,
In fair round belly with good capon lined,
With eyes severe and beard of formal cut,
Full of wise saws and modern instances;
And so he plays his part. The sixth age shifts
Into the lean and slipper'd pantaloon,
With spectacles on nose and pouch on side;
His youthful hose, well saved, a world too wide
For his shrunk shank; and his big manly voice,
Turning again towards childish treble, pipes
And whistles in his sound. Last scene of all,
That ends this strange eventful history,
Is second childishness, and mere oblivion,
Sans teeth, sans eyes, sans taste, sans everything.

What We Need Are Facts, Sir!

Charles Dickens described an England in the throes of an industrial revolution, when change clashed with tradition and somehow humans muddled on. In *Hard Times* (1854), he takes us into a school where the goals of education seem to be mostly about the inculcation of obedience. Just listen to the insistence of Thomas Gradgrind as he addresses the schoolmaster and one other adult in a long classroom full of students. Try on the Gradgrind or the docile Bitzer roles described below. Is there any resemblance here to what you see in classes today? For example, does the use of multiple-choice and knowledge-based exams drive learning toward "facts"? Are your "best" students clones of yourself to some degree, quick to read your mind and give you back what you want? Do gender issues play out in your classes? For example, are your female students more reflective, empathetic, and articulate? Are the males more assertive about their opinions?

Now what we want is, Facts. Teach these boys and girls nothing but Facts. Facts alone are wanted in life. Plant nothing else, and root out everything else. You can only form the minds of reasoning animals upon Facts: Nothing else will ever be of any service to them. This is the principle upon which I bring up my own children, and this is the principle on which I bring up these children. Stick to Facts, sir! ...

The speaker, and the schoolmaster, and the third grown person present, all backed a little, and swept with their eyes the inclined plane of little vessels then and there arranged in order, ready to have imperial gallons of facts poured into them until they were full to the brim....

Gradgrind then turns on a student to underscore his point. The unfortunate Sissy Jupe is quizzed but panics and cannot answer:

"Girl number twenty unable to define a horse!" said Mr. Gradgrind, for the general behoof of all the little pitchers. "Girl number twenty possessed of no facts, in reference to one of the commonest of animals! Some boy's definition of a horse. Bitzer, yours."

"Quadruped. Graminivorous. Forty teeth, namely twenty-four grinders, four eye teeth, and twelve incisive. Sheds coat in spring; in marshy countries, sheds hoofs, too. Hoofs hard, but required to be shod with iron. Age known by marks in mouth." Thus (and much more) Bitzer.

"Now girl number twenty," said Mr. Gradgrind. "You know what a horse is." (Dickens 1854, 47-53)

I'm Trying to Teach You

David Mamet's *Oleana* has stirred up a good deal of controversy in its portrayal of a male professor caught up in an increasingly explosive series of interactions with a female student. As the play unfolds in the professor's office, his intellectual glibness, ambition, and distractibility clash with the student's struggles to learn and her growing resentment. Power? Helplessness? Ambition? Misunderstandings? Revenge? Victimization? And then violence!

Some of the controversy revolves around the various ways either character can be played. When the professor is played as an arrogant academic type who's mostly concerned with his own career and his impending purchase of a new home, you get a more traditional victimization of a younger and less powerful female. However, when the professor is played as a relatively innocent victim of an unnamed "group's" effort to confront an "oppressive academic patriarchy," you get a reversal of traditional roles and, understandably, more controversy.

In this first scene, Carol (the student) has come to talk to John (the professor) about her answer on an exam that received a very low grade. The continuation marks indicate interruptions and unfinished comments so that the characters' lines should overlap. Try each scene from the two different perspectives described above: one in which the student is impossibly helpless, and the other in which the professor is too caught up in his own role as expert to care about a struggling student. Are there other ways to play it?

The scene begins in John's office, where he sits behind his desk. The student is seated across from him. John is expecting a call about the house he and his wife are planning to buy now that he seems sure of being granted tenure. Carol has come to him to discuss her poor grade:

John: What don't you understand? (Pause)

Carol: Any of it. What you're trying to say. When you talk about ...

Try different inflections—i.e., on the "any," the "it," and the "you've" or the "trying." How do meanings or inferences shift? How does learning intersect with authority here? with age? What if John were right out of graduate school and Carol was a nontraditional student—a single mom with two kids and limited income who's back in school to complete her degree? What happens when the professor is female and the student is male?

The Calling

In *Angels Fall* by Lanford Wilson, Niles is a college professor of Art History who has a crisis of faith over the responsibility to educate students to think for themselves and not just accept his word—or anyone's word—as gospel. After rethinking his own role as expert, he rips up his own books in front of his students and announces an end to this kind of irrelevant "brainwashing." This monologue starts his reflections on why he chose teaching.

Think of the ways you could play Niles: a true heretic, someone who is slightly crazed, an idealist, a fool, or someone who could inspire the young. Do you resonate with any one of these lines?

Niles: ... I was walking around out there remembering. Though my student years were in earlier and what we like to think of as easier times—centuries ago, it seems—I remember having the same romantic impression of many professors' lives. Heaven knows, I'd never have gone into such a business otherwise. An edifice not at all like an ivory tower was my ignorant and egotistical hope those centuries ago. I actually envisioned a life of quiet reflection, strolling through the groves — the lot of it. We would go, a gentle band of enlightened teachers with quiet good humor, exchanging ideas with those younger minds entrusted to us, in a lively, perhaps even elegant symposium, with, we hoped, something like grace (Wilson 86).

Educating Rita

In a movie starring Michael Caine, Frank is a professor of Literature who takes to Rita, a commoner and hairdresser, and attempts to tutor her through the university. Think of the various ways you could play each character depending on the background and motivations you invent. When the scene begins, Frank has asked Rita to come to his office to discuss her very brief, one-line response on an assigned essay about *Peer Gynt*:

Rita: Is it wrong?

Frank: No, it's not wrong, it's just ...

Rita: See. I know it's too short. But I thought it was the right answer.

Frank: It's the basis for an argument, Rita, but one line is hardly an essay.

Rita: I know, but I didn't have much time this week, so I sort of, y' know, encapsulated all the ideas in one line.

Frank: But it's not enough.

Rita: Why not?

Frank: It just isn't.

Rita: But that's bleedin' stupid, cos you say — you say, don't y' — that one line of exquisite poetry says more than a thousand pages of second-rate prose?

Frank: But you're not writing poetry. What I'm trying to make you see is that whoever was marking this would want more than, "Do it on the radio." (He gets up and moves around to the other side of Rita's chair.) There is a way of answering examination questions that is expected. It's a sort of accepted ritual, it's a game, with rules. And you must observe those rules. (Act I, Scene 4)

Who's Afraid of Virginia Woolf?

Richard Burton and Elizabeth Taylor took Edward Albee's play and electrified the screen with their portrayal of George, a History professor at a small college whose president is the father of his wife, Martha. Their relationship smolders in a mix of alcohol, abuse, frustration, ambition, hurt, anger, sexuality, and dependency replete with periodic and public explosions. Their "son" is imagined. Nick is a junior faculty member who's new to the college with his wife, Honey. Everyone has already had a substantial amount of alcohol to drink.

The tension builds in this scene as some of the history that's personal to Martha and George plays out. Although the scene has very little reference to the classroom, it does capture some of the stories and politics that underlie every campus community. Explore your own range as you try these lines and their emotional subtext. How will different *back stories* (background experiences and information you can make up) affect the way you act? In this scene near the end of the play, Martha vents her anger at George, goading him for his failures, her own lost ambitions, and his loyalty to her father.

George: (Very quietly) I warn you.

Nick: Do you really think we have to go through … ?

Martha: I stand warned! (Pause … then to Honey and Nick) So, anyway, I married the S.O.B. and I had it all planned out. … He was the groom … he was going to be groomed. He'd take over some day … first, he'd take over the History Department, and then, when Daddy retired, he'd take over the college … you know? That's the way it was supposed to be. (To George, who is at the portable bar with his back to her.) You getting angry, baby? Huh? (Now back) That's the way it was supposed to be. Very simple. And Daddy seemed to think it was a pretty good idea, too. For a while. Until he watched for a couple of years! (To George again.) You getting angrier? (Now back) Until he watched for a couple of years and started thinking maybe it wasn't such a good idea after all … that maybe Georgie boy didn't have the stuff … that he didn't have it in him!

George: (Still with his back to them all.) Stop it, Martha.

Martha: (Viciously triumphant) The hell I will! You see, George didn't have that much … push … he wasn't particularly … aggressive. In fact, he was sort of a … (Spits the word at George's back) … a FLOP! A great …

big ... fat ... FLOP! (CRASH! Immediately after FLOP! George breaks a bottle against the portable bar and stands there, still with his back to them all, holding the remains of the bottle by the neck. There is a silence, with everyone frozen.)

References with Annotations

Abel, Lionel. 1963. *Metatheatre: A New View of Dramatic Form.* New York: Hill & Wang.

Andrew, Desley, William M. Timpson, and Duncan Nulty. 1994. Feedback on and assessment of tertiary instruction. *Tertiary Education News* 4(3): 9-16.

> A review of the published literature on student evaluation of teaching in higher education. In general, there is overwhelming support for students as reliable and fair judges of a teacher's effectiveness. This conclusion strengthens our case for audience (student) awareness and feedback.

Ausubel, David. 1963. *The Psychology of Meaningful Verbal Learning.* New York: Guine and Stratton.

> Basic verbal learning research with groundbreaking work on the advance organizer, a concept which can help you focus student attention on the underlying conceptual structure of a topic. The advance organizer is accordingly very similar to the through-line in the theatre, the theme which underlies the story and explains the actions and motivations in a coherent manner.

Barish, Jonas. 1981. *The Anti-theatrical Prejudice.* Berkeley, CA: University of California Press.

Barton, Robert. 1989. *Acting: Onstage and Off.* New York: Holt, Rinehart and Winston.

> As Barton points out, "Acting is one of the best ways to learn about being alive " (vii). In this text chock-full of helpful exercises, Barton explores the relationship between acting and daily life, demonstrating not only how the actor draws upon his or her personal experience in creating a character but how the acting process can facilitate personal growth.

Barton, Robert. 1993. *Style for Actors.* Mountain View, CA: Mayfield.

> This award-winning book, written in a style that engages the student's imagination, is intended to help student actors enter the "world" of plays from different historical periods. The methodology outlined here could be adapted by teachers of History or Literature to bring an historical period alive for their students, too.

Bates, Brian. 1987. *The Way of the Actor: A Path to Knowledge and Power.* Boston: Shambhala.

For readers who want to probe deeper into the ways in which acting can provide a path for self-development; contains quotes from numerous actors including Meryl Streep, Marlon Brando, Glenda Jackson, Liv Ullmann, and Jack Nicholson.

Belenky, Mary F., Blythe M. Clinchy, Nancy R. Goldberger, and Jill R. Tarule, eds. 1986. *Women's Ways of Knowing.* New York: Basic Books.

Along with books by Gilligan and Tobias, and fueled by a steady flow of research on the differences between men and women which run along some hypothe-sized sociobiological continuum, Belenky et al. make a persuasive claim for a more student-centered approach to teaching. Whatever your own beliefs about a very complex issue, our lessons from the stage can at the very least help equip you with a range of ideas for organizing and managing instruction.

Benedetti, Robert. 1976. *The Actor at Work.* Englewood Cliffs, NJ: Prentice-Hall.

Excellent acting textbook with lots of exercises to help you develop vocal and physical expressiveness.

Berman, Paul, and Milbrey McLaughlin. 1975. *Federal Programs Supporting Educational Change, Vol. VI: The Findings in Review.* Santa Monica, CA: The Rand Corporation.

A now classic study of the federal efforts at promoting educational change. A number of principles emerged which have served as guides for others since then: e.g., the importance of understanding the local context and involving key personnel at that level; a reaffirmation of the value of high expectations or "nothing ventured, nothing gained."

Bloom, Benjamin, ed. 1985. *Developing Talent in Young People.* New York: Ballantine.

A very important treatise on the nature of coaching and mentoring in the development of talent across a range of disciplines and activities including several with performance aspects, i.e., Mathematics, Music, Sports. If you want to model your own professional development after processes common to the stage and solicit more feedback and coaching (direction) about your own teaching, then this book may prove quite useful for explaining the underlying dynamics. Moreover, you will have much to ponder as you think about the relationships you yourself have with your own students.

Bloom, Benjamin and R. Clift. 1984. The phoenix agenda: Essential reform in teacher education. *Educational Researcher* 13: 5-18.

Bloom, Benjamin, et al. 1956. *Taxonomy of Educational Objectives. Handbook I: Cognitive Domain.* New York: Longman Green.

Perhaps the most cited of Bloom's work, this hierarchy for cognitive functioning can be a very useful reference for both planning and teaching. At the lowest level, students are asked to master particular knowledge but then move up through intellectually more demanding expectations with understanding, application, analysis, synthesis and evaluation. In a similar way, good scripts do more than just tell the details of a story but instead leave audience members with some central question or issue to ponder.

Boal, Augusto. 1979. *Theatre of the Oppressed.* Translated by Charles A and Maria Odilla Leal McBride. New York: Urizen.

Boal's now classic adaptation of the work of fellow Brazilian Paulo Freire to the theatre. Here, audience members become the subjects ("spect-actors") of the actors skills. The "production" is no longer about a written script, but is developed instead out of the lived experiences of those in attendance. Everyone, actors and audience members alike, joins in exploring possible solutions.

Boal, Augusto. 1992. *Games for Actors and Non-actors.* Translated by Adrian Jackson. New York: Routledge.

Building on the work of Paulo Freire (*Pedagogy of the Oppressed*), Boal has developed a form of interactive theatre aimed at empowering the audience and facilitating social change. Includes a brief description of the history of Boal's work in exploring real life issues through the use of theatre exercises as well as numerous exercises which can be adapted for classroom use.

Boal, Augusto. 1995. *Rainbow of Desire: The Boal Method of Theatre and Therapy.* Translated by Adrian Jackson. New York: Routledge.

A summary of Boal's theatre work as applied to education and therapy. Includes references to earlier work as cited above as well as new exercises. Again the focus is on increased awareness, personal empowerment, developing new skills and attitudes, exploring new possibilities through group support and assistance, gaining new insights via nonverbal representations, and more.

Boyer, Ernest. 1990. *The Professoriate Reconsidered.* Princeton, NJ: Carnegie Commission.

This report was commissioned by the Carnegie Commission to address the long-standing tensions between research and teaching and offer some new ideas. On many campuses and especially large research universities, growing expectations to publish and compete for external funding have imbalanced the reward system and discouraged ongoing commitment to quality teaching. In a set of recommendations which have received a great deal of attention world wide, Boyer calls for an expanded notion of scholarship which goes beyond basic research to recognize contributions across a range of activities including the writing of texts, research on teaching and learning, and various instructional innovations such as videotapes and computer software. Until the creative work which renews and energizes teaching is rewarded, Boyer insists, undergraduates in large classes in particular will continue to be exploited to support research and graduate studies.

Brecht, Bertolt. 1964. *Brecht on Theatre: The Development of an Aesthetic.* Edited and translated by John Willett. New York: Hill & Wang.

Bruner, Jerome. 1966. *Toward a Theory of Instruction.* Cambridge, MA: Harvard University Press.

Important reference by a scholar who produced some of the most frequently cited research on student learning, in particular, on the processes by which students discover and understand concepts. We see much potential here for applying various lessons from the stage whereby drama is utilized to help inspire interest and promote active, deep learning.

Burnaford, Gail, and David Hobson. 2001. *Responding to Reform: Images for Teaching in the New Millenium.*

In *Images of Schoolteachers in America.* 2nd ed. edited by Pamela Bolotin Joseph and Gail E. Burnaford Mahwah, NJ: Lawrence Erlbaum.

Burns, Morris, and Porter Woods. 1991. *Teacher as Actor.* Dubuque, IA: Kendall-Hunt.

Two theatre professors draw on their experiences with leading workshops for faculty to describe lessons from the stage which are relevant to postsecondary teaching. An easy read with lots of stories from the theatre and the classroom.

Bybee, Roger, and Robert Sund. 1982. *Piaget for Educators.* Columbus, OH: Merrill.

Sifting through a very dry, academic and dense prose which was translated from French into English makes any reading of Piaget's original work difficult. Bybee and Sund have written an accessible interpretation for teachers at all levels.

Campbell, Duane. 1996. *Choosing Democracy.* Upper Saddle River, NJ: Prentice-Hall.

Going beyond the more traditional arguments for multicultural education, Campbell argues for the centrality of diversity to our democratic principles and vitality. With an emphasis on communication skills, cooperative learning and critical thinking, in particular, teachers at all levels can model inclusive, accepting and democratic practices in their classrooms.

Cohen, Robert. 1984. *Acting One.* Palo Alto, CA: Mayfield.

Good, basic acting text by a popular acting teacher, with exercises for vocal development and inflection which should be especially useful for teachers.

Cole, David. 1982. *Acting as Reading: The Place of the Reading Process in the Actor's Work.* Ann Arbor, MI: University of Michigan Press.

Clurman, Harold. 1972. *On Directing.* New York: Collier.

A founding member of the influential Group Theatre in the 1930s, Harold Clurman helped to introduce the Stanislavski system of acting to the U.S. This book provides valuable examples of directorial analysis of a script, particularly the use of spines (superobjectives).

Cross, K. Patricia, and Mimi Harris Steadman. 1996. *Classroom Research: Implementing the Scholarship of Teaching.* San Francisco: Jossey-Bass.

Davis, Barbara Gross. 1993. *Tools for Teaching*. San Francisco: Jossey-Bass.

Evolving from a series of papers for instructors at the University of California-Berkeley, this book is intended to be a source book of practical ideas with little formal attention to underlying theories.

Davis, Robert, Carolyn Maher, and Nel Noddings. 1990. *Constructivist Views on the Teaching and Learning of Mathematics*. Reston, VA: National Council of Teachers of Mathematics.

There is a growing and rich literature on constructivist approaches to teaching and learning, three of which are featured in our text through discussions about the interrelationships between lessons from the stage and ideas about development, discovery and creativity. Mathematics education, in particular, suffers from enduring indictments of irrelevance and abstractions. Constructivist notions support more active approaches, which in turn promote deeper learning that are grounded in hands-on, concrete experience, with manipulables for example.

Delgado, Ramon. 1986. *Acting with Both Sides of Your Brain*. Cincinnati, OH: International Thomson Publishing.

Ideas about brain hemisphere functioning applied to the acting process. Includes an interesting section on conscious and unconscious role playing, with specific examples drawn from university life.

Denham, Carolyn, and Ann Lieberman. 1980. *Time to Learn*. Washington, DC: National Institute of Education.

A work which summarizes what is known about engaged learning, an important concept when looking at teaching from the perspective of the stage. Beginning with the time that is allotted and then subtracting what is lost to tardiness or announcements and the like, teachers then have a subset of time defined as "instructional." Subtracting time when students are off task, however, produces another subset labeled here as "engaged time." Subtracting the time when students are *not* learning produces the final inner subset when they are indeed successful. An even smaller subset could include those times when students are challenged to go from surface to deep learning. Much described in our text about the various lessons from the stage point toward an expansion of these inner two subsets where students are more engaged and learning at a deeper level.

Dickens, Charles. 1854. *Hard Times*. Edited by David Craig. New York: Penguin.

Some classic scenes of an earlier era of schooling where the mastery of facts meant everything. Fun to portray. Potentially provocative as a stimulus for discussion. Portraying an extreme position can allow for more open and frank exchange of opinions and beliefs.

Dreikurs, Rudolf. 1968. *Psychology in the Classroom: A Manual for Teachers*. New York: Harper & Row.

Parallel to the benefits which the actor gets from a study of a character's motivations, teachers can get much from understanding student motivations and how to channel potentially disruptive intentions into constructive directions that support learning.

Eble, Kenneth. 1994. *The Craft of Teaching.* San Francisco: Jossey-Bass

One of the most cited books on teaching in higher education. Readable. Lots of good ideas and solid recommendations. This is not a heavily referenced academic style text.

Erikson, Erik. 1974. *Dimensions of a New Identity.* New York: Norton.

No discussion of development could be complete without some mention of Erik Erikson and the crises that we all confront in our movement across the lifespan. For teachers in higher education, advanced stages have special relevance as wisdom and skills are passed on to the next generation.

Felman, Jyl Lynn. 2001. *Never a Dull Moment: Teaching and the Art of Performance.* London: Routledge.

Frank, Arthur W. 1995. Lecturing and transference: The uncover work of pedagogy. In *Pedagogy: The Question of Impersonation: Theories of Contemporary Culture,* edited by J. Gallop. Bloomington, IN: University of Indiana Press.

Freire, Paulo.1970. *Pedagogy of the Oppressed.* New York: Seabury.

A classic work that describes a paradigm, a philosophy and various practices which promote student empowerment. Recognizable in the spectacularly successful national literacy campaigns which were mounted in Nicaragua and Cuba, Freire's work extols active and cooperative learning, building blocks for many of the principles and techniques in the performing arts.

Fullan, Michael. 2001. *The New Meaning of Educational Change.* New York: Teacher's College Press.

The most referenced review of the literature on educational change, although with a primary focus on elementary and secondary schools. Most of the conclusions still hold for higher education, however. Easy to understand why tradition is so difficult to change. Although most relevant from a system's perspective, there are lots of findings which can help you plan your own program for professional development; i.e., the importance of feedback, of local models, support and assistance.

Gardner, Howard. 1983. *Frames of Mind.* New York: Basic Books.

Gardner, Howard. 1999a. *The Disciplined Mind: What All Students Should Understand.* New York: Simon and Schuster.

Gardner, Howard. 1999b. *Intelligence Reframed: Multiple Intelligences for the 21st Century.* New York: Basic Books.

Howard Gardner has become popular with teachers at all levels by arguing for a broader conceptualization of intelligence from the traditional, psychometric measurement of memory and reasoning. Like Dan Goleman (1994), he wants more recognition for the understanding that underlies our own self-awareness and self-efficacy *(intrapersonal intelligence)* as well as those skills that determine our effectiveness in interaction with others *(interpersonal intelligence)*. The six other intelligences which he defines are as follows: Linguistic, logical-mathematical, musical, spatial, bodily-kinesthetic, spiritual/environmental. Note how each could have an important place in the application of performance training to teaching.

Gilligan, Carol. 1982. *In a Different Voice.* Cambridge, MA: Harvard University Press.

A very important critique of the dominant Kohlberg model of moral development and one which offers an alternative view for women. Gilligan's work and the larger discussions about the role of gender and diversity in learning become especially important given the emphasis in a developmental perspective on instruction that is stimulating and challenging, requires active student involvement, and is sensitive to individual student needs.

Glasser, William. 1969. *Schools without Failure.* New York: Harper and Row.

Although his focus is on elementary and secondary school teaching, Glasser's arguments stand out as a treatise on the centrality of student self-worth and use of non-judgmental acceptance by teachers. As performers — and teachers — explore new roles and stretch to develop new skills, the importance of a non-judgmental professional climate becomes more important.

Glasser, William. 1975. *Reality Therapy: A New Approach to Psychiatry.* New York: Harper and Row.

Gleick, Janet. 1987. *Chaos: Making a New Science.* New York: Viking Penguin.

A difficult but important description of the origins of chaos theory. Even if you can't follow all the math, the story reaffirms the place for what is nonlinear, unpredictable. It's truly humbling what we don't know. Take the weather—even with very big and fast supercomputers and despite all that is riding on accurate weather predictions (e.g., agriculture, flooding, storms), there is a very large element of uncertainty here. Should humility have a bigger role in your classes?

Goffman, Erving. 1959. *The Presentation of Self in Everyday Life.* New York: Doubleday Anchor.

Goleman, Daniel. 1994. *Emotional Intelligence.* New York: Bantam.

An argument for recognizing the central role feelings play in our lives, how much of our traditional sense of intelligence (i.e., memory, reasoning and expression) can be squandered when we are overcome by frustrations and anger, neediness or despair. Goleman emphasizes the understanding and practical skills we need to navigate these emotional challenges, our own and others. For example, each of us can benefit from having more self-awareness, in the sense of recognizing feelings and building a vocabulary for them, and seeing the links between thoughts, feelings, and reactions. We can know about the ways in which thoughts or feelings are ruling a decision. We can analyze what is behind a feeling (for example, the hurt that triggers anger). We can learn ways to handle anxieties, anger, and sadness. In a world grown smaller by media and telecommunication, we can do better with the diversity we encounter by learning how to empathize, understand the feelings and perspectives of others, how to be a good listener and question-asker. We can learn how to distinguish between what someone says or does and our own reactions and judgments. We can become more assertive rather than angry or passive. We can study the arts of cooperation, conflict resolution, and negotiating compromise.

Gordon, William J.J. 1961. *Synectics: The Development of Creative Capacity*. New York: Harper.

Groundbreaking work which has helped to demystify the nature and development of creativity. Using the nonrational, analogies and regular practice, individuals and groups in any area can learn to stretch their thinking and inspire fresh insights.

Grant, Barbara and Dorothy Hennings. 1971. *The Teacher Moves: An Analysis of Nonverbal Activity*. New York: Teachers College Press.

Important analysis of the interrelationships between teaching and movement—the prevalence of teacher distractions for students and the potential for using gestures and movements generally to enhance learning.

Gressler, Thomas. 2002. Theatre as the Essential Liberal Art in the American University. Lewiston, NY: Mellon.

Gressler reviews the scholarship on active, experiential, and cooperative learning, Gardner's multiple intelligences, etc., and explains how theatre in higher education provides a complete, integrated learning experience for students — one that fulfills criteria articulated by the most recent learning theories.

Grotowski, Jerzy. 1968. *Towards a Poor Theatre*. New York: Simon and Schuster.

Hagen, Uta. 1973. *Respect for Acting*. New York: Macmillan.

A first person description of the acting process by a major American actress/teacher.

Hornby, Richard. 1986. *Drama, Metadrama, and Perception*. Lewisburg PA: Bucknell University Press.

Hunter, Madeline. 1982. *Mastery Teaching*. El Segundo, CA: TIP Publications.

Written for teachers at all levels as a concise summary of relevant research on teaching effectiveness, this book has proven particularly poplar among elementary and secondary teachers. Indeed, the concepts described here can serve as a common language as teachers from different disciplines discuss common problems, share ideas and plan collaborative improvement activities. You will find much support here for various recommendations from the stage, in particular, using multimodal approaches and "teaching to both sides of the brain."

Jackson, Linda, and Michael Murray. 1997. *What Students Really Think of Professors.* Lewiston, NY: Edwin Mellon Press.

Johnson, David, and Roger Johnson. 1994. *Learning Together and Alone.* Needham Heights, MA: Allyn and Bacon.

Summarizing years of research and numerous studies, the Johnson brothers make a very strong case for cooperative learning. Bubbling with the confidence of near-zealots, these authors attack competitive and individualized learning as anachronistic, ineffective and divorced from the real world. Although written primarily for elementary and secondary teachers, there are many practical ideas described here that are quite relevant for higher education. Because performances are necessarily collaborative, this material provides another strong link between the classroom and the stage.

Johnson, David, Roger Johnson, and Karl Smith. 1989. *Cooperative Learning: Cooperation and Competition, Theory and Research.* Edina, MN: Interaction Book Co.

An excellent reference, full of references on the value and use of cooperative learning in higher education.

Johnstone, Keith. 1979. *Impro: Improvisation and the Theatre.* New York: Theatre Arts Books.

A pioneer in British educational theatre, Johnstone explores the use of improvisational exercises to free the creative imagination from what he sees as the numbing effects of social conditioning. He recounts: "As I grew up, everything started getting gray and dull. I could still remember the amazing intensity of the world I'd lived in as a child, but I thought the dulling of perception was an inevitable consequence of age—just as the lens of the eye is bound gradually to dim. I didn't understand that clarity is in the mind. I've since found tricks that can make the world blaze up again in about fifteen seconds, and the effects last for hours...In a normal education everything is designed to suppress spontaneity, but I wanted to develop it " (13, 15).

Joyce, Bruce, and Beverly Showers. 1978. The coaching of teaching. *Educational Leadership* 40: 4-10.

Critiquing the professional isolation that encases teaching at every level, these authors categorize the different kinds of coaching which can improve teaching. From providing basic support and feedback to offering expert advice, Joyce and Showers describe processes which mirror what performers undergo during the rehearsal process.

Joyce, Bruce and Marsha Weil. 2000. *Models of Teaching*. Needham Heights, MA: Allyn and Bacon.

One of the most popular books for K-12 teachers since its first release in 1972, Joyce and Weil give concise and useful descriptions of a range of approaches to instruction organized into four "families": i.e., the "social family" including inquiry, group learning, role playing; the "information-processing family" including inductive thinking, concept learning, memorization, creativity, and cognitive development; the "personal family" including nondirective communication and learner-centered instruction; and the "behavioral systems family" including mastery learning, direct instruction and simulations.

Kohlberg, Lawrence. 1981. *The Philosophy of Moral Development*. New York: Harper and Row.

Although controversial in its presumed hierarchy and generalizability, many teachers continue to find much value here. In his call for dilemmas as catalysts for classroom discussions, Kohlberg makes a strong case for the use of the dramatic to engage the minds and feelings of students and, thereby, promote higher levels of moral judgment.

Kounin, Jacob. 1970. *Discipline and Group Management in Classrooms*. New York: Holt.

First classification of the term "with it" to describe those teachers who were ever aware of what was happening in their classes — which students were struggling, who was disengaged, when a change was needed. An important concept for the discussion of spontaneity, creativity and "audience awareness" in teaching.

Kuhn, Thomas. 1970. *The Structure of Scientific Revolutions*. Chicago, Illinois: University of Chicago Press.

The now classic description of the paradigm shifts that occur in every discipline when new ideas shift the way people think. For example, before Galileo both science and the church insisted that the world was indeed the center of the universe. For us, promoting the value of the performing paradigm for education often has the feel of heresy.

Levinson, Daniel. 1978. *The Seasons of a Man's Life*. New York: Ballantine.

Along with his book, *The Seasons of a Woman's Life*, Levinson describes the stages and markers for adult development. While actors must study their characters to understand underlying motivations, teachers often neglect formal attention to their own developmental needs. Through coaching, for example, experienced teachers can offer much of value to new recruits. Indeed, this kind of mentoring is quite evident, both formally and informally, during the rehearsal process for staged productions. But most importantly, actors must know themselves, how best to draw on their strengths and overcome their weaknesses. Lifelong learning is a necessary foundation for staying alert to what is in the world, to what can be used on stage. We believe that the same is true for teachers.

Lortie, Dan C. 1975. *Schoolteacher*. Chicago: University of Chicago Press.

Lowman, Joseph. 1995. *Mastering the Techniques of Teaching*. San Francisco: Jossey-Bass.

In one of the best books on teaching in higher education, Lowman provides much practical advice along with a conclusion which boils a teacher's effectiveness in the classroom down to two primary factors — intellectual excitement and interpersonal rapport. As such the link to the stage is obvious and compelling. Great teaching will indeed require much more than expertise and the transmission of knowledge

Marsh, Herbert W. 1987. Students' evaluations of university teaching: Research findings, methodological issues, and directions for future research. *International Journal of Educational Research* 11: 253-388.

Often cited summary of the existing research. Much evidence is reported here for the essential reliability and validity of student evaluations of teaching. Given certain weightings for class size and level of students enrolled, student judgments prove quite fair.

Maslow, Abraham. 1954. *Motivation and Personality*. New York: Harper and Row.

Maslow remains another seminal figure in the area of human motivation. Whether the focus is on your own needs as a teacher or those of your students, you may find it useful to understand more about the hierarchy which begins with a preoccupation with survival needs and proceeds upwards toward self-actualization where individuals are relatively free to pursue self-development. It will be at the highest levels where you may find more value from these lessons from the stage as you attempt to develop more creative and engaging approaches that promote deeper learning.

McGaw, Charles, and Larry Clark. 1992. *Acting Is Believing: A Basic Method*. Fort Worth: Harcourt Brace Jovanovich.

We find this a very useful text for teachers, ascribing much success on stage to an actor's ability to understand a character at a deep level. This, then, will make a character believable. At another level, we like this text because of what it implies about the teacher's role, how your care for the subject combines with a core belief in student abilities to energize instruction and empower learning.

McKeachie, Wilbert J., et al. 2002. *McKeachie's Teaching Tips*. St. Charles, IL: Houghton Mifflin.

One of the classics, already through multiple printings. Very little theory and lots of specific ideas and suggestions. The nuts and bolts of teaching in higher education.

McLaren, Peter. 1988. The liminal servant and the ritual roots of critical pedagogy. *Language Arts* 65: 164-179.

McLaughlin, Milbury W. 1990. The Rand Change Agent Study revisited: Macro perspectives and micro realities. *Educational Researcher* 19: 11-16.

Revisiting an extensive study of the impact of federal efforts at educational change, McLaughlin reaffirms the power of credible, local role models as catalysts for changing teacher behaviors and attitudes. Accordingly, the peer feedback/coaching model we recommend here employs teaching colleagues and classroom observations and closely parallels the rehearsal/direction process essential for staged productions.

McLaughlin, Milbury W., R. Scott Pfeifer, Deborah Seanson-Ownes, and Sylvia Yee. 1986. Why teachers won't teach. *Phi Delta Kappan* 67: 420-426.

Miller, Arthur. 1967. The American Theatre. In *Death of a Salesman: Text and Criticism*, edited by G. Weales. New York: Viking.

Moore, Sonia. 1984. *The Stanislavski System: The Professional Training of an Actor*. New York: Penguin.

A concise introduction to the acting principles developed by Stanislavski, the founder of modern acting theory and practice.

Perry, William. 1981. Cognitive and ethical growth: The making of meaning. In *The Modern American College: Responding to the new Realities of Diverse Students and a Changing Society*, edited by Arthur Chickering. San Francisco: Jossey-Bass.

Perhaps the most frequently cited reference about the cognitive development of college-aged students, Perry's work describes the shifts which allow the twenty-two year old to understand a greater diversity of opinion and handle increasing levels of complexity. In contrast to the neatly packaged pieces of information so typical of the lecture format, we see much value for teachers in higher education especially through lessons from the stage where great theatre can offer a range of characters and conflicts, multiple levels of meaning, and much for audience members to contemplate.

Perry, William. 1999. *Forms of Intellectual and Ethical Development in the College Years*. San Francisco: Jossey-Bass.

Peters, Thomas, and Robert Waterman. 1982. *In Search of Excellence*. New York: Harper & Row.

Although you may feel that this work is misplaced in a volume on university teaching, we are impressed with the conclusions here, which match with many of the arguments we make about relevant lessons from the stage — "staying close to the knitting" (student learning/audience engagement), "management by walking around" (close monitoring of student reactions/direction and feedback through rehearsal).

Peters, Thomas, and Nancy Austin. 1985. *A Passion for Excellence*. New York: Warner

After re-evaluating their data and adding a third author, Peters et al. sifted the evidence down to two qualities which seem to drive successful companies — caring for the customer and innovation. It is of great interest to us that these two qualities also drive stage performances but are all too often made secondary to teaching in higher education when the focus is primarily on course coverage.

Peters, Thomas. 1987. *Thriving on Chaos.* New York: Knopf.

With an environment intended to promote innovation comes a need for a more dynamic management and leadership style, one that is less hierarchical and more dependent on good communication.

Piaget, Jerome. 1952. *The Origins of Intelligence in Children.* New York: International Universities Press.

Although the bulk of his research focused on children, Piaget identified several principles and concepts which have relevance for the college- aged student and our arguments for the theatre analogy. Often overlooked are those factors that impact the learning of the very young and that continue to play a role, albeit diminished, throughout life. For example, infants learn primarily through touch, taste and smell while most of higher education is encased in language. Yet, science teachers in particular recognize the importance of labs in giving students hands-on experiences. Thus, active and experiential learning can be important at every level of schooling. As such, the theatre certainly offers more of a slice of life than a verbal description of life.

Pineau, Elyse Lamm. 1994. Teaching Is performance: reconceptualizing a problematic metaphor. *American Educational Research Journal* 31: 3-25.

Polsky, Milton. 1980. *Let's Improvise: Becoming Creative, Expressive and Spontaneous through Drama.* Englewood Cliffs, NJ: Prentice-Hall.

A highly accessible introduction to unleashing one's creativity through dramatic improvisation. Polsky includes a chapter on the use of role-playing as a teaching tool in the classroom.

Postlewait, Thomas, and Bruce McConachie, eds. 1989. *Interpreting the Theatrical Past: Essays in the Historiography of Performance.* Iowa City, IA: University of Iowa Press.

Ramsden, Paul. 1992. *Learning to Teach in Higher Education.* London: Routledge.

An especially popular book in the United Kingdom and Australia where Brisbane-based Ramsden makes a simple and direct appeal to shift the focus from teaching to the needs of the learner. However, you may still want to go to Timpson and Bendel-Simso or McKeachie for other ways to conceptualize and improve your teaching.

Rogers, Carl. 1951. *Client-Centered Therapy: Its Current Practices, Implications, and Theory.* Boston: Houghton Mifflin.

A classic relevant to any student-centered focus for instruction. Given the experiential and developmental emphasis of many of the lessons from the stage described here, where feedback from students and others becomes so vital, Rogers' emphasis on acceptance, listening and empathy proves very valuable.

Rogoff, Barbara. 1990. *Apprenticeship in Thinking.* New York: Oxford University Press.

A good argument for "conversations" over "teaching" when the focus is deep learning (i.e., understanding, what is constructed and made meaningful).

Sarason, Seymour. 1984. *The Nature of Schools and the Problem of Change.* Boston: Allyn and Bacon.

Often cited in the literature on educational change, Sarason is a clinical psychologist who has catalogued the stress which isolation makes for teachers in the classroom. If nothing else, an experience in the theatre with rehearsal and direction builds a sense of community among cast members. Utilizing peer feedback and coaching can do the same for teachers in higher education.

Sarason, Seymour. 1999. *Teaching as a Performing Art.* New York: Teachers College Press.

Schechner, Richard. 1985. *Between Theatre and Anthropology.* Philadelphia: University of Pennsylvania Press.

Schon, Donald. 1983. *The Reflective Practitioners.* New York: Basic Books.

Seldin, Peter. 1993. *The Teaching Portfolio.* Bolton, MA: Anker.

A practical and concise volume which describes the advantages and possible components of portfolios for teaching. Here individuals can document and analyze their own performance in teaching, including their attempts at innovation (e.g., writing new materials, utilizing new software, creating new television programs), curricula revision or new course development as well as any success they have had in securing external funds or writing for publication on instruction. As the portfolio becomes more accepted for purposes of promotion and tenure, it should promote greater support for utilizing lessons from the stage.

Showalter, Elaine. 2001. Teaching in public: A modest proposal. *Pedagogy: Critical Approaches to Teaching Literature, Language, Composition, and Culture* 1(3): 449-455.

Shurtleff, Michael. 1978. *Audition.* New York: Bantam.

Smiley, Sam. 1971. *Playwriting: The Structure of Action.* Englewood Cliffs, NJ: Prentice-Hall.

If you want to explore the possibility of structuring your lectures like plays, then this text by master playwriting teacher Sam Smiley can give you insight into how playwrights do it.

Smith, Ralph. 1979. Is teaching really a performing art? *Contemporary Education* 51: 31-35.

Spolin, Viola. 1983. *Improvisation for the Theatre*. Evanston, IL: Northwestern University Press.

> Perhaps a bible for those wanting to explore the issue of spontaneity. Lots of good exercises that are both fun and revealing. Often quoted by performers, this book is quite accessible to teachers.

Spolin, Viola. 1985. *Theatre Games for Rehearsal: A Director's Handbook*. Evanston, IL: Northwestern University Press.

> More exercises and improvisations from the "mother" of American improvisational theatre.

Swanson, Charles H. 1980. Our medium is our message: Potentials for educational theatre. *Theatre Quarterly* 9: 61-65.

Takaki, Ronald. 1993. *A Different Mirror*. Boston: Little, Brown and Company.

> In one of the most celebrated and readable books on American diversity, students wake up to the impact of economic exploitation and racism, in particular, on various immigrant groups. History comes alive through the stories of individuals—African slaves and Jewish sweatshop workers, Irish 'savages' and dispossessed Native tribes, Mexican and Asians—whose struggles reflect some of our darkest moments as a country as well as some of our brightest examples of struggles endured.

Tharp, Roland., and Ronald Gallimore. 1988. *Rousing Minds to Life*. New York: Cambridge University Press.

> An acclaimed new argument for instruction which is active and engaging, emphasizing the importance of "conversations" with students and the learning that they can construct out of their involvement in their communities.

Timpson, William M., and David N. Tobin. 1982. *Teaching as Performing*. Englewood Cliffs, NJ: Prentice Hall.

> The predecessor to this current book, but with a more generalized focus on teaching at all levels. Treated as a bit heretical by those scholars who have been focused on the "science" of teaching, this short and practical book seemed to threaten those teachers who feared any discussion of the parallels between the classroom and the stage and who wanted instead to stay steadfastly focused on content.

Timpson, William M. 1988. Paulo Freire: Advocate of literacy through liberation. *Educational Leadership* 45: 62-66.

> Following study-tours to Nicaragua, Cuba and Brazil, Timpson described the literacy campaigns which were inspired by the writings of Paulo Freire. Turning traditional teaching on its head, these countries were able to inspire dramatic increases in literacy through the use of small study groups and materials which built off the skills, experiences and hopes of students.

Timpson, William M., and Paul Bendel-Simso. 1996. *Concepts and Choices for Teaching*. Madison, WI: Atwood Publishing.

In contrast to other books on teaching in higher education which focus on skills, common sense and/or anecdotal commentary, Timpson and Bendel-Simso review the most important research on teaching and learning and describe those concepts which underlie effective instruction. The range of choices can produce very different results and allow teachers to organize instruction in a variety of ways.

Timpson, William M. 1999. *Metateaching and the Instructional Map*. Madison, WI: Atwood Publishing.

Building from the concept of *metacognition* or thinking about thinking, Timpson constructs a parallel concept for teachers and, then, offers an idea for a visual/conceptual "map" to help track major classroom factors, i.e., an instructor's focus along the continua from *product* (information, skills) to *process* (thinking, creating), from *teacher-directed* (lecture) to *student-centered* (discussion), and from *individual* to *group* learning.

Tobias, Sheila. 1990. *They're Not Dumb, They're Different*. Tucson, AZ: Research Corporation.

In what is quickly becoming a classic study of learning in higher education, Tobias interviewed students who quit as science majors but then found much success in other disciplines. Given that she was analyzing a talented population, her resulting indictments of the ways in which large introductory science classes are typically taught has proven quite telling. In particular, large numbers of female and minority students reported feeling discouraged when classes were impersonal, competitive and judgmental. Here again we see benefits from the stage where the cast and crew tackle a production as an ensemble. Grading on the curve and traditional teacher-directed instruction can be altered to incorporate more cooperative learning with its emphasis on peer support and assistance.

Tobin, Kenneth. 1983. The influence of wait-time on classroom learning. *European Journal of Science Education* 5: 35-48.

Teachers can overcome some problems with student participation by using greater patience in waiting for responses to questions. For example, counting silently to five can provide the needed opportunity for some students to formulate their own ideas and contribute to the general group discussion.

Toffler, Alvin. 1974. *Learning for Tomorrow: The Role of the Future in Education*. New York: Random House.

Turner, Victor. 1982. *From Ritual to Theatre: The Human Seriousness of Play*. New York: PAJ.

von Oech, Roger. 1986. *A Kick in the Seat of the Pants*. New York: Warner.

Various roles play out as humans create and then attempt to act on those creations. The *Explorer* in you is willing to investigate new possibilities, is daring, adventurous. While your *artist* persona can see aesthetic values, your *judge* has to make some decisions and then your *warrior* puts these into action. Another fun, light and easy read with some lasting value—for you and your students.

von Oech, Roger. 1983 *A Whack on the Side of the Head.* New York: Warner.

Fun. Accessible for you and your students. Once you accept the importance of creativity in teaching, a whole world can open up. From mind locks to myths, a quick skip through the terrain. Lots of activities to try. The first of two volumes.

Wilsey, Cathy, and Joellen Killion. 1982. Making staff development programs work. *Educational Leadership* 40: 36-43.

Wilshire, Bruce. 1982. *Role Playing and Identity: The Limits of Theatre as Metaphor.* Bloomington: Indiana University Press.

Wirth, Jeffery. 1994. *Interactive Acting: Acting, Improvisation, and Interacting for Audience Participatory Theatre.* Fall Creek, OR: Fall Creek Press.

Drawing on the work of Augusto Boal, Playback Theatre, and other forms of improvisatory theatre which elicit audience participation, Wirth offers specific suggestions for actors and directors, many of which are relevant for teachers wishing to employ role playing exercises in the classroom.

Yager, R. 1991. The constructivist learning model. *The Science Teacher* 58(6): 52-57.

Another recent work on constructivist teaching. Much work in science education is now pointing toward more attention to active, hands-on and engaged learning as a foundation for shifting from a surface learning of terminology and facts toward a deeper understanding of more abstract and theoretical constructs. (See Davis et al. cited above.)

Young, T.R. 1990. *The Drama of Social Life: Essays in Post-Modern Social Psychology.* New Brunswick, NJ: Transaction.

Zukav, Gary. 1984. *The Dancing Wu Li Masters: An Overview of the New Physics.* London: Fontana.

A wonderful read about research in physics and the ways in which Eastern ideas about intuition and wonder can be vital companions to a more reductionist approach to science and discovery. Drawing an analogy from the arts, Zukav describes the best teaching as a dance where learners are led through the material in an intimate series of turns and steps.

Index